GOLD &

palates

Telephone
of Pioneers
America

ANSWERING THE CALL OF THOSE IN NEED

REGION 2

ACKNOWLEDGEMENTS

As Project Chairperson for the Region 2 *Gold & Silver Palates*, I would like to give special recognition and thanks for their dedication and time in making this become a reality.

Administrative Members

* ★ **Nick Trisch** - John I. Sabin Chapter Pioneer Administrator
* ★ **Joanne Rossi** and **Carol Holmes** - John I. Sabin Staff Associates
* ★ **Marie Johnson** - Associate Member

Committee Members

* ★ **Linda Lim** - Los Amigos
* ★ **Dorothy Hamata** - Mission
* ★ **Janet Turner** - De Anza
* ★ **Linda Rowe** - George S. Ladd
* ★ **John Sobol** - Sierra Pacific
* ★ **Lin Fox-Norris** - Silver State

Thanks to all the Pioneers, friends and co-workers who contributed their favorite recipe.

It is our sincere wish that *Gold & Silver Palates* gives you many years of pleasure.

Evelyn Mess, Project Chairperson
John I. Sabin Chapter

This cookbook is a collection of our favorite recipes
which are not necessarily original recipes.

Published by: Favorite Recipes® Press
P.O. Box 305142
Nashville, Tennessee 37230

Copyright© 1992 by: Telephone Pioneers of America Region 2
140 New Montgomery Street, Room 1822
San Francisco, California 94105

Manufactured in the United States of America
First Printing: 1992   13,500 copies

Library of Congress Catalog Number: 92-8852
ISBN: 0-87197-329-4

WELCOME TO REGION 2!

You've just made a purchase that will bring years of pleasure. The recipes were gathered from two states, California and Nevada. In Pioneer language, that equates to all of Region 2.

What makes this recipe book unique, is that it encompasses all chapters in the region, there are seven. Their names and office location are:

* **George Ladd** – San Francisco
* **Sierra Pacific** – Santa Clara
* **Los Amigos** – Los Angeles
* **De Anza** – San Diego
* **Mission** – Alhambra
* **Silver State** – Reno
* **John I. Sabin** – Sacramento

Total membership in Region 2 is 69,896 with 29,961 regular members and 39,935 life members.

The Pioneers in Region 2 are not simply Pioneers in name. The membership recorded 195,010 participation hours in the first three months of 1991. This equates to an incredible 2.79 hours per member per month.

The truth be known, no one is really from California or Nevada. Everyone is a transplant from some other part of the country. They moved west for a host of reasons. Some seeking fortune and fame others merely escaping the law. Once they arrived most fell in love with the beauty and the mild weather and set down roots.

These transplanted residents didn't forget their original roots nor their original favorite recipes. What they did was sprinkle some West Coast flavor on them making them better than ever. Being human, they gave no credit to the recipe's origin, claiming instead, that they were the originator. You be the judge, you decide. We have every confidence you'll be delighted with the outcome and will find yourself pulling this book off the shelf again and again.

From all of us in California and Nevada Region 2, *bon appetite!*

LIST OF CONTRIBUTORS

Acard, Rose
Adams, Beverly
Albury, Brenda
Allen, Carolyn
Allen, Joyce
Allen, Pamela
Arroyos, Rachel
Atkinson-McKinney, Mary
Auffhammer, Bonna
Austin, Arvetta
Austin, Sue
Aznoe, Karolyn Tillisch
Babcock, Marian
Bailey, Jo
Bailey, Terry
Bambas, Ruth P.
Bauman, Diana
Bell, Ann
Benavidez, Helen
Bernhardt, E.
Berta, Helen
Biondi, Mary
Birdsall, Bess
Blissitt, Martha
Boatright, Donna Sue
Bocage, Charlotte
Bodle, Edna
Boelens, Bonnie
Bogue, Audrey
Bolz, Diane
Booker, Sharon
Borges, Pat
Bostdorff, Laurie
Bowman, T. J.
Boyles, Georgina
Bresee, Janice
Brown, Shelly
Buehler, Bruce
Buehler, Mary
Burke, Leone
Byrd, Marsha
Cameron, Gwen
Campbell, Chris
Campbell, Yolanda

Capitani, Vincent
Carlin, Debbie
Carpenter, Pauline K.
Catley, Clara
Celaya, Karen
Chadwick, Katherine
Chagonjian, Mavis
Chandler, Iris
Chapman, Gina
Chargois, Marlene
Chrystal, Marjorie
Church, Joan
Clark, Alice
Coats, Dorothy
Colon, Linda
Colyer, Deborah
Combs, Diane
Combs, Rick
Connor, Faith
Coonradt, Hettie
Corocco, Renee
Cortez, Margaret
Cousins, Sharon
Cramer, Sheryl
Crane, Jennifer
Crane, Michelle
Crowder, Carol
Cuthbert, Robin
Dahl, Doris
Dahl, Lori
Danielson, Mrs. E. C.
Davis, Lorraine
Davis, Winifred
De Bernardi, Joan
De Cou, Aundrea
De Jardins, Mildred
Derett, Lucille
Desjardins, Linda
DiBenedetto, Bonnie
Dodge, Marion
Dunkleberger, Jann
Durkton, Eve
Earl, Toni
Eckels, Betty

Elliott, Eleanor
Ellis, Madelene Jeane
Eringer, Helen
Evans, Joan
Favre, Joseph E.
Ferrucci, Marilyn
Flores, Ruth
Fox-Norris, Lynn
Frame, Anne Marie
Franklin, Stacy
Frawner, Marge
Fredenburg, Shirley
Fry, Nancy
Fua, Cheryl
Fuller, Esther
Funk, Bonnie
Fuqua, Lorraine
Garcia, Alma
Garlock, Edna
Garrotto, Dorothy
Garrotto, Jim
Gist, Evelyn
Gray, Betty Menk
Greenlee, Ann
Gregg, Susan
Grimm, Linda
Haller, Shirley
Hamata, Dorothy
Hansen, Georgia
Hanson, Doris
Harper, Cathy
Harris, Norma
Hearn, Jo
Henry, Theresa
Henry, Yvette
Hermance, Marjorie
Hightower, Ethel
Hillman, Leona
Hoffman, Cindy
Holmes, Carol
Hunsicker, Dorothy
Huysentruyt, Stephen J.
Irving, Lorraine
Jacobs, Julia
Jagara, Angle
Jaramillo, Dorothy
Jarrett, Barbara

Johnson, Bettie
Johnson, Sharleen
Johnson, Shirley
Jones, Deanie
Jordan, Dyane
Juarez, Barbara
Kamman, Rusty
Karch, Carole
Keirn, Ruth
Keirn, Susan
Keller, Thelma
Kennedy, Charlene
King, Val
Kirk, Lenora
Kotoulas, Norma
Ladd, George S. Chapter
Lange, Henrietta
Latasa, Hallie
Laughlin, Edythe
Lewis, Anna
Lim, Linda
Lindborg, Marie
Little, Margaret F.
Lorenzo, Nita
Maben, Karen
Maple, Helen
Marchant, Gladys
Marcovecchio, John
Marinborich, Erika
Marks, Jean
Martin, Mary E.
Mathieu, Pamela
Matias, Bettina
McCalmont, Carol
McCarthy, Lucille
McCoy, Brenda
McCoy, Harold
McDonald, Gretchen
McFarland, Cathy
McNeil, Lois
Meeker, Judy
Mensey, Ursula
Mercier, Gloria
Mess, Evelyn
Miller, Pam
Milovich, Alice
Mobraaten, Rae

Modlin, Annie
Mooney, Ramona
Moore, Jan
Moore, Jim
Moser, Barbara
Moss, Claude
Mossman, Sharon
Murdock, Nancy
Murphy, Terry
Negley, Sharon
Nemeth, Tina
Nichols, Kathy
Norris, Pat
O'Connell, Eileen
O'Hagan, Delores
O'Toole, Jim
Palacios, Rosemary
Palmer, Donna
Papillon, Connie
Parker, Karin
Pedersen, Ethel
Perkins, Diane
Peterson, Corabell C.
Pierini, Dawn
Pincus, Connie
Plummer, Debra
Powell, Ellie
Reckewey, Rosemary
Regley, Sharon
Rezak, Bob
Rideout, Emma
Riley, Beatrice
Ritchie, Sally
Robinson, Lorraine
Rocha, Shirley
Rosas, Onita G.
Rossi, Joanne
Rowe, Linda
Rubio, Karen
Ruddy, Shari
Sabins, Chris
Sadler, Catherine M.
Sanchez, Toni
Sanders, Girtha
Sanders, Martha
Schelb, June
Schomburg, Florence

Seedborg, Ruth
Sheets, Elinor
Sherman, Paula
Silva, Brenda
Silva, Rita
Silveria, Roxy
Simmerson, Elaine
Slack, Ted
Sloane, Carol
Smith, Debbie
Smith, Priscilla
Sobol, John
Stancil, Lucille
Stevens, Lee
Stockstill, Juanita
Summers, Arlis
Swanson, Cathy A.
Syhre, Hilda
Syme, Dolores
Taubitz, Barbara
Thomas, Jerry
Thompson, Kelli
Tompson, Jim & Holly
Trisch, Nick
Turner, Connie
Turner, Lucille
Twomey, Mary T.
Van Roggen, Betty
Vickers, Pat
Von Dohlen, Barbara
Vultaggio, Sherri
Wardell, Elinor
Weaver, Beverly
Weekes, Chris
Welch, Lori
Wheatly, Ed
Wheeler, Velda
White, Gwendolyn
Widdifield, Wanita
Williams, Mickey
Williams, Joy
Williams, Stella
Willyard, Cindy
Wolfe, Grace
Woods, Albert
Wright, Linda
Yanez, Janie

TABLE OF CONTENTS

Nutritional Analysis Guidelines

The editors have attempted to present these family recipes in a form that allows approximate nutritional values to be computed. Persons with dietary or health problems or whose diets require close monitoring should not rely solely on the nutritional information provided. They should consult their physicians or a registered dietitian for specific information.

Abbreviations for Nutritional Analysis

Cal — Calories	Dietary Fiber — Fiber	Sod — Sodium
Prot — Protein	T Fat — Total Fat	gr — gram
Carbo — Carbohydrates	Chol — Cholesterol	mg — milligrams

Nutritional information for these recipes is computed from information derived from many sources, including materials supplied by the United States Department of Agriculture, computer databanks and journals in which the information is assumed to be in the public domain. However, many specialty items, new products and processed foods may not be available from these sources or may vary from the average values used in these analyses. More information on new and/or specific products may be obtained by reading the nutrient labels. Unless otherwise specified, the nutritional analysis of these recipes is based on all measurements being level.

* **Artificial sweeteners** vary in use and strength so should be used "to taste," using the recipe ingredients as a guideline.
* **Artificial sweeteners** using aspartame (NutraSweet and Equal) should not be used as a sweetener in recipes involving prolonged heating which reduces the sweet taste. For further information on the use of these sweeteners, refer to package information.
* **Alcoholic ingredients** have been analyzed for the basic ingredients, although cooking causes the evaporation of alcohol thus decreasing caloric content.
* **Buttermilk, sour cream** and **yogurt** are the types available commercially.
* **Cake mixes** which are prepared using package directions include 3 eggs and 1/2 cup oil.
* **Chicken,** cooked for boning and chopping, has been roasted; this method yields the lowest caloric values.
* **Cottage cheese** is cream-style with 4.2% creaming mixture. Dry-curd cottage cheese has no creaming mixture.
* **Eggs** are all large.
* **Flour** is unsifted all-purpose flour.
* **Garnishes,** serving suggestions and other optional additions and variations are not included in the analysis.
* **Margarine** and **butter** are regular, not whipped or presoftened.
* **Milk** is whole milk, 3.5% butterfat. Lowfat milk is 1% butterfat. Evaporated milk is whole milk with 60% of the water removed.
* **Oil** is any type of vegetable cooking oil. Shortening is hydrogenated vegetable shortening.
* **Salt** and other ingredients to taste as noted in the ingredients have not been included in the nutritional analysis.
* If a choice of ingredients has been given, the nutritional analysis information reflects the first option.

Appetizers
and Beverages

PINEAPPLE CHEESE BALL

Yield:
12 servings
Utensil:
bowl

16 ounces cream cheese,
  softened
1 8-ounce can crushed
  pineapple, well drained
2 tablespoons chopped
  onion

¼ cup chopped green
  bell pepper
Salt and pepper to taste
2 cups chopped pecans

Approx Per
Serving:
Cal 275
T Fat 27 g
84% Calories
from Fat
Prot 4 g
Carbo 7 g
Fiber 2 g
Chol 41 mg
Sod 112 mg

Combine cream cheese, pineapple, onion, green pepper, salt, pepper and 1 cup pecans in bowl; mix well. Chill overnight. Shape into cheese ball. Roll in remaining 1 cup pecans, coating well. Chill until serving time.

Tina Nemeth, Silver State Chapter

ROQUEFORT LOG

Yield:
8 servings
Utensil:
bowl

8 ounces cream cheese,
  softened
2 ounces Roquefort
  cheese, crumbled
2 tablespoons finely
  chopped celery

1 tablespoon finely
  chopped onion
Tabasco sauce and
  cayenne pepper to taste
¾ cup finely chopped
  walnuts

Approx Per
Serving:
Cal 198
T Fat 19 g
84% Calories
from Fat
Prot 5 g
Carbo 3 g
Fiber 1 g
Chol 37 mg
Sod 215 mg

Combine cream cheese and Roquefort cheese in bowl; mix well. Add celery, onion, Tabasco sauce and cayenne pepper; mix well. Chill in refrigerator. Shape into log 1½ inches in diameter. Roll in walnuts, coating well. Chill, wrapped in waxed paper, until firm. Slice to serve with assorted crackers.

Carole Karch, Los Amigos Chapter

CRAB MOLD

Yield:
8 servings
Utensil:
mold

Approx Per Serving:
Cal 341
T Fat 32 g
84% Calories from Fat
Prot 9 g
Carbo 5 g
Fiber 1 g
Chol 62 mg
Sod 603 mg

1 envelope unflavored gelatin
1 tablespoon cold water
1 10-ounce can cream of mushroom soup
6 ounces cream cheese, softened
1 7-ounce can crab meat
3 green onions, chopped
3 stalks celery, chopped
1 2-ounce can chopped pimento
1 cup mayonnaise
Tabasco sauce to taste

Soften gelatin in cold water in small bowl. Heat soup in saucepan. Stir in gelatin until dissolved. Cool to room temperature. Add cream cheese, crab meat, green onions, celery, pimento, mayonnaise and Tabasco sauce; mix well. Spoon into mold. Chill until set. Unmold onto serving plate. May use imitation crab meat or omit pimento.

**Anne Marie Frame and Rachel Arroyos,
Los Amigos Chapter**

SHRIMP MOLD

Yield:
12 servings
Utensil:
mold

Approx Per Serving:
Cal 248
T Fat 22 g
79% Calories from Fat
Prot 10 g
Carbo 3 g
Fiber <1 g
Chol 84 mg
Sod 394 mg

1 envelope unflavored gelatin
1 10-ounce can cream of mushroom soup
6 ounces cream cheese
1 cup mayonnaise
1 cup finely chopped celery
3 large green onions, chopped
2 7-ounce cans shrimp, coarsely chopped

Soften gelatin in soup in saucepan. Add cream cheese. Heat for 3 minutes or until gelatin dissolves and cream cheese melts, stirring to mix well. Add mayonnaise, celery, green onions and shrimp; mix well. Spoon into 4-cup mold. Chill overnight. Unmold onto serving plate. Serve with crackers. May substitute crab meat for shrimp.

Tina Nemeth, Silver State Chapter

SALMON PÂTÉ

Yield:
16 servings
Utensil:
bowl

Approx Per
Serving:
Cal 164
T Fat 14 g
76% Calories
from Fat
Prot 8 g
Carbo 2 g
Fiber <1 g
Chol 45 mg
Sod 309 mg

2 tablespoons grated onion
2 teaspoons prepared horseradish
1 tablespoon lemon juice
1 tablespoon liquid smoke
1/2 teaspoon salt
16 ounces cream cheese, softened
1   16-ounce can salmon, drained, flaked
1/2 cup finely chopped walnuts
1/2 cup parsley flakes

Mix onion, horseradish, lemon juice, liquid smoke and salt in bowl. Add cream cheese; mix well. Stir in salmon. Shape into ball. Roll in mixture of walnuts and parsley flakes, coating well. Chill, wrapped in plastic wrap, until serving time.

Toni Sanchez, Los Amigos Chapter

ARTICHOKE FRITTATA

Yield:
15 servings
Utensil:
baking dish

Approx Per
Serving:
Cal 139
T Fat 10 g
61% Calories
from Fat
Prot 6 g
Carbo 7 g
Fiber 2 g
Chol 74 mg
Sod 354 mg

2   9-ounce jars marinated artichoke hearts
1 yellow onion, chopped
24 crackers, crushed
4 eggs, beaten
2 cups shredded Cheddar cheese

Drain artichoke hearts, reserving marinade. Chop artichoke hearts. Sauté onion in reserved marinade in skillet. Add artichokes, cracker crumbs, eggs and cheese; mix well. Spoon into 9x9-inch baking dish. Bake at 325 degrees for 35 to 45 minutes or until set. Cut into squares. Serve hot or cooled.

Linda Wright, Sierra Pacific Chapter

STUFFED CELERY STICKS

Yield:
8 servings
Utensil:
bowl

Approx Per Serving:
Cal 134
T Fat 13 g
82% Calories from Fat
Prot 3 g
Carbo 4 g
Fiber 1 g
Chol 31 mg
Sod 243 mg

8 ounces cream cheese, softened
1 teaspoon mayonnaise-type salad dressing
1 envelope zesty Italian salad dressing mix
1/4 cup chopped pecans
1 bunch celery, trimmed

Combine cream cheese, salad dressing, salad dressing mix and pecans in small bowl; mix well. Cut celery into pieces. Stuff with cream cheese mixture. Chill until serving time.

Alma Garcia, John I. Sabin Chapter

CHILI-CHEESE CRACKERS

Yield:
60 servings
Utensil:
baking sheet

Approx Per Serving:
Cal 40
T Fat 3 g
66% Calories from Fat
Prot 1 g
Carbo 2 g
Fiber <1 g
Chol 8 mg
Sod 56 mg

2 cups shredded sharp Cheddar cheese
1/2 cup butter, softened
1/3 cup milk
1 teaspoon chili powder
1 teaspoon prepared mustard
1/2 teaspoon salt
1 1/2 cups masa harina

Combine cheese, butter, milk, chili powder, mustard and salt in bowl; mix well. Add masa harina; mix to form dough. Pack into cookie press. Press into desired shapes on ungreased baking sheet. Bake at 375 degrees for 10 to 12 minutes or until light brown. Remove to wire rack to cool. Store loosely covered.

Marlene Chargois, Los Amigos Chapter

CHILI RELLENO APPETIZERS

Yield:
25 servings
Utensil:
baking pan

Approx Per Serving:
Cal 93
T Fat 7 g
70% Calories from Fat
Prot 6 g
Carbo 1 g
Fiber <1 g
Chol 54 mg
Sod 150 mg

4 eggs
½ cup half and half
2 tablespoons flour
2 cups shredded Cheddar cheese
2 cups shredded Monterey Jack cheese
2 tablespoons finely chopped onion
1 4-ounce can chopped green chilies, drained

Beat eggs in bowl. Stir in half and half and flour until smooth. Add cheeses, onion and green chilies; mix well. Spoon into greased 8x8-inch or 9x9-inch baking pan. Bake at 350 degrees for 30 to 40 minutes or until knife inserted in center comes out clean. Cool in pan for 10 minutes. Cut into small squares.

Shelly Brown, George S. Ladd Chapter

MONTEREY APPETIZER PIZZA

Yield:
8 servings
Utensil:
pizza pan

Approx Per Serving:
Cal 430
T Fat 31 g
70% Calories from Fat
Prot 18 g
Carbo 12 g
Fiber 1 g
Chol 105 mg
Sod 549 mg

2 eggs
1 pound Monterey Jack cheese, shredded
1 6-count package frozen patty shells, thawed
¼ cup sliced canned mushrooms
¼ cup sliced black olives
2 tablespoons chopped onion
Salt and pepper to taste

Beat eggs in bowl. Stir in cheese. Place 3 patty shells in overlapping cloverleaf design on floured surface. Roll to fit medium pizza pan. Fit into greased pizza pan. Spread with cheese mixture. Top with mushrooms, olives and onion. Season to taste. Roll remaining patty shells in same manner. Place over filling; seal edges. Bake at 400 degrees for 20 minutes or until golden brown. Cut into wedges. Serve hot.

Doris Hanson, John I. Sabin Chapter

STUFFED MUSHROOMS

Yield:
24 servings
Utensil:
baking sheet

Approx Per Serving:
Cal 51
T Fat 2 g
33% Calories from Fat
Prot 2 g
Carbo 7 g
Fiber 1 g
Chol 3 mg
Sod 131 mg

2 tablespoons butter
2 tablespoons garlic
  spread
24 mushrooms
2 cups fresh bread crumbs

2 tablespoons dry sherry
1 teaspoon seasoned salt
¼ teaspoon seasoned
  pepper

Melt butter with garlic spread in skillet. Remove and finely chop mushroom stems. Brush mushroom caps with garlic-butter mixture. Sauté mushroom stems in remaining garlic-butter in skillet. Add bread crumbs, sherry, salt and pepper; mix well. Sauté for 2 minutes longer. Spoon into mushroom caps; place on baking sheet. Bake at 425 degrees for 10 minutes.

Bess Birdsall, Mission Chapter

STUFFED MUSHROOM CAPS

Yield:
24 servings
Utensil:
baking sheet

Approx Per Serving:
Cal 32
T Fat 2 g
46% Calories from Fat
Prot 3 g
Carbo 2 g
Fiber <1 g
Chol 15 mg
Sod 376 mg

24 large mushrooms
½ cup soy sauce
8 ounces ground beef
2 tablespoons bread
  crumbs
¼ cup minced green
  bell pepper

1 tablespoon minced
  onion
½ clove of garlic,
  minced
1 egg yolk
¼ teaspoon salt
¼ teaspoon pepper

Remove and finely chop mushroom stems. Combine mushroom caps with soy sauce in bowl. Marinate for 1 hour; drain. Combine mushroom stems with ground beef, bread crumbs, green pepper, onion, garlic, egg yolk, salt and pepper in bowl; mix well. Stuff into mushroom caps; place on baking sheet. Broil for 8 to 10 minutes or until stuffing is done to taste.

Nutritional information includes entire amount of soy sauce marinade.

Shelly Brown, George S. Ladd Chapter

TORTILLA PINWHEELS

Yield:
40 servings
Utensil:
bowl

Approx Per
Serving:
Cal 98
T Fat 8 g
66% Calories
from Fat
Prot 3 g
Carbo 6 g
Fiber 1 g
Chol 16 mg
Sod 173 mg

8 ounces cream cheese, softened
1½ cups sour cream
6 green onions, finely chopped
2 4-ounce cans chopped black olives
2 cups shredded Cheddar cheese
1 or 2 4-ounce cans chopped green chilies
1 10-count package flour tortillas

Combine cream cheese, sour cream, green onions, olives, Cheddar cheese and green chilies in bowl; mix well. Spread on tortillas. Roll tortillas tightly to enclose filling. Place close together in plastic wrap-lined dish; cover with plastic wrap. Chill for 24 hours. Cut into bite-sized pieces. Serve with salsa.

Doris Hanson, John I. Sabin Chapter

CRAB WON TONS

Yield:
72 servings
Utensil:
wok

Approx Per
Serving:
Cal 16
T Fat 1 g
71% Calories
from Fat
Prot 1 g
Carbo <1 g
Fiber <1 g
Chol 10 mg
Sod 20 mg

8 ounces cream cheese, softened
¼ teaspoon soy sauce
¼ teaspoon pepper
1¼ cups chopped chives
2 cloves of garlic, minced
8 ounces cooked crab meat
72 won ton skins
1 egg, beaten
Oil for frying

Beat cream cheese with soy sauce and pepper in mixer bowl until smooth. Add chives, garlic and crab meat; mix well. Spoon 1 teaspoon filling onto 1 corner of each won ton skin. Fold corner over filling and roll won ton to enclose filling. Moisten edges with egg and press to seal. Fry in hot oil in wok until crisp. Serve with plum sauce. May freeze fried won tons and reheat at 350 degrees for 15 minutes.

Nutritional information does not include oil for frying.

Sheryl Cramer, John I. Sabin Chapter

WON TONS

Yield:
48 servings
Utensil:
wok

**Approx Per
Serving:**
*Cal 9
T Fat <1 g
40% Calories
from Fat
Prot <1 g
Carbo <1 g
Fiber <1 g
Chol 5 mg
Sod 34 mg*

8 ounces ground pork
1 tablespoon light soy
  sauce
1 tablespoon sherry
4 water chestnuts, finely
  chopped
3 or 4 green onions,
  finely chopped
¹/₂ beaten egg
2 bok choy leaves,
  chopped
¹/₂ teaspoon salt
48 won ton skins
Oil for deep frying

Combine pork, soy sauce, sherry, water chestnuts, green onions, egg, bok choy and salt in bowl; mix well. Spoon 1 teaspoon filling into center of each won ton skin. Fold over to enclose filling; press edges to seal. Deep-fry 10 to 12 at a time in 400-degree oil in wok for 3 minutes or until golden brown; drain.

Nutritional information does not include oil for deep-frying.

Ramona Mooney, John I. Sabin Chapter

WORKING WOMAN'S APPETIZER

Yield:
20 servings
Utensil:
electric skillet

**Approx Per
Serving:**
*Cal 81
T Fat 2 g
21% Calories
from Fat
Prot 3 g
Carbo 13 g
Fiber <1 g
Chol 11 mg
Sod 165 mg*

1 16-ounce package
   chicken drumettes
1 tablespoon oil
³/₄ cup packed brown
   sugar
3 tablespoons soy sauce
1 6-ounce can frozen
   orange juice
   concentrate

Rinse chicken and pat dry. Brown in oil in electric skillet. Mix brown sugar, soy sauce and orange juice concentrate in small bowl. Spoon over chicken. Cook at 375 degrees for 40 minutes or until golden brown. Garnish with sesame seed to serve.

Sheryl Cramer, John I. Sabin Chapter

CAN'T-JUST-EAT-ONE CRACKERS

Yield:
16 servings
Utensil:
baking sheet

Approx Per
Serving:
Cal 214
T Fat 14 g
56% Calories
from Fat
Prot 3 g
Carbo 21 g
Fiber 1 g
Chol 0 mg
Sod 477 mg

³/₄ cup oil
1 envelope ranch salad
  dressing mix
¹/₄ teaspoon garlic
  powder

¹/₂ teaspoon lemon
  pepper
1 16-ounce package
  oyster crackers

Combine oil, salad dressing mix, garlic powder and lemon pepper in bowl; whisk until smooth. Add crackers, mixing to coat evenly. Spread on baking sheet. Bake at 275 degrees for 15 to 20 minutes or until golden brown.

Sheryl Cramer, John I. Sabin Chapter

PUPPY CHOW

Yield:
16 servings
Utensil:
bowl

Approx Per
Serving:
Cal 452
T Fat 22 g
41% Calories
from Fat
Prot 8 g
Carbo 62 g
Fiber 3 g
Chol 0 mg
Sod 358 mg

2 cups chocolate chips
1 cup peanut butter
¹/₂ cup margarine

1 16-ounce package
  Crispix cereal
3 cups confectioners' sugar

Melt chocolate chips, peanut butter and margarine in saucepan, stirring to mix well. Pour over cereal in bowl, stirring to coat well. Combine with confectioners' sugar in sack or large covered bowl; shake to coat well.

Marian Babcock, John I. Sabin Chapter

HOT BEAN DIP

Yield:
8 servings
Utensil:
baking dish

Approx Per Serving:
Cal 324
T Fat 26 g
74% Calories from Fat
Prot 12 g
Carbo 8 g
Fiber <1 g
Chol 73 mg
Sod 687 mg

8 ounces cream cheese, softened
1 10-ounce can bean dip
20 drops of hot pepper sauce
1/2 cup sliced green onions
1 cup sour cream
1/2 envelope taco seasoning mix
1 cup shredded Cheddar cheese
1 cup shredded Monterey Jack cheese

Combine cream cheese, bean dip, pepper sauce, green onions, sour cream and taco seasoning mix in mixer bowl or food processor; mix until smooth. Layer bean dip mixture, Cheddar cheese and Monterey Jack cheese 1/2 at a time in 1½-quart baking dish. Bake at 350 degrees for 20 minutes. Serve warm with corn chips or tortilla chips. May microwave on High for 3 to 5 minutes if preferred.

Mary Biondi, Mission Chapter

CHILI DIP

Yield:
12 servings
Utensil:
slow cooker

Approx Per Serving:
Cal 160
T Fat 14 g
70% Calories from Fat
Prot 6 g
Carbo 7 g
Fiber 2 g
Chol 25 mg
Sod 746 mg

1 16-ounce can chili without beans
1 cup sour cream
1 cup shredded Cheddar cheese
2 tomatoes, chopped
1 4-ounce can chopped green chilies
1 4-ounce can sliced black olives
1 cup chopped green olives

Combine chili, sour cream and cheese in slow cooker. Cook until heated through, stirring occasionally to mix well. Add tomatoes, green chilies, black olives and green olives; mix well. Serve with tortilla chips.

Barbara Juarez, Los Amigos Chapter

CHIPPED BEEF DIP

Yield:
8 servings
Utensil:
glass dish

Approx Per Serving:
Cal 149
T Fat 13 g
80% Calories from Fat
Prot 5 g
Carbo 2 g
Fiber <1 g
Chol 38 mg
Sod 405 mg

1 2¹/₂-ounce jar chipped beef, shredded
8 ounces cream cheese, softened
¹/₂ cup (or more) sour cream
¹/₄ cup chopped green bell pepper
3 green onions, chopped
2 tablespoons milk
¹/₂ teaspoon garlic powder
¹/₄ teaspoon pepper

Combine chipped beef, cream cheese, sour cream, green pepper, green onions, milk, garlic powder and pepper in bowl; mix well. Spread in shallow glass dish. Serve with crackers. May garnish with chopped pecans or paprika.

Shirley Johnson, Silver State Chapter

CINNAMON DIP

Yield:
8 servings
Utensil:
bowl

Approx Per Serving:
Cal 114
T Fat 10 g
78% Calories from Fat
Prot 2 g
Carbo 4 g
Fiber 0 g
Chol 32 mg
Sod 87 mg

8 ounces cream cheese, softened
2 tablespoons milk
1 teaspoon cinnamon
2 tablespoons brown sugar
¹/₄ teaspoon nutmeg
1 teaspoon vanilla extract

Combine cream cheese, milk, cinnamon, brown sugar, nutmeg and vanilla in bowl; beat until smooth. Serve with sliced apples or cookies.

Martha Sanders, Los Amigos Chapter

Cottage Cheese Dip

Yield:
16 servings
Utensil:
bowl

2 cups cottage cheese
2 tablespoons
  mayonnaise

1 envelope ranch salad
  dressing mix
Chopped parsley to taste

Combine cottage cheese, mayonnaise, salad dressing mix and parsley in bowl; mix well. Serve with chips or crackers.

Carol Holmes, John I. Sabin Chapter

Approx Per
Serving:
Cal 43
T Fat 2 g
52% Calories
from Fat
Prot 3 g
Carbo 2 g
Fiber 0 g
Chol 5 mg
Sod 238 mg

Dill Dip

Yield:
16 servings
Utensil:
bowl

1 cup mayonnaise
1 cup sour cream
2 green onions, thinly
  sliced

1½ teaspoons dillweed
1½ teaspoons seasoned
  salt

Combine mayonnaise, sour cream, green onions, dillweed and seasoned salt in bowl; mix well. Chill until serving time. Serve with vegetable dippers.

Dorothy Hamata, Mission Chapter

Approx Per
Serving:
Cal 130
T Fat 14 g
95% Calories
from Fat
Prot 1 g
Carbo 1 g
Fiber <1 g
Chol 15 mg
Sod 208 mg

RED BELL PEPPER RELISH

Yield:
48 servings
Utensil:
saucepan

**Approx Per
Serving:**
*Cal 27
T Fat <1 g
1% Calories
from Fat
Prot <1 g
Carbo 7 g
Fiber <1 g
Chol 0 mg
Sod 45 mg*

6 medium red bell
  peppers
1½ cups sugar

¾ cup cider vinegar
1 tablespoon cornstarch
1 teaspoon salt

Chop or grind bell peppers in food processor. Combine with sugar, vinegar, cornstarch and salt in saucepan. Cook for 6 minutes. Store in refrigerator. Serve over cream cheese with crackers.

Arvetta Austin, George S. Ladd Chapter

SALSA

Yield:
*192
tablespoons*
Utensil:
saucepan

**Approx Per
Tablespoon:**
*Cal 10
T Fat 1 g
59% Calories
from Fat
Prot <1 g
Carbo 1 g
Fiber <1 g
Chol 0 mg
Sod 300 mg*

9 tablespoons oil
9 tablespoons vinegar
10 cloves of garlic
20 jalapeño peppers
2 28-ounce cans
  tomatoes

3 large onions, chopped
2 8-ounce cans tomato
  sauce
3 tablespoons MSG
2 tablespoons salt

Combine oil, vinegar, garlic, peppers, tomatoes, onions, tomato sauce, MSG and salt in blender or food processor container; process until smooth. Bring to a boil in large saucepan. Simmer for 30 minutes. Spoon into three sterilized 1-quart jars. Seal with 2-piece lids. Process in boiling water bath for 5 minutes.

Janie C. Yanez, John I. Sabin Chapter

SEVEN-LAYER DIP

Yield:
20 servings
Utensil:
dish

Approx Per
Serving:
Cal 262
T Fat 24 g
76% Calories
from Fat
Prot 6 g
Carbo 11 g
Fiber 6 g
Chol 23 mg
Sod 538 mg

1   16-ounce can spicy
  refried beans
3 avocados
Juice of 1 lemon
1 cup mayonnaise
1 cup sour cream
1 envelope taco
  seasoning mix
3 tomatoes, chopped

1 bunch green onions,
  chopped
3   4-ounce cans pitted
  black olives, drained
1 cup shredded
  Monterey Jack cheese
1 cup shredded Cheddar
  cheese

Spread beans in rectangular dish. Mash avocados with lemon juice in small bowl. Spread over beans. Combine mayonnaise, sour cream and taco seasoning mix in bowl; mix well. Spread over avocado layer. Layer tomatoes, green onions, olives, Monterey Jack cheese and Cheddar cheese over sour cream layer. Chill for 2 hours. Serve with tortilla chips.

Rosemary Palacios, Los Amigos Chapter

HOT BREAD CLAM DIP

Yield:
16 servings
Utensil:
baking sheet

Approx Per
Serving:
Cal 303
T Fat 25 g
66% Calories
from Fat
Prot 12 g
Carbo 17 g
Fiber <1 g
Chol 98 mg
Sod 364 mg

1 round loaf unsliced
  shepherd's bread
4   8-ounce cans minced
  clams

32 ounces cream cheese,
  softened
Garlic salt and pepper to
  taste

Slice off top of bread; hollow out and reserve bread from center. Drain clams, reserving liquid. Combine clams with cream cheese, garlic salt and pepper in bowl; mix well. Add enough reserved clam juice to make of desired consistency; mixture should be stiff. Spoon into bread shell; replace top. Wrap with foil; place on baking sheet. Bake at 325 degrees for 1½ hours. Serve with reserved bread cubes for dipping.

Helen Eringer, Los Amigos Chapter

HOT CRAB DIP

Yield:
20 servings
Utensil:
double boiler

Approx Per Serving:
Cal 182
T Fat 17 g
82% Calories from Fat
Prot 7 g
Carbo 1 g
Fiber 0 g
Chol 58 mg
Sod 282 mg

2 7-ounce cans crab meat
24 ounces cream cheese
1/2 cup mayonnaise
2 teaspoons confectioners' sugar
1/2 teaspoon garlic powder
2 teaspoons dry mustard
1/2 teaspoon onion salt
1/2 teaspoon seasoned salt
1/4 cup Sauterne

Combine crab meat, cream cheese, mayonnaise, confectioners' sugar, garlic powder, dry mustard, onion salt and seasoned salt in double boiler. Heat until cream cheese melts, stirring to mix well. Stir in wine. Serve hot with cubes of French bread. May substitute 12 ounces fresh crab meat for canned crab meat.

Ruth Flores, Sierra Pacific Chapter

CRAB LOAF DIP

Yield:
16 servings
Utensil:
baking sheet

Approx Per Serving:
Cal 179
T Fat 9 g
46% Calories from Fat
Prot 9 g
Carbo 15 g
Fiber <1 g
Chol 43 mg
Sod 281 mg

1 round loaf unsliced sourdough bread
8 ounces cream cheese, softened
1 cup sour cream
4 green onions, chopped
12 ounces crab meat

Slice off top of bread; hollow out and reserve bread from center. Combine cream cheese, sour cream, green onions and crab meat in bowl; mix well. Spoon into bread shell; replace top. Wrap with heavy-duty foil; place on baking sheet. Bake at 350 degrees for 1 1/2 hours. Serve hot with reserved bread, toast squares or crackers. May use shepherd's bread or imitation crab meat if preferred.

Stacy Franklin, Los Amigos Chapter

CRAB AND SHRIMP DIP

Yield:
12 servings
Utensil:
mold

Approx Per
Serving:
Cal 261
T Fat 24 g
80% Calories
from Fat
Prot 10 g
Carbo 3 g
Fiber <1 g
Chol 75 mg
Sod 435 mg

1 envelope unflavored
  gelatin
1 tablespoon cold water
1   10-ounce can cream
  of mushroom soup
8 ounces cream cheese,
  softened

1 cup mayonnaise
3 green onions, chopped
1   7-ounce can crab meat
1   7-ounce can shrimp

Soften gelatin in water in bowl. Heat soup in saucepan. Add gelatin, stirring to dissolve. Add cream cheese; mix well. Stir in mayonnaise, green onions, crab meat and shrimp. Spoon into mold. Chill until set. Unmold onto serving plate. May use fresh crab meat and fresh shrimp if preferred.

Sue Austin, George S. Ladd Chapter

SHRIMP DIP

Yield:
8 servings
Utensil:
bowl

Approx Per
Serving:
Cal 156
T Fat 13 g
75% Calories
from Fat
Prot 8 g
Carbo 2 g
Fiber <1 g
Chol 76 mg
Sod 147 mg

1   7-ounce can tiny
  shrimp, drained
8 ounces cream cheese,
  softened
2 tablespoons mayonnaise

¹/₂ small onion, finely
  chopped
4 or 5 drops of hot
  pepper sauce

Mash shrimp with fork in bowl. Add cream cheese; mix well. Stir in mayonnaise, onion and pepper sauce; mix well. Chill for 1 hour. Serve with chips or crackers.

Pamela Mathieu, Los Amigos Chapter

PINK SHRIMP DIP

Yield:
8 servings
Utensil:
bowl

Approx Per
Serving:
Cal 197
T Fat 19 g
84% Calories
from Fat
Prot 6 g
Carbo 2 g
Fiber <1 g
Chol 59 mg
Sod 213 mg

6 ounces cream cheese,
  softened
1/2 cup mayonnaise
2 tablespoons catsup
1 tablespoon lemon juice
1/4 teaspoon Tabasco
  sauce
1/4 teaspoon pepper
1 tablespoon finely
  chopped onion
1 cup canned or frozen
  cooked shrimp,
  chopped

Blend cream cheese and mayonnaise in medium bowl.
Add catsup, lemon juice, Tabasco sauce and pepper; mix
well. Stir in onion and shrimp. Chill until serving time.
Serve with crackers or mini bagels.

Doris Dahl, George S. Ladd Chapter

SPINACH ONION DIP

Yield:
12 servings
Utensil:
bowl

Approx Per
Serving:
Cal 90
T Fat 8 g
78% Calories
from Fat
Prot 2 g
Carbo 3 g
Fiber 1 g
Chol 17 mg
Sod 93 mg

1 10-ounce package
   frozen chopped
   spinach, thawed, well
   drained
2 cups sour cream
1 envelope onion soup
  mix

Combine spinach, sour cream and soup mix in bowl; mix
well. Chill, covered, for 2 hours or longer.

Carol Holmes, John I. Sabin Chapter

SPINACH DIP

Yield:
12 servings
Utensil:
bowl

Approx Per Serving:
Cal 222
T Fat 21 g
82% Calories from Fat
Prot 3 g
Carbo 8 g
Fiber 1 g
Chol 24 mg
Sod 411 mg

1 10-ounce package frozen chopped spinach, thawed, well drained
1 envelope vegetable soup mix
1 7-ounce can water chestnuts, drained, chopped
3 green onions, chopped
1¹/₂ cups sour cream
1 cup mayonnaise

Combine spinach, soup mix, water chestnuts, green onions, sour cream and mayonnaise in bowl; mix well. Chill, covered, until serving time.

Diana Bauman, Los Amigos Chapter

APRICOT LIQUEUR

Yield:
32 servings
Utensil:
jar

Approx Per Serving:
Cal 259
T Fat <1 g
0% Calories from Fat
Prot 1 g
Carbo 34 g
Fiber 2 g
Chol 0 mg
Sod 7 mg

1¹/₂ pounds dried apricots
1¹/₂ pounds rock candy
¹/₂ gallon vodka

Combine apricots, candy and vodka in 1-gallon jar; mix well. Cover tightly. Let stand in cool dark place for 60 days. Drain liquid into small decanters. Cheap vodka works well in this recipe.

Nutritional information includes apricots.

Marian Babcock, John I. Sabin Chapter

APRICOT CORDIAL

Yield:
13 servings
Utensil:
jar

Approx Per
Serving:
Cal 344
T Fat <1 g
1% Calories
from Fat
Prot 1 g
Carbo 58 g
Fiber 2 g
Chol 0 mg
Sod 6 mg

1 cup sugar
2½ cups Reisling

¾ cup brandy
12 ounces dried apricots

Combine sugar, wine and brandy in wide-mouth 1½-quart jar. Add apricots. Cover tightly. Let stand for 2 days to 3 months. Drain, reserving apricots and cordial. Serve cordial at room temperature or over ice. Serve apricots as dessert topping.

Barbara Taubitz, John I. Sabin Chapter

CRANBERRY-CANTALOUPE SHAKE

Yield:
4 servings
Utensil:
blender

Approx Per
Serving:
Cal 111
T Fat 1 g
6% Calories
from Fat
Prot 4 g
Carbo 24 g
Fiber 1 g
Chol 2 mg
Sod 47 mg

3 cups chopped
  cantaloupe, chilled
¼ cup frozen cranberry
  juice concentrate

½ cup skim milk
½ cup vanilla low-fat
  yogurt

Combine cantaloupe, cranberry juice concentrate, milk and yogurt in blender container; process for 30 seconds. Serve in tall glasses. Garnish with sprinkle of nutmeg and cantaloupe chunks.

Lucille Derett, Sierra Pacific Chapter

KAHLUA

Yield:
24 servings
Utensil:
jar

**Approx Per
Serving:**
Cal 138
T Fat <1 g
*0% Calories
from Fat*
Prot <1 g
Carbo 28 g
Fiber <1 g
Chol 0 mg
Sod 2 mg

2 cups water
2 cups sugar
¼ cup instant coffee
  granules

½ cup water
1 fifth of brandy
½ vanilla bean

Boil 2 cups water and sugar in saucepan for 5 minutes. Stir in coffee dissolved in ½ cup water. Cool to room temperature. Add brandy and vanilla bean. Pour into jar; cover tightly. Let stand for 6 days or longer. Do not use freeze-dried coffee in this recipe.

Marian Babcock, John I. Sabin Chapter

BANANA PUNCH

Yield:
60 servings
Utensil:
punch bowl

**Approx Per
Serving:**
Cal 91
T Fat <1 g
*1% Calories
from Fat*
Prot <1 g
Carbo 23 g
Fiber <1 g
Chol 0 mg
Sod 8 mg

2 cups sugar
1 46-ounce can
  unsweetened
  pineapple juice
5 bananas, mashed

2 12-ounce cans frozen
  orange juice
  concentrate, thawed
4 1-liter bottles of 7-Up

Combine sugar, pineapple juice, bananas and orange juice concentrate in bowl; mix well. Spoon into 4 freezer containers. Freeze until firm. Combine each container of mix with 1 liter of 7-Up in punch bowl at serving time; mix until slushy.

Bess Birdsall, Mission Chapter

CHAMPAGNE PUNCH

Yield:
16 servings
Utensil:
punch bowl

Approx Per
Serving:
Cal 144
T Fat <1 g
0% Calories
from Fat
Prot 1 g
Carbo 16 g
Fiber <1 g
Chol 0 mg
Sod 8 mg

2　6-ounce cans frozen
　orange juice
　concentrate, thawed
1　6-ounce can frozen
　lemonade concentrate,
　thawed

1¹/₂ quarts ice water
2 quarts champagne,
　chilled

Mix orange juice concentrate and lemonade concentrate with water in punch bowl. Add champagne; mix gently. Garnish with orange slices. May add 1 pint of orange sherbet if desired.

Dorothy Hamata, Mission Chapter

PARTY PUNCH

Yield:
24 servings
Utensil:
glasses

Approx Per
Serving:
Cal 155
T Fat <1 g
0% Calories
from Fat
Prot <1 g
Carbo 29 g
Fiber <1 g
Chol 0 mg
Sod 10 mg

1　12-ounce can frozen
　orange juice
　concentrate, thawed
1　12-ounce can frozen
　lemonade concentrate,
　thawed

4　12-ounce cans water
2 cups vodka
1 cup diluted tea
1 cup sugar
2　1-liter bottles of 7-Up

Combine orange juice concentrate, lemonade concentrate, water, vodka, tea and sugar in bowl; mix well. Pour into freezer container. Freeze until slushy. Place 2 scoops frozen mixture into each glass. Fill glass with 7-Up.

Shirley J. Haller, John I. Sabin Chapter

HOLIDAY SLUSH PUNCH

Yield:
18 servings
Utensil:
glasses

Approx Per Serving:
Cal 132
T Fat <1 g
0% Calories from Fat
Prot <1 g
Carbo 25 g
Fiber <1 g
Chol 0 mg
Sod 13 mg

3½ cups water
½ cup sugar
½ cup water
2 tea bags
1   6-ounce can frozen
   lemonade concentrate,
   thawed

1   6-ounce can frozen
   orange juice
   concentrate, thawed
1¼ cups dry gin
2 liters 7-Up

Bring 3½ cups water and sugar to a boil in saucepan. Cook until sugar is dissolved, stirring frequently. Cool to room temperature. Bring ½ cup water to a boil in saucepan. Add tea bags. Steep until cool. Combine sugar syrup, tea, lemonade concentrate, orange juice concentrate and gin in large plastic container. Freeze for 24 hours. Place 3 or 4 heaping spoonfuls of slush in each glass. Fill glasses with 7-Up.

Barbara Von Dohlen, John I. Sabin Chapter

HOT SPICED TEA

Yield:
70 servings
Utensil:
jar

Approx Per Serving:
Cal 40
T Fat 0 g
0% Calories from Fat
Prot 0 g
Carbo 10 g
Fiber 0 g
Chol 0 mg
Sod 3 mg

2 cups instant orange
   breakfast drink mix
1 cup instant tea
1   3-ounce envelope
   lemonade mix

2½ cups sugar
1 teaspoon ground cloves
1 teaspoon cinnamon

Combine orange breakfast drink mix, instant tea, lemonade mix, sugar, cloves and cinnamon in jar; mix well. Place 1 tablespoon spiced tea mix in cup for each serving. Fill with boiling water.

Velda Wheeler, John I. Sabin Chapter

HOT SPICED WINE

Yield:	
50 servings	
Utensil:	
saucepan	

2 cups sugar
2 teaspoons cinnamon
2 teaspoons ground
  cloves
1 teaspoon allspice
¼ teaspoon nutmeg
50 cups wine

*Approx Per
Serving:
Cal 189
T Fat 0 g
0% Calories
from Fat
Prot <1 g
Carbo 9 g
Fiber 0 g
Chol 0 mg
Sod 10 mg*

Combine sugar, cinnamon, cloves, allspice and nutmeg in jar; seal tightly. Combine 2 teaspoons mix with ½ cup water for each serving in saucepan. Bring to a boil. Add 1 cup wine for each serving. Heat to serving temperature; do not boil. Ladle into cups.

Marian Babcock, John I. Sabin, Chapter

THANK GOD FOR DIRTY DISHES

Thank God for dirty dishes.

They have a tale to tell.

While others are going hungry

We're eating very well.

With home and health and happiness

I shouldn't want to fuss,

For by this stack of evidence,

God's very good to us.

Brenda McCoy, John I. Sabin Chapter

Soups

BLACK BEAN SOUP

Yield:
8 servings
Utensil:
stockpot

Approx Per Serving:
Cal 268
T Fat 1 g
4% Calories from Fat
Prot 17 g
Carbo 50 g
Fiber 18 g
Chol 0 mg
Sod 348 mg

1 pound dried black beans
2 quarts water
1½ cups chopped onions
1½ cups chopped celery
1 large green bell pepper, chopped
1½ cups chopped carrots
1 tablespoon minced garlic
¼ cup water
1   15-ounce can tomato sauce
8 cups water
1 bay leaf
Salt and pepper to taste
1 teaspoon thyme
3 tablespoons cumin
1½ teaspoons oregano
¼ teaspoon cayenne pepper
½ to 1 tablespoon liquid smoke
¼ cup fresh lime juice

Soak beans in 2 quarts water in saucepan overnight; drain. Combine next 6 ingredients in nonstick stockpot sprayed with nonstick cooking spray. Cook until vegetables are tender. Add beans, tomato sauce and next 9 ingredients. Bring to a boil; reduce heat. Simmer over medium heat for 2 to 2½ hours or until beans are tender. Remove bay leaf. Ladle into soup bowls. Serve with lime juice.

Nutritional information does not include liquid smoke.

Joan De Bernardi, John I. Sabin Chapter

SPANISH BASQUE GARBANZO BEAN SOUP

Yield:
8 servings
Utensil:
stockpot

Approx Per Serving:
Cal 359
T Fat 17 g
41% Calories from Fat
Prot 17 g
Carbo 37 g
Fiber 11 g
Chol 10 mg
Sod 696 mg

1 pound dried garbanzo beans
1 teaspoon baking soda
8 cups cold water
1 onion, chopped
Chopped garlic, salt and pepper to taste
8 ounces pepperoni, sliced
1 teaspoon olive oil

Soak beans with baking soda in water to cover in saucepan overnight; drain. Combine beans with 8 cups cold water in large stockpot. Bring to a boil. Add onion, garlic, salt and pepper. Simmer for 1 hour. Add pepperoni and olive oil. Simmer for 3 hours longer or until beans are tender, stirring occasionally and adding additional water if needed for desired consistency. May cook in slow cooker for 6 hours if preferred.

Hallie Latasa, Mission Chapter

Portuguese Bean Soup

Yield:
8 servings
Utensil:
saucepan

Approx Per Serving:
Cal 316
T Fat 10 g
28% Calories from Fat
Prot 16 g
Carbo 42 g
Fiber 13 g
Chol 27 mg
Sod 1134 mg

2 ham hocks
1 12-ounce linguica or Portuguese sausage, chopped
3 medium potatoes, chopped
2 medium onions, chopped
3 stalks celery with leaves, chopped
2 medium green bell peppers, chopped
1 medium bunch parsley, chopped
2 15-ounce cans kidney beans, drained, rinsed
1 teaspoon oregano
1 teaspoon cumin
1 teaspoon hot pepper sauce
1 bay leaf
1 teaspoon salt
1 teaspoon pepper

Sauté ham hocks and linguica in large saucepan over medium heat for 4 minutes. Add remaining ingredients and water to cover. Bring to a boil. Skim surface and reduce heat. Simmer for 2 hours. Remove ham hocks. Cut meat from bones and discard bones. Return meat to soup. Cook until heated through. Discard bay leaf. Ladle into soup bowls.

Brenda Silva, George S. Ladd Chapter

Broccoli Soup

Yield:
6 servings
Utensil:
saucepan

Approx Per Serving:
Cal 193
T Fat 17 g
75% Calories from Fat
Prot 6 g
Carbo 7 g
Fiber 2 g
Chol 47 mg
Sod 536 mg

1/4 cup chopped onion
1 tablespoon margarine
8 ounces cream cheese, chopped
1 cup milk
1 chicken bouillon cube
3/4 cup boiling water
12 ounces fresh broccoli, cooked, drained
1/2 teaspoon lemon juice
1/2 teaspoon salt
Pepper to taste

Sauté onion in margarine in saucepan. Stir in cream cheese and milk. Cook until cream cheese melts, stirring constantly. Add bouillon dissolved in boiling water. Stir in broccoli, lemon juice, salt and pepper. Cook until heated through. Garnish servings with toasted slivered almonds. May substitute one 10-ounce package cooked and drained spinach for broccoli.

Ruth Flores, Sierra Pacific Chapter

Chili Soup

Yield:
8 servings
Utensil:
saucepan

1 28-ounce can
  tomatoes, chopped
2 16-ounce cans red
  beans
Chili powder to taste

Salt to taste
4 cups water
1½ pounds ground beef
1 small onion, chopped

Approx Per
Serving:
Cal 289
T Fat 13 g
39% Calories
from Fat
Prot 23 g
Carbo 22 g
Fiber 10 g
Chol 56 mg
Sod 604 mg

Combine tomatoes, red beans, chili powder, salt and water in large saucepan. Brown ground beef with onion in skillet, stirring frequently; drain. Add to soup. Cook until heated through.

Carol Holmes, John I. Sabin Chapter

Mohave Chili

Yield:
24 servings
Utensil:
slow cooker

1 16-ounce can pinto
  beans with onions
1 16-ounce can kidney
  beans
1 16-ounce can
  ranch-style beans
1 16-ounce can
  tomatoes, chopped
1 16-ounce can tomato
  sauce
2 envelopes chili mix
2 green bell peppers,
  chopped

3 onions, chopped
1 tablespoon oil
3 pounds lean ground
  beef
1½ pounds bulk
  sausage with sage
2 pounds sweet Italian
  sausage, sliced
2 tablespoons hot
  pepper sauce
Cayenne pepper to taste
1 cup water

Approx Per
Serving:
Cal 303
T Fat 19 g
56% Calories
from Fat
Prot 20 g
Carbo 13 g
Fiber 2 g
Chol 62 mg
Sod 784 mg

Combine beans, tomatoes, tomato sauce and chili mix in 12-quart slow cooker. Sauté green peppers and onions in oil in skillet until light brown. Add to soup. Brown ground beef, bulk sausage and sliced sausage in skillet, stirring frequently; drain. Add to soup. Stir in pepper sauce, cayenne pepper and water. Cook on Low for 12 hours.

Ed Wheatly, Los Amigos Chapter

CHILI

Yield:
8 servings
Utensil:
skillet

Approx Per
Serving:
Cal 501
T Fat 21 g
37% Calories
from Fat
Prot 36 g
Carbo 43 g
Fiber 16 g
Chol 83 mg
Sod 1140 mg

2 pounds ground beef
1 large onion, finely
  chopped
1/2 small green bell
  pepper, finely chopped
Salt and pepper to taste
2 tablespoons chili
  powder
1 28-ounce can tomatoes
2 or 3 16-ounce cans
  small red beans
1 8-ounce can beer
1 small onion, thinly
  sliced
1 small green bell
  pepper, thinly sliced
Onion powder and
  cumin to taste
1 teaspoon cayenne
  pepper
1 tablespoon sugar
1 16-ounce can chili
  con carne

Brown ground beef with chopped onion and chopped green pepper in large skillet, stirring frequently; drain. Season with salt and pepper. Add chili powder, tomatoes, beans and half the beer. Simmer for 30 minutes. Add sliced onion, sliced green pepper, onion powder, cumin, cayenne pepper, sugar, chili and remaining beer. Simmer for 1 hour longer, adding hot water if necessary for desired consistency.

Lorraine Fuqua, Los Amigos Chapter

CREAMY CLAM CHOWDER

Yield:
8 servings
Utensil:
saucepan

Approx Per
Serving:
Cal 451
T Fat 36 g
66% Calories
from Fat
Prot 12 g
Carbo 31 g
Fiber 2 g
Chol 131 mg
Sod 639 mg

2 or 3 6-ounce cans
  minced clams
2 cups finely chopped
  potatoes
1 cup finely chopped
  celery
1 cup finely chopped
  onion
3/4 cup flour
3/4 cup melted butter
1 quart half and half
1/2 teaspoon sugar
1 1/2 teaspoons salt
1/4 teaspoon pepper

Drain clams, reserving liquid. Combine reserved liquid with potatoes, celery and onion in saucepan. Add enough water to just cover. Cook for 10 minutes or until tender. Blend flour into melted butter in large saucepan. Stir in half and half. Cook until thickened, stirring constantly. Add clams and undrained vegetables. Cook until heated through. Season with sugar, salt and pepper.

Dyane Jordan, John I. Sabin Chapter

Soups

CLAM CHOWDER

Yield:
8 servings
Utensil:
saucepan

*Approx Per
Serving:*
Cal 348
T Fat 17 g
41% Calories
from Fat
Prot 14 g
Carbo 42 g
Fiber 3 g
Chol 71 mg
Sod 750 mg

4 medium potatoes,
chopped
1 stalk celery, chopped
4 slices bacon, chopped
1 medium onion,
chopped
1/4 cup butter
6 tablespoons flour
3 cups milk

1 12-ounce can
evaporated milk
2 6-ounce cans minced
clams
Thyme to taste
1/2 teaspoon garlic
powder
2 teaspoons salt
1/2 teaspoon pepper

Cook potatoes and celery in water to cover in medium saucepan until tender. Fry bacon until crisp in large saucepan. Remove bacon. Sauté onion in bacon drippings in saucepan. Stir in butter and flour. Add milk. Cook until thickened, stirring constantly. Add evaporated milk. Cook just until heated through; do not boil. Add potatoes with cooking liquid, undrained clams, bacon, thyme, garlic powder, salt and pepper. Cook just until heated through.

Marge Frawner, John I. Sabin Chapter

NEW ENGLAND CLAM CHOWDER

Yield:
6 servings
Utensil:
saucepan

*Approx Per
Serving:*
Cal 475
T Fat 40 g
70% Calories
from Fat
Prot 10 g
Carbo 28 g
Fiber 2 g
Chol 160 mg
Sod 182 mg

4 ounces salt pork,
chopped
1 cup finely chopped
onion
3 cups cold water
4 cups 1/4-inch potato
cubes

2 6-ounce cans minced
clams
2 cups cream
1/8 teaspoon thyme
Salt and pepper to taste
2 tablespoons butter,
softened

Render salt pork in 2-quart saucepan over high heat; reduce heat. Add onion. Sauté until light brown. Add water and potatoes. Cook just until potatoes are tender. Add undrained clams, cream and thyme. Heat just to the simmering point. Season with salt and pepper. Top each serving with 1 teaspoon butter; garnish with paprika.

Shelly Brown, George S. Ladd Chapter

CLAM AND CORN CHOWDER

Yield:
4 servings
Utensil:
saucepan

Approx Per
Serving:
Cal 221
T Fat 11 g
37% Calories
from Fat
Prot 10 g
Carbo 31 g
Fiber 3 g
Chol 47 mg
Sod 471 mg

1 small yellow onion, chopped
2 tablespoons butter
1 6-ounce can minced clams

1 17-ounce can cream-style corn
17 ounces Equal milk
1 teaspoon dillweed
Salt and pepper to taste

Sauté onion in butter in saucepan until tender but not brown. Add clams, corn, milk, dillweed, salt and pepper. Bring to a simmer. Simmer for 5 minutes.

Aundrea DeCou, Los Amigos Chapter

CORN CHOWDER

Yield:
6 servings
Utensil:
saucepan

Approx Per
Serving:
Cal 225
T Fat 1 g
5% Calories
from Fat
Prot 6 g
Carbo 55 g
Fiber 6 g
Chol 0 mg
Sod 834 mg

2 16-ounce cans whole kernel corn
2 16-ounce cans cream-style corn
2 16-ounce cans water

2 carrots, finely chopped
2 stalks celery, finely chopped
1 onion, finely chopped
Salt and pepper to taste

Combine corn, water, carrots, celery, onion, salt and pepper in large saucepan; mix well. Simmer until vegetables are tender.

Velda Wheeler, John I. Sabin Chapter

MOM'S CORN AND POTATO CHOWDER

Yield:
4 servings
Utensil:
saucepan

*Approx Per
Serving:*
Cal 435
T Fat 20 g
*39% Calories
from Fat*
Prot 12 g
Carbo 57 g
Fiber 7 g
Chol 27 mg
Sod 1712 mg

1 bay leaf
1/2 teaspoon basil
1/4 cup margarine
1/2 cup minced onion
1/3 cup chopped celery
2 cups chopped potatoes
2 cups boiling water
2 cups cream-style corn

1 1/2 cups milk
1 cup chopped tomatoes
1/2 cup shredded
　Cheddar cheese
2 teaspoons salt
1/8 teaspoon pepper
1 tablespoon minced
　parsley

Tie bay leaf and basil in cheesecloth bag. Combine with margarine, onion, celery, potatoes and water in saucepan. Cook until potatoes are tender. Remove seasoning bag. Add corn, milk, tomatoes, cheese, salt and pepper. Cook just until cheese melts. Sprinkle servings with parsley. Serve with toasted muffins.

Evelyn Mess, John I. Sabin Chapter

OVEN FISH CHOWDER

Yield:
8 servings
Utensil:
Dutch oven

*Approx Per
Serving:*
Cal 356
T Fat 15 g
*44% Calories
from Fat*
Prot 30 g
Carbo 26 g
Fiber 1 g
Chol 100 mg
Sod 676 mg

2 pounds cod or halibut
　filets
1　7-ounce package au
　gratin potatoes
4 cups water
1/2 cup white wine
1 clove of garlic,
　chopped

3 onions, thinly sliced
1 bay leaf
4 whole cloves
1/4 teaspoon thyme
1/4 teaspoon pepper
1/4 cup butter
2 cups half and half

Place fish in Dutch oven. Add potatoes with seasonings, water, wine, garlic, onions, bay leaf, cloves, thyme, pepper and butter. Bake at 350 degrees for 1 1/2 hours. Stir in half and half. Simmer on stove top just until heated through. Discard bay leaf. May add peas or mixed vegetables if desired. May substitute lowfat milk for half and half.

Diane Combs, Silver State Chapter

FRENCH ONION SOUP GRATINÉ

Yield:
4 servings
Utensil:
saucepan

Approx Per Serving:
Cal 399
T Fat 21 g
51% Calories from Fat
Prot 19 g
Carbo 28 g
Fiber 3 g
Chol 34 mg
Sod 1031 mg

3 onions, sliced
3 tablespoons margarine
2¹/₄ cups water
¹/₂ cup white wine
2   10-ounce cans beef broth
Thyme and Italian seasoning to taste
Salt and pepper to taste
4 slices French bread, toasted
1 cup shredded Swiss cheese
¹/₂ cup grated Parmesan cheese

Sauté onions in margarine in saucepan over medium heat until transparent. Add water, wine and broth. Bring to a boil. Stir in thyme, Italian seasoning, salt and pepper. Simmer, covered, for 15 minutes. Ladle into 4 ovenproof bowls. Place 1 slice toasted bread on each serving; sprinkle with cheeses. Place on baking sheet. Broil until cheese is melted and brown.

Diane Bolz, George S. Ladd Chpater

FRENCH ONION SOUP

Yield:
4 servings
Utensil:
casserole

Approx Per Serving:
Cal 409
T Fat 22 g
47% Calories from Fat
Prot 19 g
Carbo 31 g
Fiber 3 g
Chol 46 mg
Sod 1810 mg

4 red onions, thinly sliced
1 tablespoon olive oil
2 tablespoons butter
1 teaspoon sugar
1 teaspoon salt
1 teaspoon cayenne pepper
1 quart chicken stock
4 slices French bread, toasted
1 cup shredded Monterey Jack cheese
¹/₄ cup grated Parmesan cheese

Sauté onions in olive oil and butter in saucepan until tender. Stir in sugar, salt and cayenne pepper. Spoon into casserole. Stir in chicken stock. Place toasted bread on top of soup; sprinkle with Monterey Jack cheese. Bake at 350 degrees for 20 minutes. Sprinkle with Parmesan cheese.

Charlotte Bocage, Los Amigos Chapter

HAMBURGER STEW

<table>
<tr><td>

Yield:
6 servings
Utensil:
saucepan

</td></tr>
</table>

1 pound ground beef
4 onions, chopped
2   8-ounce cans tomato
   sauce
1   8-ounce bottle of
   catsup
1 catsup bottle of water
2 to 4 carrots, chopped
6 potatoes, chopped
1 head cabbage, chopped
Chili powder, salt and
   pepper to taste

<table>
<tr><td>

*Approx Per
Serving:*
Cal 504
T Fat 12 g
20% Calories
   from Fat
Prot 23 g
Carbo 81 g
Fiber 11 g
Chol 49 mg
Sod 937 mg

</td></tr>
</table>

Brown ground beef with onions in saucepan, stirring frequently; drain. Stir in tomato sauce, catsup, water and carrots. Simmer for 20 minutes. Add potatoes and cabbage. Simmer until vegetables are tender. Add chili powder, salt and pepper. Simmer for 10 minutes.

Marilyn Ferrucci, George S. Ladd Chapter

BAKED MINESTRONE

<table>
<tr><td>

Yield:
8 servings
Utensil:
saucepan

</td></tr>
</table>

1 1/2 pounds lean stew beef
1 cup coarsely chopped
   onion
2 cloves of garlic, crushed
1 teaspoon salt
1/4 teaspoon pepper
2 tablespoons olive oil
3   10-ounce cans
   condensed beef broth
1 1/2 teaspoons mixed
   herbs
2 soup cans water
1   16-ounce can tomatoes
1   16-ounce can kidney
   beans
1   6-ounce can pitted
   olives
1 1/2 cups thinly sliced
   carrots
1 cup small uncooked
   shell macaroni
2 cups sliced zucchini

<table>
<tr><td>

*Approx Per
Serving:*
Cal 286
T Fat 14 g
42% Calories
   from Fat
Prot 23 g
Carbo 21 g
Fiber 7 g
Chol 48 mg
Sod 1095 mg

</td></tr>
</table>

Combine first 5 ingredients in Dutch oven. Add olive oil, stirring to coat well. Bake at 400 degrees for 30 minutes or until beef is brown, stirring occasionally. Reduce oven temperature to 350 degrees. Add broth, herbs and water; mix well. Bake, covered, for 1 hour or until beef is tender. Stir in tomatoes, undrained beans and olives, carrots and macaroni. Top with zucchini. Bake, covered, for 30 to 40 minutes or until carrots are tender. Serve with grated Parmesan cheese.

Kelli Thompson, John I. Sabin Chapter

MINESTRONE

Yield:
12 servings
Utensil:
saucepan

Approx Per Serving:
Cal 98
T Fat 3 g
28% Calories from Fat
Prot 3 g
Carbo 16 g
Fiber 3 g
Chol <1 mg
Sod 139 mg

2 large onions, chopped
4 medium carrots, sliced
2 cups shredded cabbage
2 cloves of garlic, minced
3 tablespoons margarine
1   16-ounce can tomatoes
2 cups chopped spinach
1/4 cup instant beef bouillon
2 small potatoes, chopped
3 quarts water
2 small zucchini, chopped
1/4 cup uncooked elbow macaroni
1/4 cup broken uncooked spaghetti
12 uncooked rigatoni
1/2 teaspoon each pepper, basil, thyme and oregano

Sauté onions, carrots, cabbage and garlic in margarine in large saucepan for 20 minutes or until tender. Add remaining ingredients; mix well. Bring to a boil; reduce heat. Simmer until vegetables and pasta are tender. Garnish servings with Parmesan cheese. Serve with French bread.

Shirley J. Haller, John I. Sabin Chapter

MUSHROOM SOUP

Yield:
4 servings
Utensil:
saucepan

Approx Per Serving:
Cal 227
T Fat 15 g
58% Calories from Fat
Prot 11 g
Carbo 13 g
Fiber 3 g
Chol 224 mg
Sod 956 mg

1 medium onion, minced
1 clove of garlic, cut into halves
1 tablespoon butter
1 tablespoon olive oil
1 pound mushroom caps, sliced
3 tablespoons tomato paste
3 cups chicken stock
2 tablespoons sweet vermouth
1/2 teaspoon salt
Pepper to taste
4 egg yolks
2 tablespoons finely chopped parsley
2 1/2 tablespoons grated Parmesan cheese

Sauté onion and garlic in butter and olive oil in heavy 3-quart saucepan until garlic is brown. Discard garlic. Add mushrooms. Sauté for 5 minutes. Stir in tomato paste, chicken stock, wine, salt and pepper. Simmer for 10 minutes. Beat egg yolks, parsley and cheese in bowl. Add to soup gradually, stirring constantly. Serve immediately. Serve with toasted French bread.

Laurie Bostdorff, Sierra Pacific Chapter

BASQUE OXTAIL SOUP

Yield:
8 servings
Utensil:
stockpot

Approx Per Serving:
Cal 103
T Fat <1 g
3% Calories from Fat
Prot 3 g
Carbo 24 g
Fiber 5 g
Chol 0 mg
Sod 40 mg

1 pound oxtails
8 cups water
2 cloves of garlic, chopped
1 onion, chopped
5 or 6 carrots, chopped
2 stalks celery, chopped
1 small head cabbage, sliced
2 or 3 tomatoes, sliced
2 potatoes, sliced
1 teaspoon parsley flakes
Salt and pepper to taste

Rinse oxtails. Bring to a boil in water in large stockpot; skim surface. Add garlic, onion, carrots, celery, cabbage, tomatoes, potatoes, parsley flakes, salt and pepper. Simmer for 3 to 4 hours or until meat falls from bones, adding additional water as needed and stirring occasionally. May cook in slow cooker for 6 hours if preferred.

Nutritional information does not include oxtails.

Hallie Latasa, Mission Chapter

QUICK AND EASY OYSTER SOUP

Yield:
4 servings
Utensil:
saucepan

Approx Per Serving:
Cal 340
T Fat 46 g
87% Calories from Fat
Prot 6 g
Carbo 9 g
Fiber 1 g
Chol 148 mg
Sod 829 mg

¼ cup chopped green onions
½ cup butter
24 fresh oysters
1 10-ounce can cream of mushroom soup
1 soup can milk
Salt and pepper to taste

Sauté green onions in butter in saucepan for 5 minutes. Add oysters. Cook just until oysters curl at edges. Stir in mushroom soup and milk. Heat just to the simmering point. Season with salt and pepper to taste. May use skim milk if preferred.

Leona Hillman, Los Amigos Chapter

SOPA DE MAIZ

Yield:
4 servings
Utensil:
saucepan

Approx Per Serving:
Cal 489
T Fat 28 g
49% Calories from Fat
Prot 30 g
Carbo 34 g
Fiber 6 g
Chol 110 mg
Sod 580 mg

3½ cups fresh corn kernels
1 cup chicken broth
¼ cup butter
2 cups milk
1 clove of garlic, chopped
1 teaspoon oregano

Salt and pepper to taste
1 or 2 tablespoons chopped green chilies
1 chicken breast, cooked, chopped
1 cup chopped tomatoes
1 cup shredded Monterey Jack cheese

Process corn and chicken broth in blender until smooth. Combine with butter in saucepan. Simmer for 5 minutes. Add milk, garlic, oregano, salt and pepper. Bring to a boil; reduce heat. Stir in green chilies. Simmer for 5 minutes. Sprinkle chicken, tomatoes and cheese into 4 soup bowls. Ladle soup into bowls. Garnish with parsley and fried tortilla squares.

Helen H. Maple, John I. Sabin Chapter

OLD-FASHIONED CREAM OF TOMATO SOUP

Yield:
6 servings
Utensil:
saucepan

Approx Per Serving:
Cal 360
T Fat 34 g
82% Calories from Fat
Prot 4 g
Carbo 13 g
Fiber 2 g
Chol 119 mg
Sod 454 mg

1 32-ounce can tomatoes, chopped
1 cup chicken broth
1 tablespoon chopped onion

2 tablespoons butter
2 tablespoons sugar
⅛ teaspoon baking soda
2 cups cream

Combine tomatoes, chicken broth, onion, butter, sugar and baking soda in medium saucepan. Simmer for 1 hour. Heat cream in double boiler. Add to soup. Serve immediately.

Elinor M. Wardell, John I. Sabin Chapter

Hearty Vegetable Chowder

Yield:
6 servings
Utensil:
saucepan

Approx Per Serving:
Cal 270
T Fat 10 g
32% Calories from Fat
Prot 11 g
Carbo 37 g
Fiber 3 g
Chol 29 mg
Sod 913 mg

4 ounces bacon, coarsely chopped
1 cup diagonally sliced celery
1 cup chopped potato
1 cup thinly sliced carrot
1 cup cut green beans
1 16-ounce can whole kernel corn, drained
1/2 cup thinly sliced onion
2 cups boiling water
1/2 teaspoon garlic powder
1 1/2 teaspoons salt
2 cups evaporated milk
2 tablespoons flour
1/4 cup water

Fry bacon in 3 to 4-quart saucepan until crisp; remove with slotted spoon. Add celery, potato, carrot, beans, corn, onion, 2 cups boiling water, garlic powder and salt to drippings in saucepan; mix well. Bring to a boil; reduce heat. Simmer, covered, for 20 minutes or until vegetables are tender. Stir in evaporated milk. Add mixture of flour and 1/4 cup water; mix well. Simmer for 5 minutes or until thickened, stirring constantly. Stir in bacon.

Ruth Flores, Sierra Pacific Chapter

Vidalia Onion Soup

Yield:
6 servings
Utensil:
saucepan

Approx Per Serving:
Cal 339
T Fat 18 g
48% Calories from Fat
Prot 15 g
Carbo 21 g
Fiber 2 g
Chol 49 mg
Sod 1179 mg

4 large Vidalia onions, thinly sliced
1/4 cup butter
2 10-ounce cans beef broth
1 1/4 tablespoons Worcestershire sauce
1 cup white Zinfandel
1 teaspoon garlic salt
4 slices French bread, toasted
1 cup grated Parmesan cheese
4 slices Swiss cheese

Sauté onions in butter in 5-quart saucepan over low heat for 15 minutes. Add broth, Worcestershire sauce, wine and garlic salt. Simmer for 45 minutes. Place toasted French bread in 6 ovenproof bowls. Ladle soup over bread; top with cheeses. Place on baking sheet. Bake at 375 degrees for 10 minutes or until cheeses melt.

John Sobol, Sierra Pacific Chapter

Salads

Cinnamon Apple Salad

Yield:
8 servings
Utensil:
saucepan

2 cups water
½ cup red cinnamon
  candies
¼ cup sugar
4 apples, peeled, cut
  into halves, cored

Simmer water, cinnamon candies and sugar in saucepan until candies dissolve. Add apples. Simmer just until tender. Remove apples from syrup and cool. Serve on lettuce leaves.

Katherine Chadwick, Los Amigos Chapter

Approx Per
Serving:
Cal 122
T Fat <1 g
1% Calories
from Fat
Prot <1 g
Carbo 31 g
Fiber 1 g
Chol 0 mg
Sod 3 mg

Apricot Salad

Yield:
15 servings
Utensil:
dish

1   29-ounce can apricots
1   29-ounce can crushed
    pineapple
1   6-ounce package
    orange gelatin
2 cups boiling water
1 cup miniature
  marshmallows

Drain apricots and pineapple, reserving 1 cup mixed juices. Dissolve gelatin in boiling water in bowl. Stir in reserved juice. Chill until partially set. Stir in apricots, pineapple and marshmallows. Spoon into 9x13-inch dish. Chill until set. Garnish with walnuts.

Angle Jagara, Los Amigos Chapter

Approx Per
Serving:
Cal 127
T Fat <1 g
1% Calories
from Fat
Prot 2 g
Carbo 32 g
Fiber 1 g
Chol 0 mg
Sod 43 mg

APRICOT-PINEAPPLE SALAD

Yield:
15 servings
Utensil:
dish

Approx Per Serving:
Cal 244
T Fat 6 g
21% Calories from Fat
Prot 3 g
Carbo 48 g
Fiber 1 g
Chol 18 mg
Sod 68 mg

1 29-ounce can apricots
1 29-ounce can crushed
   pineapple
2 3-ounce packages
   orange gelatin
2 cups boiling water
2 cups miniature
   marshmallows
¹/₂ cup sugar
2 tablespoons flour
2 tablespoons butter
1 egg
8 ounces whipped
   topping

Drain apricots and pineapple, reserving 2 cups mixed juices. Chop or mash apricots. Dissolve gelatin in boiling water in bowl. Stir in 1 cup reserved juices. Chill until syrupy. Stir in apricots, pineapple and marshmallows. Spoon into 9x13-inch dish. Chill until firm. Combine remaining 1 cup reserved juice, sugar, flour, butter and egg in saucepan. Cook until thickened, stirring constantly. Chill in refrigerator. Fold in whipped topping. Spread over congealed layer. Chill for 1 hour or longer. May top with shredded cheese if desired.

Evelyn Mess, John I. Sabin Chapter

CRANBERRY SALAD

Yield:
15 servings
Utensil:
dish

Approx Per Serving:
Cal 362
T Fat 17 g
41% Calories from Fat
Prot 3 g
Carbo 53 g
Fiber 2 g
Chol 44 mg
Sod 56 mg

1 29-ounce can crushed
   pineapple
3 cups ground
   cranberries
1¹/₂ cups sugar
1 cup coarsely chopped
   pecans
2 cups miniature
   marshmallows
1 6-ounce package
   raspberry gelatin
2 cups whipping cream,
   whipped

Drain pineapple, reserving juice. Combine cranberries, sugar, pineapple, pecans and marshmallows in bowl; mix well. Add enough water to reserved pineapple juice to measure 2 cups. Bring to a boil in saucepan. Stir in gelatin until dissolved. Chill until partially set. Add cranberry mixture; mix gently. Fold in whipped cream. Spoon into 9x13-inch dish. Chill until set. May substitute two 16-ounce cans whole cranberry sauce for ground cranberries if preferred.

Bess Birdsall, Mission Chapter

FROZEN CRANBERRY SALAD

Yield:
8 servings
Utensil:
muffin pan

*Approx Per
Serving:*
Cal 321
T Fat 20 g
*53% Calories
from Fat*
Prot 4 g
Carbo 35 g
Fiber 2 g
Chol 33 mg
Sod 123 mg

8 ounces cream cheese,
  softened
2 tablespoons sugar
2 tablespoons
  mayonnaise
1/2 cup chopped walnuts

1 16-ounce can whole
  cranberry sauce
1 8-ounce can crushed
  pineapple
1 cup whipped topping

Beat cream cheese with sugar and mayonnaise in mixer bowl until smooth. Add walnuts, cranberry sauce and pineapple; mix well. Fold in whipped topping. Spoon into paper-lined muffin cups. Freeze until firm. Let stand at room temperature for 10 to 15 minutes before serving. May freeze in 5x9-inch pan if preferred.

Sheryl Cramer, John I. Sabin Chapter

CRANBERRY SAUCE GELATIN

Yield:
8 servings
Utensil:
mold

*Approx Per
Serving:*
Cal 226
T Fat 6 g
*23% Calories
from Fat*
Prot 3 g
Carbo 42 g
Fiber 1 g
Chol 13 mg
Sod 99 mg

1 6-ounce package
  flavored gelatin
2 cups boiling water
1 teaspoon lemon juice

1 16-ounce can whole
  cranberry sauce
1 cup sour cream

Dissolve gelatin in boiling water in bowl. Stir in lemon juice. Chill until syrupy. Stir cranberry sauce in bowl. Add to gelatin; mix well. Stir in sour cream. Pour into mold. Chill overnight. Unmold onto serving plate.

Arliss Summers, Mission Chapter

HOLIDAY FRUIT SALAD

Yield:
12 servings
Utensil:
dish

Approx Per Serving:
Cal 306
T Fat 16 g
45% Calories from Fat
Prot 2 g
Carbo 41 g
Fiber 1 g
Chol 90 mg
Sod 44 mg

1 20-ounce can
  pineapple chunks
2 eggs, beaten
3 tablespoons cornstarch
2/3 cup sugar
Salt to taste
Juice of 1 lemon

1 4-ounce jar
  maraschino cherries,
  drained, chopped
8 ounces miniature
  marshmallows
2 cups whipping cream,
  whipped

Drain pineapple, reserving juice. Combine reserved juice with eggs, cornstarch, sugar and salt in saucepan; mix well. Cook over medium heat until thickened, stirring constantly. Stir in lemon juice. Let stand until cool. Fold in cherries, pineapple, marshmallows and whipped cream. Spoon into serving dish. Chill overnight.

Joy Williams, John I. Sabin Chapter

LEMON-GRAPE NUTS SALAD

Yield:
15 servings
Utensil:
dish

Approx Per Serving:
Cal 151
T Fat 3 g
16% Calories from Fat
Prot 3 g
Carbo 31 g
Fiber 2 g
Chol 0 mg
Sod 142 mg

1 6-ounce package
  lemon gelatin
1 8-ounce can crushed
  pineapple

2 cups Grape Nuts
1/2 cup chopped raisins
1/2 cup chopped pecans

Prepare gelatin using package directions. Stir in pineapple, cereal, raisins and pecans. Spoon into 9x13-inch dish. Chill until set. Serve with salad dressing. May also serve with whipped cream as dessert.

Dorothy Hunsicker, Mission Chapter

LEMON-LIME GELATIN SALAD

Yield:
15 servings
Utensil:
dish

Approx Per Serving:
Cal 215
T Fat 10 g
42% Calories from Fat
Prot 6 g
Carbo 26 g
Fiber 1 g
Chol 13 mg
Sod 181 mg

1 3-ounce package lemon gelatin
1 3-ounce package lime gelatin
2 cups boiling water
1 cup cold water
2 cups cottage cheese
1 cup sour cream
3 tablespoons mayonnaise
1 20-ounce can crushed pineapple
1/2 to 3/4 cup chopped walnuts
2 cups miniature marshmallows

Dissolve gelatins in boiling water in bowl. Stir in cold water. Cool to room temperature. Combine cottage cheese, sour cream and mayonnaise in bowl; mix well. Add undrained pineapple, walnuts and gelatin; mix well. Sprinkle marshmallows into dish. Spoon gelatin mixture over marshmallows. Chill until set.

Marlene Chargois, Los Amigos Chapter

PINEAPPLE AND CHEESE SALAD

Yield:
15 servings
Utensil:
dish

Approx Per Serving:
Cal 244
T Fat 11 g
37% Calories from Fat
Prot 4 g
Carbo 35 g
Fiber 1 g
Chol 66 mg
Sod 105 mg

1 1/2 cups shredded Cheddar cheese
1 16-ounce package miniature marshmallows
1 29-ounce can crushed pineapple, well drained
3 tablespoons egg yolks
3 tablespoons sugar
3 tablespoons cider vinegar
1 cup whipping cream, whipped

Combine cheese, marshmallows and pineapple in bowl; mix well. Combine egg yolks, sugar and vinegar in small saucepan; mix well. Cook over medium heat until thickened, stirring constantly. Cool to room temperature. Fold into whipped cream in bowl. Fold in pineapple mixture. Spoon into 9x13-inch dish. Chill for 2 hours to overnight.

Toni Earl, Silver State Chapter

PINEAPPLE DAIQUIRI SALAD

Yield:
8 servings
Utensil:
mold

Approx Per
Serving:
Cal 119
T Fat <1 g
1% Calories
from Fat
Prot 2 g
Carbo 21 g
Fiber 1 g
Chol 0 mg
Sod 2 mg

1 15-ounce can crushed
   pineapple
2 envelopes unflavored
   gelatin
1/2 cup light rum

1 6-ounce can frozen
   limeade concentrate,
   thawed
8 to 10 ice cubes

Drain pineapple, reserving juice. Add enough water to reserved juice to measure 1 cup. Combine 1/2 cup reserved juice and gelatin in blender container. Process for 30 seconds. Let stand for 1 minute. Bring remaining 1/2 cup juice to a boil in saucepan. Add to gelatin mixture. Process for 30 seconds or until gelatin dissolves. Add rum, limeade concentrate and ice cubes. Process until smooth. Stir in pineapple. Spoon into oiled 4-cup mold. Chill until firm. Unmold onto serving plate.

Marian Babcock, John I. Sabin Chapter

SEVEN-UP SALAD

Yield:
8 servings
Utensil:
dish

Approx Per
Serving:
Cal 258
T Fat 11 g
37% Calories
from Fat
Prot 3 g
Carbo 40 g
Fiber 1 g
Chol 12 mg
Sod 97 mg

1 20-ounce can pears
1 1/2 3-ounce packages
   lime gelatin
3 ounces cream cheese,
   chopped

1 cup 7-Up
8 ounces whipped
   topping

Drain pears, reserving 1 cup juice. Bring reserved juice to a boil in saucepan. Stir in gelatin until dissolved. Stir in cream cheese. Add 7-Up. Chill until set. Whip gelatin until smooth. Add pears and whipped topping. Spoon into dish. Chill until firm. May mash pears if preferred.

Mary Atkinson-McKinney, Los Amigos Chapter

STRAWBERRY GELATIN

Yield:
9 servings
Utensil:
dish

Approx Per Serving:
Cal 194
T Fat 5 g
24% Calories from Fat
Prot 3 g
Carbo 36 g
Fiber 2 g
Chol 11 mg
Sod 82 mg

1 6-ounce package strawberry gelatin
2 cups boiling water
1 10-ounce package frozen strawberries
1 16-ounce can applesauce
1 cup sour cream
1 cup miniature marshmallows

Dissolve gelatin in boiling water in bowl. Add strawberries and applesauce; mix well. Spoon into 8x8-inch dish. Chill until firm. Combine sour cream and marshmallows in bowl; mix well. Chill overnight, stirring occasionally. Spread over congealed layer.

Bonna Auffhammer, Sierra Pacific Chapter

STRAWBERRY MOLD

Yield:
8 servings
Utensil:
mold

Approx Per Serving:
Cal 182
T Fat 6 g
29% Calories from Fat
Prot 3 g
Carbo 31 g
Fiber 2 g
Chol 13 mg
Sod 84 mg

1 6-ounce package strawberry gelatin
1 cup boiling water
1 16-ounce package frozen sliced strawberries
1 8-ounce can crushed pineapple
1 cup sour cream, at room temperature

Dissolve gelatin in boiling water in bowl. Add strawberries and undrained pineapple, stirring rapidly to mix well. Spoon half the mixture into 4-cup mold. Spread with sour cream. Add remaining gelatin mixture. Chill until set.

Alice Milovich, Silver State Chapter

STRAWBERRY PRETZEL SALAD

Yield:
15 servings
Utensil:
dish

Approx Per Serving:
Cal 359
T Fat 18 g
43% Calories from Fat
Prot 5 g
Carbo 47 g
Fiber 2 g
Chol 50 mg
Sod 425 mg

2²/₃ cups coarsely chopped pretzels
³/₄ cup melted butter
12 ounces cream cheese, softened
1¹/₄ cups sugar
2 cups pineapple juice
1 6-ounce package strawberry gelatin
2 10-ounce packages frozen strawberries

Mix pretzels and butter in bowl. Press into 9x13-inch baking dish. Bake at 400 degrees until light brown. Cool to room temperature. Beat cream cheese and sugar in mixer bowl until light. Spread over crust. Chill for 1 hour. Bring pineapple juice to a boil in saucepan. Stir in gelatin until dissolved. Cool to room temperature. Spread strawberries over cream cheese layer. Spoon gelatin over strawberries. Chill overnight.

Martha Blissitt, John I. Sabin Chapter

WATERGATE FRUIT SALAD

Yield:
10 servings
Utensil:
bowl

Approx Per Serving:
Cal 215
T Fat 10 g
38% Calories from Fat
Prot 1 g
Carbo 33 g
Fiber 1 g
Chol 0 mg
Sod 88 mg

1 20-ounce can crushed pineapple
1 4-ounce package pistachio instant pudding mix
1 cup miniature marshmallows
¹/₂ cup chopped walnuts
8 ounces whipped topping

Mix pineapple and pudding mix in medium bowl; mix well. Add marshmallows and walnuts; mix well. Fold in whipped topping. Chill for 1 hour or longer.

Rusty Kamman, Mission Chapter

STIR-FRY FAJITA SALAD

Yield:
4 servings
Utensil:
wok

Approx Per Serving:
Cal 248
T Fat 12 g
43% Calories from Fat
Prot 24 g
Carbo 12 g
Fiber 4 g
Chol 64 mg
Sod 119 mg

1 pound flank steak
Fajita Marinade
1 tablespoon oil
1 medium red bell pepper, sliced
2 medium green chilies, seeded, chopped

³/₄ cup sliced green onions
2 cups chopped peeled tomatoes
3 cups torn leaf lettuce
3 cups torn romaine lettuce

Place steak in Fajita Marinade in shallow dish, turning to coat well. Marinate, covered, for 8 hours to overnight, turning steak occasionally; drain. Freeze steak partially. Slice diagonally cross grain into thin strips. Coat wok or skillet with nonstick cooking spray; add 1 tablespoon oil. Heat to 325 degrees for 2 minutes. Add bell pepper, green chilies and green onions. Stir-fry for 2 minutes. Remove with slotted spoon. Stir-fry steak ½ at a time in drippings in skillet for 3 to 5 minutes. Return stir-fried vegetables to wok; add tomatoes. Stir-fry for 1 minute. Arrange leaf lettuce and romaine lettuce on 4 serving plates. Spoon fajita mixture onto prepared plates. May remove wok or skillet from heat, add lettuce and stir for 1 minute to wilt lettuce if preferred.

Fajita Marinade

Nutritional information for entire amount of Fajita Marinade is included above.

2 tablespoons lime juice
1 tablespoon vinegar
1½ teaspoons oil
1 clove of garlic, sliced

1 tablespoon minced fresh cilantro
¹/₈ teaspoon salt
¹/₄ teaspoon pepper

Combine lime juice, vinegar, 1½ teaspoons oil, garlic, cilantro, salt and pepper in bowl; mix well.

Lynn Fox-Norris, Silver State Chapter

CHINESE CHICKEN AND ALMOND SALAD

Yield:
4 servings
Utensil:
dish

Approx Per Serving:
Cal 636
T Fat 46 g
63% Calories from Fat
Prot 28 g
Carbo 32 g
Fiber 5 g
Chol 54 mg
Sod 2508 mg

3 chicken breasts
Garlic salt, salt and pepper to taste
¹/₄ cup vinegar
¹/₄ cup sugar
1 teaspoon MSG
2 teaspoons salt
¹/₂ teaspoon pepper
1 head lettuce, shredded
Noodles of 1 package ramen noodles, crushed
4 green onions, chopped
¹/₂ cup slivered almonds
¹/₄ cup sesame seed, lightly toasted
¹/₂ cup oil

Rinse chicken well. Combine with water to cover and seasonings to taste in saucepan. Cook for 20 minutes or until tender. Drain and cool. Chop chicken, discarding skin and bone. Combine vinegar and next 4 ingredients in saucepan. Cook over low heat until sugar dissolves, stirring well. Cool completely. Combine chicken and next 5 ingredients in serving dish. Add oil to dressing in jar; shake to mix well. Pour over salad; toss to mix well.

Bonnie DiBenedetto, John I. Sabin Chapter

CHINESE CHICKEN SALAD

Yield:
6 servings
Utensil:
bowl

Approx Per Serving:
Cal 406
T Fat 27 g
59% Calories from Fat
Prot 30 g
Carbo 13 g
Fiber 2 g
Chol 72 mg
Sod 1493 mg

1 package mung bean threads (saifun)
Oil for deep frying
6 green onions
3 chicken breasts, cooked, shredded
1¹/₂ heads lettuce, finely shredded
¹/₄ cup sliced almonds, roasted
¹/₄ cup sesame seed, roasted
¹/₂ cup oil
¹/₂ cup cider vinegar
¹/₄ cup sugar
4 teaspoons salt
1 teaspoon pepper

Deep-fry bean threads a small amount at a time in hot oil using package directions; drain and break into pieces. Cut green onions into 1-inch pieces; slice into thin strips. Combine with chicken, lettuce, bean threads, almonds and sesame seed in serving bowl. Add mixture of remaining ingredients; toss gently to mix.

Nutritional information does not include mung bean threads or oil for deep frying.

Catherine M. Sadler, Sierra Pacific Chapter

CRUNCHY CHINESE CHICKEN SALAD

Yield:
4 servings
Utensil:
bowl

Approx Per
Serving:
Cal 351
T Fat 24 g
59% Calories
from Fat
Prot 15 g
Carbo 22 g
Fiber 2 g
Chol 32 mg
Sod 419 mg

1 tablespoon sesame oil
1/4 cup vegetable oil
3 tablespoons rice
   vinegar
2 teaspoons soy sauce
2 tablespoons sugar
1/2 teaspoon dry mustard
2 cups shredded lettuce

2 cups shredded Napa
   cabbage
1 cup chopped cooked
   chicken breast
2 green onions, sliced
1   3-ounce can chow
   mein noodles

Mix sesame oil, vegetable oil, vinegar, soy sauce, sugar and dry mustard in small bowl. Combine lettuce, cabbage, chicken and green onions in serving bowl; mix well. Add dressing and noodles; toss to mix well.

Mary Biondi, Mission Chapter

SPECIAL CHINESE CHICKEN SALAD

Yield:
6 servings
Utensil:
bowl

Approx Per
Serving:
Cal 213
T Fat 12 g
51% Calories
from Fat
Prot 18 g
Carbo 8 g
Fiber 1 g
Chol 48 mg
Sod 225 mg

9 won ton wrappers
Oil for deep frying
1/2 package mung bean
   threads
1/4 cup white or rice
   vinegar
3 tablespoons sugar
1/4 teaspoon MSG
Salt and pepper to taste

4 chicken breasts,
   cooked, shredded
1 large head lettuce, torn
1/2 bunch green onions,
   thinly sliced
   diagonally
1/4 cup vegetable oil
1 teaspoon sesame oil

Deep-fry won ton wrappers in hot oil until crisp; drain. Cut bean threads into small sections. Deep-fry a few at a time until crisp; drain. Combine vinegar, sugar, MSG, salt and pepper in small saucepan. Heat until sugar dissolves. Cool to room temperature. Combine chicken, lettuce and green onions in serving bowl. Add vegetable oil and sesame oil to dressing; mix well. Pour dressing over salad. Add won ton wrappers and bean threads; toss lightly. May add roasted sesame seed if desired.

Nutritional information does not include oil for deep frying.

Joanne Rossi, John I. Sabin Chapter

MEXICAN SALAD

Yield:
4 servings
Utensil:
dish

Approx Per Serving:
Cal 777
T Fat 47 g
54% Calories from Fat
Prot 35 g
Carbo 56 g
Fiber 6 g
Chol 135 mg
Sod 1271 mg

1 pound ground beef
1 small onion, chopped
1/4 cup chopped green bell pepper
2 8-ounce cans tomato sauce
1/2 cup water
Hot pepper sauce to taste
1 teaspoon chili powder
1 cup shredded Cheddar cheese
1/4 cup butter
1/2 cup water
4 cups corn chips
2 cups cooked rice
3 cups chopped lettuce
2 tomatoes, chopped

Combine ground beef, onion, green pepper, tomato sauce, 1/2 cup water, pepper sauce and chili powder in saucepan. Simmer for 30 minutes. Melt cheese and butter with 1/2 cup water in double boiler over low heat. Layer corn chips, rice, ground beef mixture, lettuce and tomatoes in 9x13-inch dish. Pour cheese mixture over layers. Serve at once.

Lucille Turner, Los Amigos Chapter

TACO SALAD

Yield:
12 servings
Utensil:
bowl

Approx Per Serving:
Cal 338
T Fat 22 g
57% Calories from Fat
Prot 14 g
Carbo 23 g
Fiber 6 g
Chol 35 mg
Sod 573 mg

1 pound lean ground beef
1 head lettuce, chopped
3 tomatoes, chopped
5 green onions, chopped
1 avocado, chopped
4 ounces longhorn cheese, shredded
1 8-ounce jar green taco sauce
1/2 8-ounce bottle of Catalina salad dressing
1 16-ounce can kidney beans, drained, rinsed
1 8-ounce package tortilla chips, crushed

Brown ground beef in skillet, stirring until crumbly; drain. Combine lettuce, tomatoes, green onions and avocado in large bowl; mix well. Add cheese, taco sauce and salad dressing; toss to mix well. Add ground beef and beans; toss lightly. Top with chips.

Dorothy Hunsicker, Mission Chapter

EASY TACO SALAD

Yield:
8 servings
Utensil:
bowl

**Approx Per
Serving:**
Cal 602
T Fat 42 g
*61% Calories
from Fat*
Prot 22 g
Carbo 39 g
Fiber 3 g
Chol 71 mg
Sod 1054 mg

1 pound ground beef
1 cup mild taco sauce
1 head lettuce, torn
1 or 2 tomatoes, chopped
1 small green bell
 pepper, chopped
8 ounces American
 cheese, shredded

½ cup olives
1 8-ounce bottle of
 Thousand Island salad
 dressing
1 14-ounce package
 taco-flavored tortilla
 chips, crushed

Brown ground beef in skillet, stirring until crumbly; drain. Stir in taco sauce. Cook until heated through. Combine lettuce, tomatoes, green pepper, cheese, olives and salad dressing in bowl; mix well. Spoon ground beef mixture over salad; top with chips.

Carol Holmes, John I. Sabin Chapter

CRAB SALAD MOLD

Yield:
4 servings
Utensil:
mold

**Approx Per
Serving:**
Cal 719
T Fat 69 g
*86% Calories
from Fat*
Prot 16 g
Carbo 10 g
Fiber 1 g
Chol 133 mg
Sod 1224 mg

1 envelope unflavored
 gelatin
1 tablespoon cold water
1 10-ounce can cream
 of mushroom soup
8 ounces cream cheese,
 softened
1 cup mayonnaise

1 cup chopped celery
3 green onion bulbs,
 chopped
1 6-ounce can crab meat
Worcestershire sauce to
 taste
Salt to taste

Soften gelatin in cold water in saucepan. Add soup; mix well. Cook until gelatin dissolves. Cool for 10 minutes. Add cream cheese, mayonnaise, celery, green onions, crab meat, Worcestershire sauce and salt; mix well. Spoon into mold. Chill overnight. Unmold onto serving plate. May freeze in individual molds if preferred.

Velda Wheeler, John I. Sabin Chapter

FAR EASTERN TUNA SALAD

Yield:
8 servings
Utensil:
bowl

Approx Per Serving:
Cal 323
T Fat 24 g
64% Calories from Fat
Prot 13 g
Carbo 17 g
Fiber 4 g
Chol 27 mg
Sod 411 mg

1 7-ounce can tuna, drained
1 10-ounce package frozen peas, thawed
1 cup thinly sliced celery
3/4 cup sliced green onions
1 5-ounce can sliced water chestnuts, drained
3/4 cup mayonnaise
1 teaspoon lemon juice
1 teaspoon soy sauce
1/4 teaspoon garlic powder
1/4 teaspoon curry powder
1 3-ounce can chow mein noodles
1/2 cup slivered almonds

Combine tuna, peas, celery, green onions and water chestnuts in serving bowl; mix well. Mix mayonnaise, lemon juice, soy sauce, garlic powder and curry powder in small bowl. Add to salad; mix well. Add almonds and noodles; toss lightly. May cook peas if preferred.

Henrietta Lange, Mission Chapter

ANTIPASTO SALAD

Yield:
6 servings
Utensil:
bowl

Approx Per Serving:
Cal 408
T Fat 35 g
70% Calories from Fat
Prot 4 g
Carbo 30 g
Fiber 9 g
Chol 0 mg
Sod 2367 mg

2 8-ounce jars marinated artichoke hearts
1 red onion, sliced
1 green bell pepper, thinly sliced
1 6-ounce can pitted black olives, drained
1 6-ounce jar green olives, drained
1/2 cup olive oil
1/4 cup wine vinegar
1/2 cup sugar
1 tablespoon salt
1/2 teaspoon pepper
2 cups cherry tomatoes
8 ounces fresh mushrooms, sliced

Combine artichokes and marinade with onion, green pepper and olives in bowl; mix well. Add olive oil, vinegar, sugar, salt and pepper. Marinate in refrigerator overnight. Add tomatoes and mushrooms at serving time.

Sharleen Johnson, George S. Ladd Chapter

FOUR-BEAN SALAD

Yield:
10 servings
Utensil:
bowl

Approx Per
Serving:
Cal 170
T Fat 1 g
4% Calories
from Fat
Prot 6 g
Carbo 38 g
Fiber 5 g
Chol 0 mg
Sod 710 mg

1 15-ounce can garbanzo beans
1 15-ounce can kidney beans
1 15-ounce can green beans
1 15-ounce can wax beans
2 stalks celery, chopped
1 red onion, chopped
1 2-ounce can chopped pimento, drained
¾ cup vinegar
¾ cup sugar
1 teaspoon salt
¼ teaspoon pepper

Drain beans. Combine with celery, onion and pimento in large bowl. Combine vinegar, sugar, salt and pepper in small saucepan. Cook until mixture steams. Pour over salad; mix well. Chill for several hours to 2 weeks.

Ruth Keirn, John I. Sabin Chapter

KIDNEY BEAN SALAD

Yield:
6 servings
Utensil:
bowl

Approx Per
Serving:
Cal 530
T Fat 36 g
60% Calories
from Fat
Prot 18 g
Carbo 37 g
Fiber 16 g
Chol 235 mg
Sod 1139 mg

3 15-ounce cans kidney beans, drained
6 hard-boiled eggs, chopped
½ cup chopped celery
3 tablespoons sweet pickle relish
2 tablespoons prepared mustard
1 cup mayonnaise

Combine beans and eggs in serving bowl. Add celery, relish, mustard and mayonnaise; mix well. Chill until serving time.

Debra Plummer, Silver State Chapter

RED CABBAGE SALAD

Yield:
8 servings
Utensil:
bowl

Approx Per
Serving:
Cal 141
T Fat 14 g
84% Calories
from Fat
Prot 1 g
Carbo 5 g
Fiber 1 g
Chol 0 mg
Sod 7 mg

1 medium head red cabbage, shredded
1 medium onion, chopped
1/4 cup red wine vinegar
1/2 cup extra-virgin olive oil
1 tablespoon sugar
2 tablespoons tarragon

Combine cabbage, onion, vinegar, olive oil, sugar and tarragon in serving bowl; mix well. Chill overnight.

Gina Chapman, Los Amigos Chapter

CABBAGE CRUNCH

Yield:
15 servings
Utensil:
bowl

Approx Per
Serving:
Cal 256
T Fat 22 g
74% Calories
from Fat
Prot 4 g
Carbo 14 g
Fiber 2 g
Chol 0 mg
Sod 173 mg

1/4 cup sesame seed
1 cup slivered almonds
2 packages ramen noodles
1/4 cup sugar
1 cup oil
6 tablespoons red wine vinegar
1 teaspoon pepper
1 head cabbage, shredded
4 green onions, chopped

Sprinkle sesame seed and almonds in shallow pan. Bake at 350 degrees for 20 minutes, stirring every 5 minutes. Combine seasoning packets from noodles, sugar, oil, vinegar and pepper in small bowl; mix well. Store in refrigerator. Combine cabbage and green onions in bowl; mix well. Chill for several hours to overnight. Crush ramen noodles. Add to salad with sesame seed, almonds and dressing; toss to mix well. May add chopped cooked turkey or chicken if desired.

Iris Chandler, Silver State Chapter

Freezer Slaw

<table>
<tr><td>

Yield:
8 servings
Utensil:
freezer containers

</td></tr>
</table>

1 medium head cabbage, shredded
1 teaspoon salt
1 cup vinegar
¼ cup water
2 cups sugar
1 teaspoon celery seed
1 teaspoon mustard seed
1 medium carrot, grated
1 medium green bell pepper, finely chopped

<table>
<tr><td>

Approx Per Serving:
Cal 213
T Fat <1 g
1% Calories from Fat
Prot 1 g
Carbo 55 g
Fiber 1 g
Chol 0 mg
Sod 278 mg

</td></tr>
</table>

Mix cabbage and salt in large bowl. Let stand for 1 hour. Combine vinegar, water, sugar, celery seed and mustard seed in small saucepan. Bring to a boil. Cook for 1 minute, stirring to mix well. Cool to lukewarm. Press moisture from cabbage mixture. Add carrot and green pepper; mix well. Add dressing; mix well. Spoon into freezer containers, leaving ½-inch head space. Freeze until needed.

Beverly Weaver, Los Amigos Chapter

Party Coleslaw

<table>
<tr><td>

Yield:
16 servings
Utensil:
bowl

</td></tr>
</table>

1 head cabbage
⅓ head purple cabbage
4 carrots
4 stalks celery
1 20-ounce can crushed pineapple
1 15-ounce package raisins
2 large apples, chopped
2 8-ounce bottles of coleslaw dressing

<table>
<tr><td>

Approx Per Serving:
Cal 248
T Fat 10 g
33% Calories from Fat
Prot 2 g
Carbo 43 g
Fiber 4 g
Chol 7 mg
Sod 224 mg

</td></tr>
</table>

Shred cabbages, carrots and celery. Combine with pineapple, raisins and apples in bowl. Add coleslaw dressing; mix well. Chill until serving time. May add walnuts, almonds, pecans, sunflower seed, pepitos, marshmallows or grapes if desired.

Beatrice Riley, Los Amigos chapter

SWEET AND SOUR CARROTS

Yield:
16 servings
Utensil:
bowl

Approx Per
Serving:
Cal 219
T Fat 14 g
53% Calories
from Fat
Prot 1 g
Carbo 25 g
Fiber 3 g
Chol 0 mg
Sod 28 mg

2 or 3 pounds carrots,
  sliced
1   6-ounce can tomato
  paste
1 large green bell
  pepper, chopped
1 large onion, chopped
1 cup sugar
1 cup oil
³/₄ cup vinegar
1 teaspoon dry mustard
Pepper to taste

Cook carrots in water to cover for 5 minutes or until tender-crisp; drain. Combine tomato paste, green pepper, onion, sugar, oil, vinegar, dry mustard and pepper in bowl; mix well. Add hot carrots; mix well. Chill, covered, overnight. May substitute tomato sauce or tomato soup for tomato paste.

Shirley J. Haller, John I. Sabin Chapter

LOUISIANA-STYLE POTATO SALAD

Yield:
12 servings
Utensil:
bowl

Approx Per
Serving:
Cal 207
T Fat 18 g
79% Calories
from Fat
Prot 5 g
Carbo 6 g
Fiber 1 g
Chol 153 mg
Sod 200 mg

8 medium potatoes
1 to 2 tablespoons
  garlic-flavored wine
  vinegar
¹/₂ red bell pepper,
  chopped
1 celery heart, chopped
2 bunches green onions,
  thinly sliced
¹/₄ cup finely chopped
  parsley
8 hard-boiled eggs,
  chopped
1 cup (or more)
  mayonnaise
¹/₄ teaspoon salt
¹/₄ teaspoon coarsely
  ground pepper

Cook potatoes in skins in water to cover in saucepan until tender. Peel and chop potatoes while hot. Combine with vinegar in bowl. Add green pepper, celery, green onions and parsley; mix well. Fold in eggs, mayonnaise, salt and pepper. Serve warm or chilled.

Cheryl A. Fua, Sierra Pacific Chapter

WALLA WALLA ONION POTATO SALAD

Yield:
12 servings
Utensil:
bowl

Approx Per Serving:
Cal 351
T Fat 23 g
57% Calories from Fat
Prot 3 g
Carbo 36 g
Fiber 4 g
Chol 16 mg
Sod 319 mg

3 pounds medium red potatoes
1 large Walla Walla onion
1 cup thinly sliced celery
1 large golden Delicious apple, chopped
12 pimento-stuffed green olives, sliced
1/3 cup chopped sweet pickle
1 1/2 cups mayonnaise
1 teaspoon Dijon mustard
2 tablespoons white vinegar
1 teaspoon steak sauce
Salt and pepper to taste

Cook potatoes in skins in 1 inch of boiling water in 4 to 5-quart saucepan for 25 to 30 minutes or until tender; drain and cool. Peel if desired and chop. Cut onion into quarters and slice thinly. Combine with potatoes, celery, apple, olives and pickle in bowl; mix well. Combine mayonnaise, mustard, vinegar and steak sauce in bowl; mix well. Add to potato mixture; mix gently. Season with salt and pepper. Chill, covered, for 2 hours to overnight. May substitute any mild red or white onion for Walla Walla onion or soy sauce for steak sauce.

Joanne Rossi, John I. Sabin Chapter

RICE SALAD

Yield:
8 servings
Utensil:
bowl

Approx Per Serving:
Cal 224
T Fat 13 g
51% Calories from Fat
Prot 4 g
Carbo 24 g
Fiber 4 g
Chol 5 mg
Sod 826 mg

1 7-ounce package chicken-flavored rice mix
6 green onions, chopped
1/4 green bell pepper, chopped
6 pimento-stuffed olives, chopped
2 9-ounce jars marinated artichoke hearts
1/3 cup mayonnaise

Cook rice using package directions and omitting butter. Cool to room temperature. Combine with green onions, green pepper and olives in bowl. Drain artichoke hearts, reserving marinade. Chop artichoke hearts. Add to salad; mix well. Whisk reserved marinade with mayonnaise in bowl. Add to salad; mix gently. Serve in lettuce-lined salad bowl. Garnish with radish roses.

Linda Grimm, John I. Sabin Chapter

THREE-BEAN RICE SALAD

Yield:
8 servings
Utensil:
bowl

Approx Per Serving:
Cal 181
T Fat 9 g
40% Calories from Fat
Prot 4 g
Carbo 26 g
Fiber 4 g
Chol 0 mg
Sod 722 mg

1 16-ounce can wax beans, drained
1 16-ounce can French-style green beans, drained
1 8-ounce can red kidney beans, drained
¼ cup thickly sliced onion
½ cup Italian salad dressing
½ teaspoon salt
⅛ teaspoon pepper
1½ cups water
½ teaspoon salt
1½ cups uncooked instant rice

Combine wax beans, green beans, kidney beans, onion, salad dressing, ½ teaspoon salt and pepper in large bowl; mix well. Let stand for several minutes. Bring water and ½ teaspoon salt to a boil in saucepan. Stir in rice. Remove from heat. Let stand, covered, for 5 minutes. Add to bean mixture; mix well. Chill, covered, until serving time. Serve on lettuce-lined plates.

Brenda McCoy, John I. Sabin Chapter

RUSSIAN SALAD

Yield:
10 servings
Utensil:
bowl

Approx Per Serving:
Cal 86
T Fat 7 g
74% Calories from Fat
Prot 2 g
Carbo 3 g
Fiber 1 g
Chol 64 mg
Sod 21 mg

5 green bell peppers, chopped
1 onion, chopped
3 hard-boiled eggs, sliced
¼ cup olive oil
Salt to taste

Combine green peppers, onion and eggs in serving bowl. Add olive oil; mix gently. Chill until serving time. Season to taste.

Margaret Cortez, Los Amigos Chapter

SAUERKRAUT SALAD

Yield:
4 servings
Utensil:
bowl

Approx Per Serving:
Cal 179
T Fat <1 g
2% Calories from Fat
Prot 1 g
Carbo 45 g
Fiber 3 g
Chol 0 mg
Sod 812 mg

1 11-ounce can sauerkraut
1 cup chopped celery
1 cup chopped green bell pepper
3 tablespoons chopped pimento

¼ cup chopped onion
¾ cup sugar
3 tablespoons vinegar
1 teaspoon celery seed
½ teaspoon salt
¼ teaspoon pepper

Drain sauerkraut for 15 minutes. Combine with celery, green pepper, pimento and onion in serving bowl. Add sugar, vinegar, celery seed, salt and pepper; mix well. Chill for 24 hours. May use 4 teaspoons sugar substitute in place of sugar.

Marie Lindborg, Los Amigos Chapter

SNOW SWEET PEA SALAD

Yield:
6 servings
Utensil:
bowl

Approx Per Serving:
Cal 140
T Fat 6 g
38% Calories from Fat
Prot 8 g
Carbo 15 g
Fiber 6 g
Chol 2 mg
Sod 111 mg

2 10-ounce packages frozen peas
½ cup crushed dry-roasted peanuts

1½ teaspoons onion flakes
2 tablespoons sour cream

Combine frozen peas with peanuts, onion flakes and sour cream in bowl; mix well. Let stand for 10 minutes for peas to thaw. Serve cold or at room temperature.

Marlene Chargois, Los Amigos Chapter

SPAGHETTI SALAD

> *Yield:*
> *6 servings*
> *Utensil:*
> *bowl*

> *Approx Per*
> *Serving:*
> *Cal 389*
> *T Fat 27 g*
> *55% Calories*
> *from Fat*
> *Prot 7 g*
> *Carbo 42 g*
> *Fiber 4 g*
> *Chol 0 mg*
> *Sod 668 mg*

1   10-ounce package vermicelli
3 stalks celery, finely chopped
2 cloves of garlic, minced
1 bunch green onions, finely chopped
1/2 cup sliced black olives
2 tablespoons chopped parsley
1   8-ounce bottle of Italian salad dressing
1/2 cup sweet pickle juice
1/2 teaspoon caraway seed
1 teaspoon poppy seed
1 teaspoon celery seed
1 teaspoon salt
Pepper to taste

Cook pasta using package directions; drain. Combine with celery, garlic, green onions, olives and parsley in serving bowl. Add salad dressing, pickle juice, caraway seed, poppy seed, celery seed, salt and pepper; mix well. Chill overnight, stirring several times.

Marian Babcock, John I. Sabin Chapter

SPINACH AND RICE SALAD

> *Yield:*
> *6 servings*
> *Utensil:*
> *bowl*

> *Approx Per*
> *Serving:*
> *Cal 218*
> *T Fat 12 g*
> *45% Calories*
> *from Fat*
> *Prot 4 g*
> *Carbo 30 g*
> *Fiber 1 g*
> *Chol 1 mg*
> *Sod 332 mg*

1 cup uncooked rice
1/2 cup Italian salad dressing
1 tablespoon soy sauce
1/2 teaspoon sugar
1/2 cup sliced celery
2 cups thinly sliced fresh spinach
1/2 cup sliced green onions
1/3 cup crumbled crisp-fried bacon

Cook rice using package directions. Cool slightly. Combine salad dressing, soy sauce and sugar in large bowl; mix well. Add warm rice. Chill, covered, in refrigerator. Add celery, spinach, green onions and bacon at serving time; mix gently.

Sue Austin, George S. Ladd Chapter

Tomato Salad

Yield: *6 servings* **Utensil:** *bowl*	

¼ cup oil
2 tablespoons vinegar
2 tablespoons prepared
  mustard
1 teaspoon sugar
Chopped parsley to taste

Garlic powder to taste
1 teaspoon salt
¼ teaspoon pepper
2 or 3 large tomatoes,
  sliced

**Approx Per
Serving:**
*Cal 100
T Fat 9 g
82% Calories
from Fat
Prot 1 g
Carbo 4 g
Fiber 1 g
Chol 0 mg
Sod 426 mg*

Combine oil, vinegar, mustard, sugar, parsley, garlic powder, salt and pepper in small bowl; mix well. Drizzle over tomatoes in serving dish.

Brenda McCoy, John I. Sabin Chapter

Twenty-Four Hour Salad

Yield:
8 servings
Utensil:
bowl

1 head lettuce, torn
1 cup sliced celery
8 ounces bacon, crisp-
  fried, crumbled
1 cup cauliflowerets
¼ cup sliced green
  onions

1 10-ounce package
   frozen green peas,
   thawed
Seasoned salt to taste
2 cups mayonnaise
1 cup shredded Cheddar
   cheese

**Approx Per
Serving:**
*Cal 537
T Fat 53 g
87% Calories
from Fat
Prot 9 g
Carbo 9 g
Fiber 3 g
Chol 55 mg
Sod 593 mg*

Layer lettuce, celery, bacon, cauliflower, green onions and peas in 2-quart salad bowl. Sprinkle with seasoned salt. Spread mayonnaise over layers, sealing to edge of bowl. Sprinkle with cheese. Chill for 24 hours or longer.

Tina Nemeth, Silver State Chapter

Vegetable Salad

Yield:
12 servings
Utensil:
bowl

Approx Per Serving:
Cal 179
T Fat 6 g
30% Calories from Fat
Prot 3 g
Carbo 30 g
Fiber 4 g
Chol 0 mg
Sod 522 mg

1 16-ounce can French-style green beans, drained
1 16-ounce can wax beans, drained
1 16-ounce cans peas, drained
1 small sweet onion, chopped
1 large bunch celery, chopped
1/3 cup chopped pimento
1 cup sugar
1 cup vinegar
1/3 cup oil
1 teaspoon salt
1 teaspoon vanilla extract

Combine green beans, wax beans, peas, onion, celery and pimento in salad bowl. Combine sugar, vinegar, oil, salt and vanilla in jar. Shake until sugar dissolves. Add to salad; mix gently. Chill overnight or up to 1 week.

Margaret F. Little, De Anza Chapter

Overnight Vegetable Salad

Yield:
16 servings
Utensil:
bowl

Approx Per Serving:
Cal 161
T Fat 7 g
38% Calories from Fat
Prot 3 g
Carbo 24 g
Fiber 3 g
Chol 0 mg
Sod 414 mg

2 16-ounce cans French-style green beans, drained
1 16-ounce can tiny peas, drained
1 16-ounce can Shoe Peg corn, drained
1 large green bell pepper, chopped
1 4-ounce jar chopped pimento, drained
1 cup finely chopped celery
1/3 red onion, chopped
3 green onions with tops, finely chopped
2 carrots, shredded
3/4 cup sugar
1/2 cup oil
3/4 cup cider vinegar
1 tablespoon water
1 teaspoon salt

Combine beans, peas, corn, green pepper, pimento, celery, red onion, green onions and carrots in large bowl; mix well. Combine sugar, oil, vinegar, water and salt in saucepan. Bring to a boil, stirring to dissolve sugar. Cool to room temperature. Add to salad; mix well. Chill overnight. Drain before serving.

Nutritional information includes entire amount of marinade.

Cathy A. Swanson, De Anza Chapter

PASTA AND VEGETABLE SALAD

Yield:
10 servings
Utensil:
bowl

Approx Per
Serving:
Cal 307
T Fat 20 g
58% Calories
from Fat
Prot 7 g
Carbo 26 g
Fiber 4 g
Chol 77 mg
Sod 321 mg

2 cups uncooked medium shell macaroni
1 cup uncooked small elbow macaroni
1 cup uncooked corkscrew macaroni
3 or 4 carrots, sliced
1 cup chopped broccoli
1 cup cauliflowerets
1 medium onion, chopped
2 or 3 stalks celery, chopped
1 or 2 large garlic dill pickles, chopped
3 or 4 green onions with tops, chopped
3 or 4 radishes, sliced
1 or 2 zucchini, sliced
1 cucumber, chopped
1 cup mayonnaise
3 hard-boiled eggs, sliced
6 to 8 cherry tomatoes, cut into halves

Cook pasta using package directions; rinse with cold water. Cook carrots in water to cover in saucepan for 3 minutes. Add broccoli and cauliflower. Cook for 2 minutes longer; drain. Combine next 7 ingredients, cooked vegetables and pasta in large serving bowl; mix well. Mix in mayonnaise. Top with sliced eggs and cherry tomatoes. Garnish with paprika and parsley flakes.

Pauline K. Carpenter, Silver State Chapter

RANCH SALAD DRESSING

Yield:
16 tablespoons
Utensil:
bowl

Approx Per
Tablespoon:
Cal 36
T Fat 4 g
89% Calories
from Fat
Prot <1 g
Carbo 1 g
Fiber <1 g
Chol 4 mg
Sod 27 mg

¼ cup mayonnaise
¼ cup buttermilk
¼ cup plain yogurt
¼ cup sour cream
1 teaspoon onion powder
¼ teaspoon garlic powder
1 teaspoon parsley flakes
Salt and pepper to taste

Combine mayonnaise, buttermilk, yogurt, sour cream, onion powder, garlic powder, parsley flakes, salt and pepper in small bowl; whisk to mix well. Chill for 1 hour. May use light mayonnaise, skim milk and light sour cream for a lighter salad dressing.

Ann Greenlee, John I. Sabin Chapter

Meats

BAKED BRISKET

Yield:
8 servings
Utensil:
roasting pan

Approx Per Serving:
Cal 321
T Fat 13 g
38% Calories from Fat
Prot 43 g
Carbo 5 g
Fiber 1 g
Chol 128 mg
Sod 638 mg

1 4-pound lean beef brisket, trimmed
1½ teaspoons salt
⅛ teaspoon pepper
⅛ teaspoon allspice
1 bay leaf, crushed
1 large carrot, thinly sliced
1 large onion, sliced into rings
1 cup diagonally sliced celery
1 envelope brown gravy mix

Rub brisket with salt, pepper and allspice. Place in roasting pan. Sprinkle with bay leaf. Arrange carrot, onion and celery around beef. Cover tightly with foil. Bake at 300 degrees for 3½ hours or until beef is very tender. Remove brisket to serving plate. Stir gravy mix into juices in roasting pan. Cook over low heat until thickened and bubbly, stirring constantly. Slice brisket cross grain. Serve with hot gravy.

Dorothy Jaramillo, De Anza Chapter

CORNED BEEF DINNER

Yield:
10 servings
Utensil:
saucepan

Approx Per Serving:
Cal 358
T Fat 11 g
27% Calories from Fat
Prot 37 g
Carbo 27 g
Fiber 5 g
Chol 102 mg
Sod 91 mg

1 4-pound corned beef brisket
4 stalks celery, coarsely chopped
6 onions, cut into quarters
4 carrots, cut into quarters
3 medium potatoes, cut into quarters
1 head cabbage, cut into quarters

Simmer brisket in water to cover in heavy saucepan for 3 hours. Remove brisket to serving platter; skim broth. Add celery, onions, carrots and potatoes to broth. Simmer for 15 minutes. Add cabbage. Simmer for 10 minutes. Slice brisket cross grain. Arrange vegetables around corned beef.

Lorraine Robinson, John I. Sabin Chapter

BARBECUED SHORT RIBS WITH RICE

Yield:
4 servings
Utensil:
baking dish

Approx Per Serving:
Cal 491
T Fat 26 g
49% Calories from Fat
Prot 28 g
Carbo 35 g
Fiber 1 g
Chol 104 mg
Sod 487 mg

2 pounds beef short ribs
Salt and pepper to taste
1/2 cup uncooked rice
1/2 cup chopped onion
4 teaspoons Worcestershire sauce
1/2 teaspoon Tabasco sauce
1/2 cup catsup
1/4 cup vinegar
1/4 cup water
4 teaspoons sugar
1 teaspoon dry mustard
1 teaspoon paprika
1/2 teaspoon pepper

Brown short ribs on all sides in saucepan. Season with salt and pepper to taste. Stir in rice. Sauté until rice is golden brown. Spoon into deep baking dish. Combine onion, Worcestershire sauce, Tabasco sauce, catsup, vinegar, water, sugar, dry mustard, paprika and 1/2 teaspoon pepper in bowl; mix well. Pour into baking dish. Bake, covered, at 325 degrees for 1 1/2 hours. May substitute round steak for short ribs and add sliced carrots.

Marian Babcock, John I. Sabin Chapter

CHEAP POT ROAST

Yield:
6 servings
Utensil:
baking pan

Approx Per Serving:
Cal 349
T Fat 17 g
44% Calories from Fat
Prot 43 g
Carbo 4 g
Fiber <1 g
Chol 128 mg
Sod 556 mg

1 3-pound blade-cut chuck or round roast
1 envelope onion soup mix
1 10-ounce can cream of mushroom soup

Tear 3-foot length of heavy-duty foil; fold double. Place roast on foil. Sprinkle with soup mix; spread with mushroom soup. Seal foil. Place in baking pan. Bake at 350 degrees for 3 hours.

Dorothy Hamata, Mission Chapter

BARBECUED BEEF

Yield:
10 servings
Utensil:
slow cooker

**Approx Per
Serving:**
*Cal 340
T Fat 14 g
38% Calories
from Fat
Prot 43 g
Carbo 8 g
Fiber <1 g
Chol 128 mg
Sod 440 mg*

1 **5-pound beef rump
roast**
1 **12-ounce can Coca-Cola**
1 **16-ounce bottle of
barbecue sauce**

Place roast fat side up in slow cooker. Add cola and half the barbecue sauce. Cook on Low for 8 hours or until beef shreds easily. Remove beef to plate; drain half the juices from cooker. Shred beef with fork; return to cooker. Stir in remaining barbecue sauce. Cook until heated through. Serve on buns.

Nutritional information includes the entire amount of roast juices.

Sherri Vultaggio, John I. Sabin Chapter

ROSEMARY RUMP ROAST

Yield:
8 servings
Utensil:
roasting pan

**Approx Per
Serving:**
*Cal 543
T Fat 40 g
68% Calories
from Fat
Prot 43 g
Carbo 0 g
Fiber 0 g
Chol 147 mg
Sod 69 mg*

1 **4-pound rump roast**
Salt and pepper to taste
Sprigs of fresh rosemary
**8 ounces suet, cut to
cover roast**

Sprinkle roast on all sides with salt and pepper. Sprinkle double layers of heavy-duty foil with rosemary; place roast on foil. Sprinkle sides and top of roast with remaining rosemary; arrange suet over top. Seal foil; place in roasting pan. Roast at 425 degrees for 30 minutes. Reduce oven temperature to 350 degrees. Bake for 45 minutes per pound or until roast is tender. May add 1 sliced clove of garlic if desired.

Nutritional information includes the entire amount of cooking suet.

Albert B. Woods, John I. Sabin Chapter

BARBECUED FLANK STEAK

Yield:
4 servings
Utensil:
grill

Approx Per Serving:
Cal 409
T Fat 28 g
61% Calories from Fat
Prot 33 g
Carbo 6 g
Fiber <1 g
Chol 96 mg
Sod 1475 mg

¹/₃ cup soy sauce
¹/₃ cup oil
3 tablespoons red wine vinegar
3 tablespoons chopped chutney
1 tablespoon instant minced onion
¹/₂ teaspoon garlic powder
1 ¹/₂-pound flank steak

Combine soy sauce, oil, vinegar, chutney, onion and garlic powder in large plastic bag; mix well. Add steak; seal bag. Marinate in refrigerator for 4 hours or longer; drain. Grill over hot coals for 5 minutes on each side. Slice cross grain ¹/₂ inch thick.

Claude Moss, De Anza Chapter

BEER BEEF

Yield:
10 servings
Utensil:
baking dish

Approx Per Serving:
Cal 321
T Fat 16 g
46% Calories from Fat
Prot 29 g
Carbo 13 g
Fiber 2 g
Chol 80 mg
Sod 326 mg

4 ounces salt pork, finely chopped, parboiled
1 tablespoon margarine
3 pounds round steak, cut into ¹/₂-inch cubes
¹/₄ cup margarine
6 medium onions, sliced
8 ounces mushrooms, thinly sliced
3 tablespoons flour
2 cups light beer
2 cups beef stock
1 teaspoon brown sugar
1 tablespoon vinegar
1 clove of garlic, minced
Salt and pepper to taste
1 leek, trimmed
3 sprigs of parsley
2 sprigs of fresh thyme
1 bay leaf

Brown pork in 1 tablespoon margarine in skillet; remove pork. Brown steak in drippings; remove to baking dish. Add ¹/₄ cup margarine and onions to drippings. Sauté until golden. Add mushrooms. Sauté for 2 minutes. Stir in flour. Cook until flour is brown. Stir in beer and stock gradually. Add brown sugar, vinegar, garlic and pork. Cook until thickened, stirring constantly. Add salt and pepper. Pour over beef. Tie remaining ingredients in cloth bag. Add to baking dish. Bake at 325 degrees for 1¹/₂ to 2 hours. Remove bag.

John A. Marcovecchio, George S. Ladd Chapter

GREEN PEPPER STEAK

Yield:
4 servings
Utensil:
skillet

Approx Per
Serving:
Cal 315
T Fat 20 g
58% Calories
from Fat
Prot 24 g
Carbo 10 g
Fiber 2 g
Chol 64 mg
Sod 1088 mg

1 pound round steak or chuck
1/4 cup soy sauce
2 cloves of garlic, chopped
1 1/2 teaspoons grated fresh ginger or 1/2 teaspoon dried ginger
1/4 cup oil

1 cup sliced green onions
1 cup 1-inch squares red or green bell pepper
2 stalks celery, sliced
1 tablespoon cornstarch
1 cup water
2 tomatoes, cut into wedges

Trim beef and pound until tender. Cut cross grain into 1/8-inch strips. Combine soy sauce, garlic and ginger in bowl. Add beef; toss to coat well. Stir-fry in oil in large skillet or wok over high heat until brown. Simmer, covered, for 30 to 40 minutes if necessary to tenderize beef. Increase heat. Add green onions, bell pepper and celery to skillet. Stir-fry for 10 minutes or until tender-crisp. Stir in mixture of cornstarch and water. Cook until thickened, stirring constantly. Add tomatoes. Cook just until heated through. Serve over rice.

Lorraine Davis, Los Amigos Chapter

BEEF STROGANOFF

Yield:
6 servings
Utensil:
skillet

Approx Per
Serving:
Cal 402
T Fat 22 g
52% Calories
from Fat
Prot 25 g
Carbo 22 g
Fiber 2 g
Chol 64 mg
Sod 381 mg

1 1/2 pounds round steak, cubed
1 cup flour
1/2 cup margarine
1/2 cup Burgundy

1   10-ounce can beef broth
2 or 3 carrots, sliced
1 onion, chopped

Coat steak with flour. Brown on all sides in margarine in large skillet. Add wine, broth, carrots and onion. Simmer for 30 minutes. Serve over rice.

Mary Buehler, John I. Sabin Chapter

Hot Tamale Loaf

Yield:
8 servings
Utensil:
baking dish

Approx Per Serving:
Cal 273
T Fat 9 g
31% Calories from Fat
Prot 24 g
Carbo 23 g
Fiber 3 g
Chol 64 mg
Sod 874 mg

2 pounds round steak
1 red pepper or 1/2 teaspoon cayenne pepper
2 small cloves of garlic, finely chopped
1 tablespoon shortening
3 or 4 tablespoons chili powder
1 tablespoon cumin seed, crushed
1 tablespoon salt
1 1/2 cups cornmeal
Salt to taste

Cook untrimmed steak in water to cover in saucepan for 30 minutes. Remove steak from cooking water. Grind steak. Return to cooking water with red pepper, garlic, shortening, chili powder, cumin seed and 1 tablespoon salt. Cook for 30 minutes, adding additional water if needed for desired consistency. Strain, reserving cooking liquid. Stir cornmeal and salt to taste into enough cold water to moisten. Add to reserved cooking liquid in saucepan. Cook until thickened. Alternate layers of cornmeal mixture and beef in baking pan until all ingredients are used. Bake, covered, at 300 degrees for 1 hour.

Ted Slack, John I. Sabin Chapter

Swiss Steak

Yield:
6 servings
Utensil:
glass dish

Approx Per Serving:
Cal 318
T Fat 13 g
36% Calories from Fat
Prot 29 g
Carbo 21 g
Fiber 1 g
Chol 95 mg
Sod 676 mg

2 tablespoons butter
2 tablespoons flour
1/4 teaspoon dry mustard
1 teaspoon salt
1/4 teaspoon pepper
1 1/2 to 2 pounds round steak
1 onion, sliced into rings
1/2 cup catsup
1/4 cup packed brown sugar

Microwave butter on High in 2-quart glass dish for 1 minute or until melted. Mix flour, dry mustard, salt and pepper in bowl. Cut steak into serving pieces. Coat well with flour mixture. Arrange in melted butter in dish. Microwave on High for 5 minutes. Turn steak over. Top with onion rings. Pour mixture of catsup and brown sugar over top. Microwave, covered, on Medium for 40 to 45 minutes or until fork tender, rearranging meat after 20 minutes. Let stand, covered, for 5 minutes.

Gladys Marchant and Esther Fuller, De Anza Chapter

MAKE-AHEAD BEEF FOR NOODLES

Yield:
4 servings
Utensil:
saucepan

2 cups beef chuck cubes
1 envelope onion soup
 mix

2 10-ounce cans cream
 of mushroom soup
¾ cup sherry

Combine beef, soup mix, soup and wine in saucepan; mix well. Simmer until tender. Serve over noodles. May substitute other wine for sherry.

Karolyn Tillisch Aznoe, John I. Sabin Chapter

Approx Per
Serving:
Cal 329
T Fat 16 g
45% Calories
from Fat
Prot 21 g
Carbo 12 g
Fiber <1 g
Chol 56 mg
Sod 1338 mg

SOUPAS

Yield:
8 servings
Utensil:
Dutch oven

2 teaspoons pickling
 spices
2 teaspoons cumin seed
1 teaspoon allspice
1 4-pound chuck roast
1½ small onions,
 chopped
3 cloves of garlic,
 chopped

1 8-ounce can tomato
 sauce
1 cup red wine
1 tablespoon salt
¼ teaspoon pepper
¼ teaspoon
 Worcestershire sauce
8 thick slices day-old
 French bread

Combine pickling spices, cumin seed and allspice in 2 tea balls or spice bags. Brown roast on all sides in large Dutch oven. Add onions, garlic, tomato sauce, wine, salt, pepper, spices and water to cover. Bake, covered, at 325 degrees for 4 hours. Stir in Worcestershire sauce. Remove spice bags. Shred or slice roast. Serve in bowls over bread slices; spoon cooking liquid over top.

Shelly Brown, George S. Ladd Chapter

Approx Per
Serving:
Cal 437
T Fat 14 g
30% Calories
from Fat
Prot 46 g
Carbo 22 g
Fiber 2 g
Chol 128 mg
Sod 1247 mg

FIVE-HOUR STEW

Yield: *8 servings* *Utensil:* *baking pan*	

Approx Per
Serving:
Cal 404
T Fat 9 g
20% Calories
from Fat
Prot 32 g
Carbo 47 g
Fiber 7 g
Chol 80 mg
Sod 1075 mg

1 28-ounce can tomatoes
2¹/2 pounds beef stew
   meat
4 potatoes, chopped
4 carrots, chopped
2 stalks celery, chopped
1 green bell pepper,
   chopped

1 onion, chopped
3 tablespoons tapioca
2 tablespoons sugar
1 tablespoon salt
¹/2 teaspoon pepper
¹/2 cup red wine
1 10-ounce package
   frozen peas

Drain tomatoes, reserving liquid. Combine beef, potatoes, carrots, celery, green pepper, onion and reserved tomato liquid in baking pan. Add tomatoes, tapioca, sugar, salt and pepper. Bake, covered, at 300 degrees for 4¹/2 hours. Add wine. Bake for 30 minutes longer. Stir in peas. May omit wine if preferred.

Ruth Seedborg, Los Amigos Chapter

MAKE AND FORGET BEEF STEW

Yield: *6 servings* *Utensil:* *baking pan*	

Approx Per
Serving:
Cal 448
T Fat 16 g
32% Calories
from Fat
Prot 53 g
Carbo 22 g
Fiber 5 g
Chol 149 mg
Sod 579 mg

3¹/2 pounds stew beef
1 onion, cut into quarters
4 carrots, cut into
   quarters
1 15-ounce can tomatoes

1 15-ounce can peas
¹/4 cup tapioca
¹/2 teaspoon celery salt
Salt and pepper to taste

Combine stew beef, onion, carrots, tomatoes, undrained peas, tapioca, celery salt, salt and pepper in heavy baking pan. Bake, covered, at 275 degrees for 10 to 12 hours.

Dorothy Hunsicker, Mission Chapter

WALDORF ASTORIA STEW

Yield:
6 servings
Utensil:
baking pan

Approx Per Serving:
Cal 368
T Fat 9 g
23% Calories from Fat
Prot 33 g
Carbo 38 g
Fiber 6 g
Chol 85 mg
Sod 237 mg

2 pounds beef, cut into 1-inch cubes
2 cups coarsely chopped potatoes
2 cups coarsely chopped carrots
2 cups coarsely chopped celery
1   15-ounce can whole tomatoes
4 medium onions, cut into quarters
1 slice bread, torn
3 tablespoons flour
1 teaspoon sugar
Salt and pepper to taste

Combine beef, potatoes, carrots, celery, undrained tomatoes, onions, bread, flour, sugar, salt and pepper in heavy baking pan. Bake, covered, at 250 degrees for 5 hours; do not remove cover during baking time.

Lorraine Irving, John I. Sabin Chapter

LIVER AND RICE CREOLE

Yield:
4 servings
Utensil:
baking dish

Approx Per Serving:
Cal 379
T Fat 12 g
29% Calories from Fat
Prot 22 g
Carbo 45 g
Fiber 2 g
Chol 307 mg
Sod 1147 mg

1 pound beef liver
1/2 cup flour
Salt and pepper to taste
2 tablespoons bacon drippings
1/2 cup uncooked brown rice
1 large onion, sliced
1 green bell pepper, chopped
Minced garlic to taste
1 teaspoon salt
1/2 teaspoon chili powder
1   10-ounce can tomato soup
1 cup hot water

Coat liver with mixture of flour and salt and pepper to taste. Brown on both sides in bacon drippings in skillet. Place in baking dish. Sprinkle with brown rice. Add onion, green pepper, garlic, 1 teaspoon salt, pepper to taste, chili powder, soup and water. Bake, covered, at 350 degrees for 1 1/2 hours. Bake, uncovered, for 30 minutes longer.

Carolyn Allen, Los Amigos Chapter

Burger Bundles

Yield:
6 servings
Utensil:
baking dish

Approx Per Serving:
Cal 404
T Fat 24 g
53% Calories from Fat
Prot 20 g
Carbo 27 g
Fiber 3 g
Chol 75 mg
Sod 1151 mg

1 package Stove Top dressing
1 pound lean ground beef
1/3 cup evaporated milk
1 10-ounce can cream of mushroom soup
1 tablespoon catsup
2 tablespoons Worcestershire sauce

Prepare dressing using package directions. Combine ground beef and evaporated milk in bowl; mix well. Shape into 6 patties. Arrange in foil-lined 9-inch baking pan. Shape dressing into balls; place on top of patties. Combine soup, catsup and Worcestershire sauce in bowl. Pour over burger bundles. Bake at 350 degrees for 45 minutes.

Henrietta Lange, Mission Chapter

Hamburgers with Sour Cream

Yield:
4 servings
Utensil:
skillet

Approx Per Serving:
Cal 547
T Fat 43 g
71% Calories from Fat
Prot 34 g
Carbo 6 g
Fiber <1 g
Chol 155 mg
Sod 185 mg

1 1/2 pounds ground sirloin
Salt and pepper to taste
1 tablespoon butter plus 1 teaspoon butter
1 tablespoon chopped shallots
2 tablespoons cognac
1 cup sour cream
1 tablespoon butter

Shape ground sirloin into 4 patties. Sprinkle with salt and pepper. Brown in 1 tablespoon butter in skillet for 3 minutes on each side; drain. Remove patties to warm platter; keep warm. Add 1 teaspoon butter to skillet. Add shallots. Sauté for 1 minute. Add cognac. Cook for 1 minute. Add sour cream and salt and pepper to taste. Cook until heated through. Strain into saucepan. Add remaining 1 tablespoon butter. Cook until heated through. Serve over patties.

Helen H. Maple, John I. Sabin

SUBSTITUTE CABBAGE ROLL

Yield:
5 servings
Utensil:
casserole

Approx Per
Serving:
Cal 246
T Fat 14 g
50% Calories
from Fat
Prot 19 g
Carbo 13 g
Fiber 2 g
Chol 59 mg
Sod 456 mg

1 pound ground beef
1 medium head cabbage, chopped
1 medium onion, chopped
1 10-ounce can cream of tomato soup

Brown ground beef in skillet, stirring until crumbly; drain. Layer 1/3 of the cabbage, 1/3 of the onion and half the ground beef in 3-quart casserole. Repeat layers. Top with remaining cabbage and onion. Pour soup over layers. Bake, covered, at 350 degrees for 1 hour. Serve with hot baked potatoes.

Bettie O. Johnson, John I. Sabin Chapter

CHINESE CASSEROLE

Yield:
8 servings
Utensil:
casserole

Approx Per
Serving:
Cal 351
T Fat 18 g
46% Calories
from Fat
Prot 17 g
Carbo 31 g
Fiber 2 g
Chol 43 mg
Sod 1096 mg

1 pound ground beef
2 medium onions, chopped
2 cups chopped celery
1/2 cup uncooked rice
1 10-ounce can cream of mushroom soup
1 10-ounce can cream of chicken soup
1 1/2 soup cans water
2 tablespoons soy sauce
1 6-ounce can Chinese noodles

Brown ground beef with onions in skillet, stirring frequently; drain. Add celery, rice, soups, water and soy sauce; mix well. Spoon into 9x13-inch casserole. Bake at 350 degrees for 1 hour. Top with noodles. Bake for 20 minutes longer.

Dorothy Hunsicker, Mission Chapter

BAKED CHOP SUEY

Yield:
6 servings
Utensil:
baking dish

Approx Per
Serving:
Cal 342
T Fat 17 g
45% Calories
from Fat
Prot 22 g
Carbo 26 g
Fiber 2 g
Chol 54 mg
Sod 2322 mg

1 pound lean ground beef
1 cup chopped celery
1 cup chopped onion
1 cup cooked rice
1 20-ounce can chop suey vegetables, drained
1 16-ounce can bean sprouts, drained
1 10-ounce can cream of mushroom soup
1 10-ounce can cream of chicken soup
1/4 cup soy sauce

Brown ground beef in skillet, stirring until crumbly; drain. Add celery, onion, rice, vegetables, soups and soy sauce; mix well. Spoon into 9x13-inch baking dish. Bake at 350 degrees for 1 hour.

Marian Babcock, John I. Sabin Chapter

BEEF AND EGGPLANT BAKE

Yield:
6 servings
Utensil:
baking dish

Approx Per
Serving:
Cal 762
T Fat 58 g
68% Calories
from Fat
Prot 40 g
Carbo 22 g
Fiber 5 g
Chol 196 mg
Sod 1263 mg

1 1/2 pounds ground chuck
1/2 cup chopped onion
1 clove of garlic, mashed
2 tablespoons butter
3 8-ounce cans tomato sauce
2 teaspoons oregano
1 teaspoon basil
1/8 teaspoon aniseed
1 1-pound eggplant, sliced 1/4 inch thick
2 eggs, beaten
1 teaspoon water
1/2 cup dried bread crumbs
1/2 cup grated Parmesan cheese
2/3 cup oil
1/2 cup grated Parmesan cheese
1 8-ounce package sliced mozzarella cheese

Brown ground chuck with onion and garlic in skillet for 5 minutes, stirring frequently; drain. Stir in butter, tomato sauce and spices. Dip eggplant in mixture of eggs and water. Coat with mixture of crumbs and 1/2 cup Parmesan cheese. Brown in hot oil in skillet; drain on paper towel. Alternate layers of eggplant, 1/2 Parmesan cheese, mozzarella cheese and sauce in greased 8x12-inch baking dish, ending with mozzarella cheese. Bake at 350 degrees for 20 minutes.

Ursula Mensey, Los Amigos Chapter

ENCHILADA CASSEROLE

Yield:
8 servings
Utensil:
casserole

Approx Per Serving:
Cal 815
T Fat 53 g
57% Calories from Fat
Prot 48 g
Carbo 42 g
Fiber 5 g
Chol 150 mg
Sod 2178 mg

1½ pounds ground beef
1 10-ounce can cream of chicken soup
2 12-ounce cans Las Palmas enchilada sauce
Salt, oregano, garlic powder and paprika to taste
12 corn tortillas, cut into strips
1 4-ounce can sliced black olives, drained
1 large onion, chopped
3 cups shredded Cheddar cheese
3 cups shredded Monterey Jack cheese
1 cup grated Parmesan cheese

Brown ground beef in skillet, stirring until crumbly; drain. Add soup, enchilada sauce and seasonings; mix well. Layer tortillas, olives, onion, Cheddar cheese, Monterey Jack cheese and ground beef mixture ½ at a time in 9x13-inch casserole. Sprinkle Parmesan cheese over top. Bake at 350 degrees for 45 minutes.

Diane Bolz, George S. Ladd Chapter

GREEN CHILIES CASSEROLE

Yield:
8 servings
Utensil:
baking dish

Approx Per Serving:
Cal 575
T Fat 36 g
55% Calories from Fat
Prot 35 g
Carbo 30 g
Fiber 4 g
Chol 117 mg
Sod 961 mg

2 pounds ground beef
2 10-ounce cans cream of mushroom soup
1 12-ounce can evaporated milk
1 4-ounce can chopped green chilies, drained
2 cups shredded Cheddar cheese
12 corn tortillas, cut into quarters

Brown ground beef in skillet, stirring until crumbly; drain. Combine soup, evaporated milk and green chilies in bowl; mix well. Alternate layers of ground beef, cheese, tortillas and soup mixture in 9x13-inch baking dish until all ingredients are used. Bake at 350 degrees for 30 to 40 minutes or until bubbly.

Marlene Chargois, Los Amigos Chapter

PINEAPPLE ORIENTAL MEATBALLS

Yield:
4 servings
Utensil:
skillet

Approx Per
Serving:
Cal 382
T Fat 20 g
46% Calories
from Fat
Prot 20 g
Carbo 34 g
Fiber 3 g
Chol 56 mg
Sod 1687 mg

12 ounces lean ground beef
1/4 cup dry bread crumbs
1/2 teaspoon ginger
1/2 teaspoon salt
2 tablespoons soy sauce
2 tablespoons oil
1 medium green bell pepper, cut into chunks
1 medium onion, sliced
1 20-ounce can pineapple chunks, drained
1 1/2 cups beef broth
2 1/2 tablespoons cornstarch
1/4 cup water
2 tablespoons soy sauce

Combine ground beef, bread crumbs, ginger, salt and 2 tablespoons soy sauce in bowl; mix well. Shape into 1 1/4-inch balls. Brown in oil in large heavy skillet, shaking skillet to brown evenly; push to 1 side. Add green pepper and onion. Sauté for 5 minutes. Add pineapple and broth. Cook, covered, for 5 minutes. Stir in mixture of cornstarch, water and remaining 2 tablespoons soy sauce. Cook over medium heat until thickened, stirring constantly.

Beverly Adams, Los Amigos Chapter

VICKERS' MEATBALLS

Yield:
4 servings
Utensil:
skillet

Approx Per
Serving:
Cal 494
T Fat 22 g
39% Calories
from Fat
Prot 25 g
Carbo 51 g
Fiber 1 g
Chol 128 mg
Sod 1023 mg

1 pound lean ground beef
1 cup soft bread crumbs
1 egg, slightly beaten
2 tablespoons minced onion
2 tablespoons milk
1 clove of garlic, minced
1/2 teaspoon salt
1/8 teaspoon pepper
1 tablespoon oil
2/3 cup chili sauce
2/3 cup grape jelly

Combine ground beef, bread crumbs, egg, onion, milk, garlic and seasonings in bowl; mix well. Shape into balls. Brown in oil in skillet; reduce heat. Cook, covered, over low heat for 5 minutes; drain. Add mixture of chili sauce and jelly. Simmer for 10 to 12 minutes or until sauce thickens. Makes 40 appetizer-sized meatballs. May keep warm in slow cooker.

Pat Vickers, George S. Ladd Chapter

Meat Loaf

Yield:
6 servings
Utensil:
loaf pan

Approx Per
Serving:
Cal 353
T Fat 20 g
51% Calories
from Fat
Prot 26 g
Carbo 17 g
Fiber 1 g
Chol 151 mg
Sod 601 mg

1¹/₂ pounds ground beef
²/₃ cup oats
1 cup milk
1 teaspoon salt
¹/₈ teaspoon pepper
¹/₄ teaspoon poultry
    seasoning
1 teaspoon
    Worcestershire sauce

2 eggs
1 small onion, finely
    chopped
¹/₄ cup catsup
2 tablespoons brown
    sugar
1 teaspoon prepared
    mustard
¹/₄ teaspoon nutmeg

Combine ground beef, oats, milk, salt, pepper, poultry seasoning, Worcestershire sauce, eggs and onion in bowl; mix well. Shape into loaf in 5x9-inch loaf pan. Spoon mixture of catsup, brown sugar, mustard and nutmeg over top. Bake at 350 degrees for 1 hour.

Jean Marks, George S. Ladd Chapter

Picadillo

Yield:
4 servings
Utensil:
skillet

Approx Per
Serving:
Cal 471
T Fat 35 g
65% Calories
from Fat
Prot 24 g
Carbo 18 g
Fiber 4 g
Chol 74 mg
Sod 360 mg

2 tablespoons oil
¹/₂ cup chopped onion
1 teaspoon chopped
    garlic
1 cup chopped celery
1 cup chopped green
    bell pepper
1 cup chopped seeded
    tomatoes
2 tablespoons tomato
    paste

¹/₂ teaspoon cinnamon
³/₄ teaspoon cumin
¹/₄ cup sliced stuffed
    green olives
¹/₄ cup raisins
¹/₄ cup chopped cashews
1 tablespoon red wine
    vinegar
1 pound ground beef
2 tablespoons oil

Heat 2 tablespoons oil in skillet. Add onion, garlic, celery and green pepper. Sauté until vegetables are tender. Add tomatoes, tomato paste and seasonings. Cook for 5 minutes. Add olives, raisins, cashews and vinegar. Cook for 2 minutes. Pour into bowl; set aside. Brown ground beef in remaining 2 tablespoons oil in skillet, stirring until crumbly; drain. Add vegetable mixture; mix well. Simmer for 10 to 15 minutes or until heated through.

Joan Evans, Los Amigos Chapter

PORTUGUESE BEANS

Yield:
12 servings
Utensil:
deep skillet

1 pound bacon, chopped
1 pound linguica, sliced
1 pound ground chuck
1 medium onion, chopped
1 pound red beans,
  cooked

4 8-ounce cans tomato
   sauce
1/4 cup picante sauce
1/4 teaspoon allspice
1 teaspoon cumin

Approx Per
Serving:
Cal 363
T Fat 17 g
42% Calories
from Fat
Prot 24 g
Carbo 30 g
Fiber 10 g
Chol 49 mg
Sod 925 mg

Fry bacon and linguica in skillet; drain. Remove to bowl. Brown ground chuck with onion in skillet, stirring frequently; drain. Add beans, tomato sauce, picante sauce, spices and bacon and linguica mixture. Simmer for 3 hours. Linguica is a Portuguese sausage. Substitute any link sausage.

Brenda Silva, George S. Ladd Chapter

EASY GROUND BEEF QUICHE

Yield:
4 servings
Utensil:
pie plate

8 ounces ground beef
1/2 cup mayonnaise
2 eggs, beaten
1/2 cup milk
1 tablespoon cornstarch

1 1/2 cups cheese
1/3 cup chopped green
  onions
1 unbaked 9-inch pie
  shell

Approx Per
Serving:
Cal 775
T Fat 63 g
73% Calories
from Fat
Prot 28 g
Carbo 25 g
Fiber 1 g
Chol 209 mg
Sod 774 mg

Brown ground beef in skillet, stirring until crumbly; drain and cool. Combine mayonnaise, eggs, milk and cornstarch in bowl; mix well. Add ground beef, cheese and green onions; mix well. Spoon into pie shell. Bake at 350 degrees for 40 minutes. May substitute crisp-fried bacon for ground beef.

Karin Parker, George S. Ladd Chapter

Spaghetti Pie

Yield:
6 *servings*
Utensil:
pie plate

Approx Per Serving:
Cal 414
T Fat 22 g
47% Calories from Fat
Prot 28 g
Carbo 27 g
Fiber 3 g
Chol 136 mg
Sod 626 mg

1 pound ground beef
½ cup chopped onion
¼ cup chopped green bell pepper
1 cup chopped undrained canned tomatoes
1 6-ounce can tomato paste
1 teaspoon sugar
1 teaspoon oregano
½ teaspoon garlic salt
3 cups hot cooked spaghetti
2 tablespoons margarine
⅓ cup grated Parmesan cheese
2 eggs, well beaten
1 cup cottage cheese
½ cup shredded mozzarella cheese

Brown ground beef with onion and green pepper in skillet, stirring frequently. Add tomatoes, tomato paste, sugar, oregano and garlic salt; mix well. Set aside. Combine hot spaghetti and margarine in bowl; mix well. Add Parmesan cheese and eggs; mix well. Shape into crust in buttered 10-inch pie plate. Spread cottage cheese over spaghetti. Top with ground beef sauce. Bake at 350 degrees for 20 minutes. Sprinkle with mozzarella cheese. Bake for 5 minutes.

Shirley J. Haller, John I. Sabin Chapter

Awesome Spaghetti Sauce

Yield:
40 *servings*
Utensil:
stockpot

Approx Per Serving:
Cal 460
T Fat 30 g
58% Calories from Fat
Prot 37 g
Carbo 13 g
Fiber 4 g
Chol 120 mg
Sod 768 mg

15 pounds lean ground beef
2 1-pound packages sweet Italian sausage
4 white onions, chopped
2 bunches green onions, chopped
3 pounds mushrooms, sliced
3 4-ounce cans sliced black olives, drained
4 carrots, finely grated
2 6-ounce cans tomato paste
5 20-ounce cans Italian tomatoes
5 16-ounce cans tomato sauce
1 tablespoon each basil, oregano and parsley flakes
10 ounces red port wine

Brown ground beef in 3-gallon stockpot, stirring until crumbly; drain. Brown sausage in skillet; drain. Cut into ¼-inch slices. Add to ground beef. Reserve 1 cup onions. Add remaining onions and next 9 ingredients; mix well. Simmer for 3 hours. Add reserved 1 cup onions and wine. Simmer for 2 to 3 hours longer or until sauce is of desired consistency. Cool. Chill for 12 hours. Reheat to serve.

Bruce Buehler, John I. Sabin Chapter

DAD'S SPAGHETTI SAUCE

Yield:
12 servings
Utensil:
stockpot

Approx Per
Serving:
Cal 256
T Fat 18 g
63% Calories
from Fat
Prot 14 g
Carbo 10 g
Fiber 2 g
Chol 75 mg
Sod 730 mg

1 onion, chopped
2 cloves of garlic, minced
1 cup chopped celery
3 tablespoons chopped
　fresh parsley
4 ounces ground beef,
　crumbled
1/4 cup oil
1 beef bouillon cube
1 1/2 cups hot water

1　16-ounce can tomatoes
　with juice, chopped
1　6-ounce can tomato
　paste
1 1/2 teaspoons salt
1/4 teaspoon pepper
1/8 teaspoon thyme
Pinch each of oregano
　and nutmeg
Parmesan Meatballs

Sauté onion, garlic, celery, parsley and ground beef in oil in stockpot, stirring frequently. Add bouillon cube dissolved in hot water, tomatoes, tomato paste and seasonings; mix well. Add Parmesan Meatballs. Simmer for 2 hours. Serve over hot cooked spaghetti.

Parmesan Meatballs

Nutritional
information for
Parmesan
Meatballs is
included above.

1 pound ground beef
2 eggs
8 ounces bulk sausage
3 slices bread
1/2 teaspoon salt
Pinch each of nutmeg
　and oregano

1/4 teaspoon pepper
1 clove of garlic, minced
1/4 cup grated Parmesan
　cheese
3 sprigs of parsley,
　chopped
2 tablespoons oil

Combine ground beef, eggs and sausage in bowl; mix well. Soak bread in a small amount of water; squeeze dry. Add to ground beef mixture with salt, nutmeg, oregano, pepper, garlic, cheese and parsley; mix well. Shape into balls. Brown in oil in skillet; drain and set aside.

Jerry Thomas, John I. Sabin Chapter

SPINACH AND BEEF CASSEROLE

Yield:
4 servings
Utensil:
casserole

Approx Per Serving:
Cal 632
T Fat 33 g
47% Calories from Fat
Prot 36 g
Carbo 45 g
Fiber 3 g
Chol 93 mg
Sod 1907 mg

1 pound ground chuck
2 tablespoons olive oil
1/2 teaspoon pepper
1 6-ounce can mushrooms
1/3 cup dry sherry
1 10-ounce package frozen chopped spinach, thawed, drained
1 16-ounce can stewed tomatoes
1 6-ounce package Italian noodles with cheese and sauce
1/2 cup shredded sharp Cheddar cheese
1/4 cup grated Parmesan cheese

Brown ground chuck in olive oil in skillet, stirring until crumbly; drain. Add pepper, mushrooms with liquid, sherry, spinach and tomatoes; mix well. Remove from heat. Add uncooked noodles, sauce mix and cheese from noodle package; mix well. Spoon into lightly greased 2-quart casserole. Sprinkle with Cheddar and Parmesan cheeses. Bake for 25 minutes or until noodles are tender. Garnish with parsley.

Ursula Mensey, Los Amigos Chapter

GROUND BEEF STROGANOFF

Yield:
5 servings
Utensil:
skillet

Approx Per Serving:
Cal 553
T Fat 30 g
50% Calories from Fat
Prot 27 g
Carbo 42 g
Fiber 2 g
Chol 80 mg
Sod 1529 mg

1/3 cup chopped onion
1 clove of garlic, minced
2 tablespoons olive oil
1 pound ground beef
2 tablespoons flour
1 beef bouillon cube
1 cup boiling water
1/4 cup red wine
2 teaspoons salt
1 cup sour cream
2 3-ounce cans mushrooms
1 8-ounce can tomato sauce
1 8-ounce package egg noodles, cooked

Brown onion and garlic in olive oil in skillet. Add ground beef. Cook until browned, stirring frequently; drain. Stir in flour and bouillon dissolved in 1 cup boiling water. Add wine, salt, sour cream, mushrooms and tomato sauce. Cook until heated through and thickened. Serve over hot cooked noodles.

Onita G. Rosas, Sierra Pacific Chapter

STROGANOFF SKILLET

Yield:
4 servings
Utensil:
skillet

Approx Per Serving:
Cal 608
T Fat 36 g
53% Calories from Fat
Prot 31 g
Carbo 40 g
Fiber 1 g
Chol 101 mg
Sod 908 mg

1 pound ground beef
1 medium onion, chopped
1 10-ounce can cream of mushroom soup
1 cup sour cream
1 10-ounce can beef broth
1/2 cup water
3 cups uncooked medium noodles

Brown ground beef with onion in skillet, stirring frequently; drain. Add soup and sour cream; mix well. Stir in broth, water and noodles. Bring to a boil; reduce heat. Cook, covered, for 10 minutes or until noodles are tender.

Shelly Brown, George S. Ladd Chapter

STUFFED BREAD

Yield:
4 servings
Utensil:
skillet

Approx Per Serving:
Cal 662
T Fat 40 g
53% Calories from Fat
Prot 41 g
Carbo 37 g
Fiber 3 g
Chol 134 mg
Sod 2241 mg

1 pound ground beef
1 medium onion, chopped
1 teaspoon garlic salt
1/4 cup chopped green bell pepper
1 4-ounce can chopped green olives, drained
1 8-ounce can tomato sauce
1 tablespoon vinegar
8 ounces Cheddar cheese, shredded
1 package sourdough French rolls

Brown ground beef in skillet, stirring until crumbly; drain. Add onion, garlic salt, green pepper, olives, tomato sauce and vinegar; mix well. Simmer for 30 minutes; remove from heat. Stir in cheese. Spoon into sliced rolls. Wrap in foil. Bake at 400 degrees for 30 minutes.

Roxy Silveria, John I. Sabin Chapter

Poor Man's Swiss Steak

Yield:
4 servings
Utensil:
skillet

Approx Per Serving:
Cal 585
T Fat 30 g
45% Calories from Fat
Prot 30 g
Carbo 52 g
Fiber 4 g
Chol 88 mg
Sod 1875 mg

1 pound ground beef, crumbled
4 ounces fresh mushrooms, sliced
1/2 cup chopped onion
2 10-ounce cans cream of mushroom soup
1 cup milk
4 cups hot mashed potatoes

Brown ground beef with mushrooms and onion in 12-inch skillet, stirring frequently; drain. Add soup and milk. Simmer for 30 minutes to 1 1/2 hours or until of desired consistency. Serve over hot mashed potatoes. May substitute wine for milk. May serve over wide noodles or rice.

Rae Mobraaten, John I. Sabin Chapter

Taco Casserole

Yield:
6 servings
Utensil:
baking dish

Approx Per Serving:
Cal 628
T Fat 46 g
63% Calories from Fat
Prot 33 g
Carbo 28 g
Fiber 3 g
Chol 106 mg
Sod 1524 mg

1 pound ground beef
1 tablespoon instant minced onion
1/2 teaspoon garlic salt
2 8-ounce cans tomato sauce
1 cup sliced black olives
1 cup sour cream
1 cup small curd cottage cheese
4 canned green chilies, chopped
1 6-ounce package nacho chips
2 cups shredded Monterey Jack cheese

Brown ground beef in skillet, stirring until crumbly; drain. Add onion, garlic salt, tomato sauce and olives; mix well and set aside. Combine sour cream, cottage cheese and chilies in bowl; mix well. Reserve several nacho chips; crush remaining chips slightly. Layer crushed chips, ground beef mixture, sour cream mixture and cheese 1/2 at a time in 13x18-inch baking pan. Top with remaining whole tortilla chips. Bake at 350 degrees for 35 to 45 minutes or until cheese melts.

Barbara Von Dohlen, John I. Sabin Chapter

TAMALE PIE

Yield:
6 servings
Utensil:
casserole

Approx Per
Serving:
Cal 361
T Fat 23 g
55% Calories
from Fat
Prot 22 g
Carbo 21 g
Fiber 4 g
Chol 69 mg
Sod 721 mg

1 pound ground beef
1 onion, chopped
Salt and pepper to taste
1 16-ounce can cream-
    style corn
1 16-ounce can tomatoes

1 4-ounce can pitted
    black olives, drained
3 large American-style
    tamales
1 cup shredded Cheddar
    cheese

Brown ground beef with onion in skillet, stirring frequently; drain. Season with salt and pepper. Add corn, tomatoes and olives; mix well. Steam tamales in hot water in saucepan for 5 minutes; cut into pieces. Add to ground beef mixture. Pour into greased casserole. Bake at 300 degrees for 1½ hours, stirring occasionally. Top with cheese. Bake for 30 minutes longer.

Pat Borges, Mission Chapter

TWENTY-MINUTE TAMALE PIE

Yield:
4 servings
Utensil:
skillet

Approx Per
Serving:
Cal 1041
T Fat 71 g
59% Calories
from Fat
Prot 46 g
Carbo 64 g
Fiber 6 g
Chol 192 mg
Sod 2448 mg

1 onion, chopped
1 pound ground beef
2 tablespoons butter
1 16-ounce can stewed
    tomatoes
1 17-ounce can whole
    kernel corn
2 cups sour cream

1 cup cornmeal
1 4-ounce can sliced
    black olives, drained
2 teaspoons salt
1 tablespoon chili
    powder
2 cups grated Monterey
    Jack cheese

Brown onion and ground beef in butter in skillet, stirring frequently; drain. Add tomatoes, undrained corn, sour cream, cornmeal, olives, salt and chili powder; mix well. Sprinkle cheese over top. Simmer, covered, for 20 minutes.

Beverly Adams, Los Amigos Chapter

TEXAS HASH

Yield:
8 servings
Utensil:
casserole

Approx Per
Serving:
Cal 229
T Fat 13 g
51% Calories
from Fat
Prot 13 g
Carbo 16 g
Fiber 2 g
Chol 37 mg
Sod 398 mg

2 large onions, sliced
2 green bell peppers,
  finely chopped
3 tablespoons shortening
1 pound ground beef

2 cups canned tomatoes
1/2 cup uncooked rice
1 teaspoon chili powder
1 teaspoon salt
1/4 teaspoon pepper

Sauté onions and green peppers in shortening in skillet until tender. Add ground beef. Cook until browned, stirring frequently. Add tomatoes, rice and seasonings. Spoon into casserole. Bake, covered, at 375 degrees for 1 hour or until rice is tender.

Ted Slack, John I. Sabin Chapter

THREE-BEAN CASSEROLE

Yield:
8 servings
Utensil:
casserole

Approx Per
Serving:
Cal 481
T Fat 15 g
28% Calories
from Fat
Prot 28 g
Carbo 62 g
Fiber 14 g
Chol 56 mg
Sod 1128 mg

1 pound ground beef
1 onion, chopped
8 ounces bacon,
  crisp-fried, crumbled
1 16-ounce can kidney
  beans, drained
1 16-ounce can butter
  beans, drained

1 3-pound can pork and
  beans
5 tablespoons brown
  sugar
3 tablespoons vinegar
1 teaspoon dry mustard

Brown ground beef with onion in skillet, stirring frequently; drain. Add bacon, beans, brown sugar, vinegar and mustard; mix well. Pour into casserole. Bake at 325 degrees for 20 minutes or until bubbly. May be simmered in skillet or warmed in slow cooker.

Kathy Nichols, George S. Ladd Chapter

Wyoming Straw Hats

Yield:
10 servings
Utensil:
skillet

**Approx Per
Serving:**
Cal 520
T Fat 34 g
*58% Calories
from Fat*
Prot 26 g
Carbo 29 g
Fiber 4 g
Chol 83 mg
Sod 1060 mg

1 cup chopped onion
2/3 cup chopped green
  bell pepper
2/3 cup chopped celery
3 tablespoons shortening
2 pounds ground beef
2 to 3 teaspoons chili
  powder
1/2 teaspoon thyme
2 6-ounce cans tomato
  paste

Dash of Tabasco sauce
2 teaspoons salt
1/4 teaspoon pepper
1/2 cup catsup
2 tablespoons
  Worcestershire sauce
1 10-ounce package
  corn chips
2 cups shredded sharp
  Cheddar cheese

Sauté onion, green pepper and celery in shortening in skillet until tender. Add ground beef. Cook until lightly browned, stirring frequently; drain. Add chili powder and thyme; mix well. Stir in tomato paste. Add Tabasco sauce, salt, pepper, catsup and Worcestershire sauce; mix well. Simmer, covered, for 1 hour, stirring occasionally. Serve over corn chips. Top with cheese.

Roxy Silveria, John I. Sabin Chapter

Zippy Beef Casserole

Yield:
4 servings
Utensil:
casserole

**Approx Per
Serving:**
Cal 621
T Fat 33 g
*48% Calories
from Fat*
Prot 33 g
Carbo 49 g
Fiber 3 g
Chol 96 mg
Sod 1816 mg

1 pound ground beef
4 ounces uncooked
  macaroni
1 10-ounce can cream
  of mushroom soup
3/4 cup milk
2/3 cup catsup
1/2 cup shredded
  Cheddar cheese

1/4 cup chopped green
  bell pepper
2 tablespoons instant
  minced onion
1 teaspoon salt
1 cup crushed potato
  chips

Brown ground beef in skillet, stirring until crumbly; drain. Cook macaroni using package directions; drain. Combine ground beef, macaroni, soup, milk, catsup, cheese, green pepper, minced onion and salt in 2-quart casserole. Bake, covered, at 350 degrees for 40 minutes. Top with potato chips. Bake, uncovered, for 5 minutes longer.

Renee Corocco, Los Amigos Chapter

PORK CHOP CASSEROLE

<table>
<tr><td>

Yield:
8 servings
Utensil:
baking dish

</td></tr>
</table>

Approx Per
Serving:
Cal 500
T Fat 18 g
34% Calories
from Fat
Prot 39 g
Carbo 43 g
Fiber 3 g
Chol 103 mg
Sod 790 mg

8 pork chops
Salt and pepper to taste
1/2 cup flour
2 tablespoons oil
2 10-ounce cans cream
  of chicken soup
4 cups cooked rice

1 16-ounce can peas
  with pearl onions
1 green bell pepper,
  chopped
1 small onion, chopped
Chopped pimento to
  taste

Sprinkle pork chops with salt and pepper; coat with flour. Brown on both sides in oil in skillet. Remove pork chops and drain most of oil from skillet. Add soup to skillet. Cook over low heat until heated through, stirring to mix well. Layer rice, peas, green pepper, onion, pimento, pork chops and soup mixture 1/2 at a time in baking dish. Bake, covered, at 350 degrees until pork chops are tender.

T. J. Bowman, Los Amigos Chapter

GLORIFIED PORK CHOPS

Yield:
6 servings
Utensil:
skillet

Approx Per
Serving:
Cal 240
T Fat 13 g
51% Calories
from Fat
Prot 24 g
Carbo 5 g
Fiber 1 g
Chol 70 mg
Sod 438 mg

6 4-ounce pork chops
1 medium onion, sliced
1 tablespoon oil

1 10-ounce can cream
  of mushroom soup
1/4 to 1/2 cup water

Cook pork chops and onion 1/2 at a time in oil in skillet for 10 minutes or until pork chops are brown on both sides; drain. Add mushroom soup and water. Simmer, covered, for 10 minutes or until pork chops are tender, stirring occasionally.

Shelly Brown, George S. Ladd Chapter

PORK MEDALLIONS

Yield:
6 servings
Utensil:
broiler pan

**Approx Per
Serving:**
*Cal 182
T Fat 10 g
49% Calories
from Fat
Prot 23 g
Carbo 0 g
Fiber 0 g
Chol 69 mg
Sod 55 mg*

**1¹/₂ pounds pork
  tenderloins
1 tablespoon olive oil**

**Basil and garlic powder
  to taste**

Rub pork tenderloins with olive oil; sprinkle with basil and garlic powder. Place on rack in broiler pan. Bake at 325 degrees for 30 minutes. Broil for 15 minutes or until brown on all sides, turning frequently. Let stand for 5 minutes. Slice ¹/₂ inch thick. Serve with mashed potatoes, asparagus and gravy prepared from mix and flavored with 1 tablespoon basil.

Lori Dahl, George S. Ladd Chapter

PORK CHOPS AND STUFFING

Yield:
6 servings
Utensil:
baking dish

**Approx Per
Serving:**
*Cal 379
T Fat 17 g
41% Calories
from Fat
Prot 36 g
Carbo 18 g
Fiber 1 g
Chol 138 mg
Sod 801 mg*

**6 pork chops
1 10-ounce can cream
  of chicken soup
1 egg
¹/₂ cup chopped celery**

**¹/₂ cup chopped onion
1 teaspoon poultry
  seasoning
1 10-count can biscuits**

Brown pork chops on both sides in skillet. Arrange in baking dish. Combine soup, egg, celery, onion and poultry seasoning in bowl; mix well. Tear each biscuit into quarters. Stir into soup mixture. Spoon over pork chops. Bake at 350 degrees for 45 to 60 minutes or until pork chops are cooked through.

Deanie Jones, Los Amigos Chapter

PORK CHOP BAKE

Yield:
4 servings
Utensil:
baking dish

Approx Per Serving:
Cal 475
T Fat 22 g
42% Calories from Fat
Prot 35 g
Carbo 34 g
Fiber 2 g
Chol 129 mg
Sod 182 mg

4 potatoes, peeled, cut
  into quarters
¼ cup melted butter

Salt and pepper to taste
4 large ½-inch thick
  pork chops

Combine potatoes, butter, salt and pepper in 9x9-inch baking dish; mix to coat well. Arrange pork chops over potatoes; season to taste. Bake, loosely covered with foil, at 350 degrees for 30 minutes. Bake, uncovered, for 30 minutes longer or until pork chops are cooked through. May turn pork chops to brown on both sides if desired.

Arliss Summers, Mission Chapter

PORK STEAKS AND CHINESE NOODLES

Yield:
6 servings
Utensil:
skillet

Approx Per Serving:
Cal 431
T Fat 9 g
19% Calories from Fat
Prot 29 g
Carbo 58 g
Fiber 1 g
Chol 49 mg
Sod 1425 mg

3 pork steaks
3 bunches green onions,
  chopped

½ cup soy sauce
1 16-ounce package
  Chinese noodles

Cut pork steaks into small pieces. Brown on all sides in skillet. Add green onions, half the soy sauce and enough water to cover. Simmer for 15 to 20 minutes, adding remaining soy sauce as needed for desired consistency. Cook noodles using package directions; drain. Add to pork mixture. Simmer for 5 minutes longer.

Nutritional information includes the entire amount of soy sauce.

Shelly Brown, George S. Ladd Chapter

COUNTRY-STYLE BARBECUED RIBS

Yield:
8 servings
Utensil:
grill

Approx Per Serving:
Cal 403
T Fat 28 g
63% Calories from Fat
Prot 26 g
Carbo 11 g
Fiber <1 g
Chol 108 mg
Sod 532 mg

4 pounds country-style ribs
Salt to taste
2 tablespoons chopped onion
1 clove of garlic, minced
1 tablespoon butter
1/2 cup catsup
1/3 cup chili sauce
2 tablespoons brown sugar
1 tablespoon Worcestershire sauce
1 tablespoon prepared mustard
3 lemon slices
1 teaspoon celery seed
1/4 teaspoon salt

Cut ribs into serving pieces. Simmer in salted water to cover in saucepan for 1 hour or until almost tender; drain. Sauté onion and garlic in butter in saucepan for 4 to 5 minutes. Add catsup, chili sauce, brown sugar, Worcestershire sauce, mustard, lemon slices, celery seed and 1/4 teaspoon salt; mix well. Grill ribs over medium coals for 10 minutes on each side, brushing with barbecue sauce. Serve with remaining sauce.

Lorraine Robinson, John I. Sabin Chapter

WONDERFUL RIBS

Yield:
20 servings
Utensil:
pressure cooker

Approx Per Serving:
Cal 714
T Fat 53 g
69% Calories from Fat
Prot 51 g
Carbo 4 g
Fiber <1 g
Chol 208 mg
Sod 530 mg

20 pounds ranch-style pork ribs
Tabasco sauce to taste
2 16-ounce bottles of spicy barbecue sauce

Cut ribs into 4-inch serving pieces. Arrange in pressure cooker, filling halfway. Pressure cook using manufacturer's instructions for 8 to 9 minutes. Remove from pressure cooker. Coat with mixture of Tabasco sauce and barbecue sauce. Chill in refrigerator. Cook on grill or smoker over low coals until light brown. Coat well with sauce. We freeze these in 2-serving portions.

Bruce Buehler, John I. Sabin Chapter

BREAKFAST HAM AND CHEESE

Yield:
10 servings
Utensil:
baking dish

Approx Per Serving:
Cal 397
T Fat 26 g
58% Calories from Fat
Prot 23 g
Carbo 18 g
Fiber 1 g
Chol 150 mg
Sod 1172 mg

1 pound ham, chopped
8 ounces Cheddar cheese, cubed
6 or 7 slices white bread, cubed
½ teaspoon dry mustard
½ teaspoon salt
½ teaspoon pepper
3 eggs, slightly beaten
2 cups milk
½ cup melted butter
1 cup crushed cornflakes
2 tablespoons melted butter

Toss ham with cheese, bread cubes, dry mustard, salt and pepper in bowl. Spread in 9x13-inch baking dish. Beat eggs with milk in bowl. Pour over ham mixture. Drizzle with ½ cup butter. Chill, covered, overnight. Let stand at room temperature for 30 minutes. Bake at 325 degrees for 30 minutes. Top with mixture of cornflakes and 2 tablespoons melted butter. Bake for 30 minutes longer.

Evelyn Mess, John I. Sabin Chapter

TAHITIAN HAM LOAF

Yield:
8 servings
Utensil:
baking dish

Approx Per Serving:
Cal 400
T Fat 9 g
20% Calories from Fat
Prot 27 g
Carbo 53 g
Fiber 1 g
Chol 97 mg
Sod 909 mg

1 pound ground smoked ham
1 pound ground fresh pork
⅔ cup coarse cracker crumbs
½ cup chopped onion
½ cup milk
1 egg, slightly beaten
1 tablespoon chopped parsley
Pepper to taste
8 slices pineapple
¼ cup pineapple juice
1 cup packed brown sugar
2 tablespoons vinegar
1 teaspoon prepared mustard

Combine ham, pork, cracker crumbs, onion, milk, egg, parsley and pepper in bowl; mix well. Shape into 9 patties. Arrange patties and pineapple slices alternately in row in 9x13-inch baking dish, pressing to form loaf. Bake at 325 degrees for 30 minutes. Blend pineapple juice, brown sugar, vinegar and mustard in bowl. Pour over loaf. Bake for 1 hour longer, basting every 20 minutes. Serve over rice.

Nancy L. Fry, Silver State Chapter

BACON AND MUSHROOM QUESADILLAS

> **Yield:**
> *5 servings*
> **Utensil:**
> *skillet*

8 ounces mushrooms, sliced
1 tablespoon margarine
10 flour tortillas
1 cup shredded Monterey Jack cheese
1 cup shredded Cheddar cheese
1 pound bacon, crisp-fried, crumbled

> **Approx Per Serving:**
> *Cal 573*
> *T Fat 36 g*
> *54% Calories from Fat*
> *Prot 26 g*
> *Carbo 41 g*
> *Fiber 3 g*
> *Chol 68 mg*
> *Sod 992 mg*

Sauté mushrooms in margarine in skillet. Remove to bowl. Soften tortillas on both sides in skillet over medium heat. Spoon cheeses onto tortillas, folding each in half to enclose cheeses. Arrange in several batches in skillet. Heat until cheese is melted. Sprinkle with bacon and mushrooms. Serve with salsa, sour cream and beer or Margaritas.

Ellie Powell, John I. Sabin Chapter

BRUNCH CASSEROLE

> **Yield:**
> *8 servings*
> **Utensil:**
> *baking dish*

1 pound sausage
1 8-count can crescent rolls
2 cups shredded mozzarella cheese
4 eggs, beaten
3/4 cup milk
1/4 teaspoon salt
1/8 teaspoon pepper

> **Approx Per Serving:**
> *Cal 332*
> *T Fat 23 g*
> *64% Calories from Fat*
> *Prot 16 g*
> *Carbo 13 g*
> *Fiber 0 g*
> *Chol 153 mg*
> *Sod 791 mg*

Brown sausage in medium skillet over medium heat, stirring until crumbly; drain. Line bottom of buttered 9x13-inch baking dish with crescent roll dough, pressing edges and perforations to seal. Layer sausage and cheese in prepared dish. Combine eggs, milk, salt and pepper in bowl; beat until smooth. Pour over layers. Bake at 425 degrees for 15 minutes or until set. Let stand for 5 minutes. Cut into squares. Serve immediately.

Anna Lewis, Los Amigos Chapter

CABBAGE AND SAUSAGE

Yield:
6 servings
Utensil:
saucepan

Approx Per Serving:
Cal 272
T Fat 12 g
37% Calories from Fat
Prot 14 g
Carbo 31 g
Fiber 9 g
Chol 29 mg
Sod 921 mg

1 pound hot Italian sausage, chopped
2 to 2¹/₂ pounds cabbage, chopped
2 carrots, chopped
2 stalks celery, chopped

1 onion, thinly sliced
1 16-ounce can stewed tomatoes, chopped
1 16-ounce can peas, drained
Pepper to taste

Brown sausage in large saucepan. Add cabbage, carrots, celery, onion and tomatoes. Add enough water to cover. Cook until vegetables are tender, adding additional water as needed for desired consistency. Add peas and pepper. May add one 8-ounce can tomato sauce and rice if desired.

Erika Marinborich, Los Amigos Chapter

HEART ATTACK SPECIAL

Yield:
4 servings
Utensil:
skillet

Approx Per Serving:
Cal 572
T Fat 25 g
41% Calories from Fat
Prot 29 g
Carbo 54 g
Fiber 2 g
Chol 661 mg
Sod 554 mg

8 ounces kielbasa
1 bunch green onions
4 ounces fresh mushrooms, sliced

9 to 12 eggs, slightly beaten
Garlic salt to taste
4 cups cooked rice

Slice sausage into ¹/₄-inch pieces; slices green onions into ¹/₂-inch pieces. Sauté sausage, green onions and mushrooms in 12-inch skillet over medium heat for 5 minutes or until green onions are tender-crisp. Stir in eggs and garlic salt. Cook until eggs are done to taste, stirring occasionally. Serve over rice. May substitute cheese-flavored rice mix if preferred.

Rae Mobraaten, John I. Sabin Chapter

ITALIAN SAUSAGE BREAKFAST BAKE

Yield:
8 servings
Utensil:
baking dish

Approx Per Serving:
Cal 396
T Fat 29 g
67% Calories from Fat
Prot 24 g
Carbo 9 g
Fiber 1 g
Chol 306 mg
Sod 1030 mg

1½ pounds Italian link sausage
1 medium onion, chopped
1   14-ounce can tomatoes, drained, chopped
1   7-ounce can chopped green chilies
1 cup shredded Monterey Jack cheese
1 cup shredded Cheddar cheese
9 eggs
1½ cups milk

Brown sausage in skillet. Remove and slice sausage; drain skillet, reserving 1 tablespoon drippings. Sauté onion in reserved drippings in skillet. Add tomatoes and green chilies. Simmer until heated through. Spoon into 10x12-inch baking dish. Spread sausage slices over top. Sprinkle with 1½ cups mixed cheeses. Beat eggs and milk in bowl. Pour over layers. Top with remaining ½ cup mixed cheeses. Bake at 350 degrees for 45 to 60 minutes or until set and light brown.

Delores J. O'Hagan, John I. Sabin Chapter

CAJUN JAMBALAYA

Yield:
10 servings
Utensil:
stockpot

Approx Per Serving:
Cal 417
T Fat 37 g
42% Calories from Fat
Prot 21 g
Carbo 38 g
Fiber 2 g
Chol 58 mg
Sod 836 mg

2 pounds pork spareribs, cut up
8 ounces hot link sausage, sliced
1 large yellow onion, chopped
1 each red and green bell pepper, chopped
3 cloves of garlic, minced
4 stalks celery, chopped
6 green onions, chopped
3 tablespoons peanut oil
1   28-ounce can whole tomatoes, crushed
3½ cups chicken broth
1 cup chopped ham
2 teaspoons Tabasco sauce
¼ cup Worcestershire sauce
1 tablespoon whole thyme
Salt and pepper to taste
2 cups uncooked rice

Place ribs in baking pan. Bake at 400 degrees for 15 minutes or until brown. Brown sausage in skillet; drain. Sauté onion, bell peppers, garlic, celery and green onions in peanut oil in skillet until tender. Combine with ribs, tomatoes and chicken broth in 12-quart stockpot. Simmer, covered, for 1 hour. Add next 6 ingredients. Simmer, covered, for 20 minutes. Add sausage and rice. Simmer for 25 minutes.

Chris Weekes, Sierra Pacific Chapter

JAMBALAYA

Yield:
8 servings
Utensil:
saucepan

Approx Per
Serving:
Cal 595
T Fat 50 g
51% Calories
from Fat
Prot 43 g
Carbo 64 g
Fiber 8 g
Chol 417 mg
Sod 968 mg

6 ounces boneless
chicken, chopped
6 tablespoons butter
6 ounces boiled ham,
chopped
6 ounces smoked pork
sausage
3 cups coarsely chopped
onions
1¹/₂ cups coarsely
chopped green bell
peppers
2 cups coarsely chopped
celery
1¹/₂ cups tomato purée

8 tomatoes, peeled,
chopped
4 bay leaves
1 tablespoon oregano
¹/₂ teaspoon cayenne
pepper
¹/₂ teaspoon thyme
3 cloves of garlic, minced
2 cups seafood stock
2¹/₂ cups rice, cooked
36 medium shrimp,
peeled, deveined
36 medium oysters
Salt and pepper to taste

Rinse chicken and pat dry. Sauté in butter in 4-quart saucepan over medium heat until no longer pink. Add ham and sausage. Cook until light brown. Add onions, green peppers and celery. Sauté until onions are tender. Add tomato purée, tomatoes, bay leaves, oregano, cayenne pepper, thyme and garlic. Simmer for 10 minutes. Add seafood stock. Bring to a boil. Stir in rice. Simmer for 6 to 8 minutes. Add shrimp and oysters. Simmer, covered, for 10 minutes. Season with salt and pepper. Remove bay leaves. May substitute water for seafood stock.

Faith Connor, Los Amigos Chapter

QUICK SEAFOOD STOCK

Nutritional
information for
Quick Seafood
Stock is
included above.

1 cup water
1 cup dry white wine
1 cup bottled clam juice

¹/₂ cup chopped celery
¹/₂ cup chopped onion
3 sprigs of parsley

Combine water, wine, clam juice and vegetables in saucepan. Simmer until reduced to 2 cups. Strain stock. This is an easy seafood stock if you are in a hurry.

Evelyn Mess, John I. Sabin Chapter

MANICOTTI

Yield:
8 servings
Utensil:
baking dish

*Approx Per
Serving:*
Cal 311
T Fat 17 g
*48% Calories
from Fat*
Prot 19 g
Carbo 21 g
Fiber 2 g
Chol 83 mg
Sod 343 mg

8 ounces Italian sausage
8 ounces ground beef
¹/₂ onion, chopped
1 6-ounce can tomato
  paste
1 8-ounce can tomato
  purée
¹/₂ cup water
1 teaspoon basil
Salt and pepper to taste

8 ounces ricotta cheese
1 cup shredded
  mozzarella cheese
1 egg, slightly beaten
2 tablespoons chopped
  parsley
8 manicotti shells
¹/₄ cup grated Parmesan
  cheese

Brown sausage and ground beef with onion in skillet, stirring frequently; drain. Stir in tomato paste, tomato purée, ¹/₂ cup water and seasonings. Simmer for 30 to 40 minutes. Mix next 4 ingredients in bowl. Cook manicotti shells in boiling water in saucepan for 4 minutes; drain and cool slightly. Stuff with cheese mixture. Spread thin layer of meat sauce in oblong baking dish. Arrange stuffed shells in prepared dish. Top with remaining meat sauce and Parmesan cheese. Bake at 375 degrees for 30 minutes.

Terri Murphy, Sierra Pacific Chapter

MEXICAN BEAN POT

Yield:
8 servings
Utensil:
saucepan

*Approx Per
Serving:*
Cal 358
T Fat 13 g
*32% Calories
from Fat*
Prot 22 g
Carbo 39 g
Fiber 14 g
Chol 32 mg
Sod 1153 mg

1 16-ounce package
  dried pinto beans
5 cups water
1 Spanish onion,
  chopped
2 teaspoons salt
1¹/₂ pounds Italian
  sausage

2 green bell peppers, cut
  into 1-inch pieces
1 16-ounce can tomatoes
1 tablespoon oregano
¹/₂ teaspoon cumin seed
¹/₂ teaspoon pepper

Bring beans and water to a boil in 4 to 5-quart saucepan. Boil for 2 minutes. Let stand for 1 hour. Add onion and salt. Simmer for 1 hour. Skin sausage and cut into 1-inch pieces. Brown sausage in large skillet. Remove with slotted spoon, reserving drippings. Sauté green peppers in drippings in skillet until tender. Stir in tomatoes, oregano, cumin and pepper. Heat until bubbly. Add to beans with sausage; mix well. Simmer for 2¹/₂ hours.

Chris Sabins, John I. Sabin Chapter

PIZZA

Yield:
4 servings
Utensil:
baking sheet

Approx Per Serving:
Cal 742
T Fat 44 g
54% Calories from Fat
Prot 55 g
Carbo 30 g
Fiber 2 g
Chol 192 mg
Sod 1198 mg

1 pound ground pork
Salt and pepper to taste
1 large round Bolla bread
1 8-ounce jar pizza sauce
8 ounces mozzarella cheese, shredded
8 ounces Cheddar cheese, shredded

Brown ground pork in skillet, stirring until crumbly; drain. Season to taste. Place bread on baking sheet. Layer pizza sauce, half the mozzarella cheese, half the Cheddar cheese, pork and remaining cheeses on bread. Bake at 350 degrees for 20 to 25 minutes or until cheese melts.

Pamela Allen, Los Amigos Chapter

PIZZA ROLL

Yield:
6 servings
Utensil:
baking sheet

Approx Per Serving:
Cal 550
T Fat 35 g
54% Calories from Fat
Prot 22 g
Carbo 45 g
Fiber 2 g
Chol 74 mg
Sod 1815 mg

1 loaf frozen bread dough, thawed
1 pound sausage
1 cup shredded Cheddar cheese
1 cup shredded mozzarella cheese
1 4-ounce can chopped black olives
1 4-ounce jar green olives, chopped
1 onion, chopped
1 4-ounce can chopped mushrooms
2 tablespoons melted butter

Let dough rise using package directions until doubled in bulk. Brown sausage in skillet, stirring until crumbly; drain. Press dough into square. Sprinkle sausage, cheeses, olives, onion and mushrooms in center of square. Fold in sides; roll to enclose filling. Press edges to seal. Place on baking sheet; brush with melted butter. Bake at 350 degrees for 30 minutes or until golden brown. May use as an appetizer.

Kathy Nichols, George S. Ladd Chapter

SAUSAGE BAKE

Yield:
10 servings
Utensil:
baking dish

Approx Per Serving:
Cal 398
T Fat 24 g
56% Calories from Fat
Prot 21 g
Carbo 22 g
Fiber 1 g
Chol 186 mg
Sod 816 mg

1½ pounds sausage
10 slices French bread, cubed
1 cup shredded Cheddar cheese
1 cup shredded Monterey Jack cheese
6 eggs
3 cups milk
2 teaspoons grated onion

Brown sausage in skillet, stirring until crumbly; drain. Layer bread cubes, sausage and cheeses ½ at a time in baking dish. Beat eggs with milk and onion in bowl. Pour over layers. Chill overnight. Bake at 350 degrees for 40 minutes or until set.

Shirley Johnson, Silver State Chapter

POLSKA KIELBASA STIR-FRY

Yield:
4 servings
Utensil:
skillet

Approx Per Serving:
Cal 359
T Fat 9 g
23% Calories from Fat
Prot 11 g
Carbo 58 g
Fiber 3 g
Chol 22 mg
Sod 358 mg

8 ounces kielbasa sausage
¼ cup coarsely chopped purple onion
1 bunch green onions, cut into ½-inch pieces
4 ounces fresh mushrooms, sliced
1 large carrot, thinly sliced
¼ cup whole kernel corn
Garlic salt to taste
½ teaspoon chili powder
4 cups cooked rice

Cut sausage into ¼-inch slices. Stir-fry sausage with onion, green onions and mushrooms in nonstick 12-inch skillet for 5 minutes. Add carrot, corn, garlic salt and chili powder; mix well. Stir-fry for 5 minutes. Serve over hot rice. May substitute baby corn for whole kernel corn or other vegetables of choice for those in recipe.

Rae Mobraaten, John I. Sabin Chapter

SMOKED SAUSAGE SKILLET SUPPER

Yield:
6 servings
Utensil:
skillet

Approx Per Serving:
Cal 293
T Fat 20 g
60% Calories from Fat
Prot 15 g
Carbo 15 g
Fiber 4 g
Chol 49 mg
Sod 1028 mg

6 slices bacon
1 2-pound head cabbage, cut into wedges
1 medium onion, chopped
1/4 cup water
2 tablespoons sugar
1 teaspoon minced garlic
2 teaspoons caraway seed
1 teaspoon seasoned salt
1 to 1 1/2 pounds kielbasa

Fry bacon in large skillet until crisp; remove bacon. Add cabbage, onion, water, sugar, garlic, caraway seed and seasoned salt to drippings in skillet. Cook, covered, over medium heat for 10 to 15 minutes, stirring occasionally. Cut sausage into 6 pieces. Add to skillet. Cook for 15 minutes longer or until sausage is heated through. Crumble bacon over servings.

Shelly Brown, George S. Ladd Chapter

TEXAS CASSEROLE

Yield:
4 servings
Utensil:
baking dish

Approx Per Serving:
Cal 737
T Fat 42 g
50% Calories from Fat
Prot 41 g
Carbo 55 g
Fiber 14 g
Chol 130 mg
Sod 2796 mg

2 slices bacon, chopped
1/2 onion, chopped
1/2 green bell pepper, chopped
1 clove of garlic, crushed
1 2-ounce jar chopped pimento
1 16-ounce can pork and beans
2 16-ounce cans chili with beans
12 ounces bologna, chopped
1 cup shredded sharp Cheddar cheese

Fry bacon in skillet until crisp. Combine with onion, green pepper, garlic, pimento, pork and beans, chili and bologna in bowl; mix well. Spoon into small baking dish; top with cheese. Bake at 400 degrees for 30 minutes.

Karolyn Tillisch Aznoe, John I. Sabin Chapter

ARMENIAN SARMA

Yield:
8 servings
Utensil:
saucepan

Approx Per
Serving:
Cal 296
T Fat 9 g
27% Calories
from Fat
Prot 29 g
Carbo 24 g
Fiber 6 g
Chol 80 mg
Sod 264 mg

2 pounds ground lamb
2 large yellow onions,
  chopped
2 large tomatoes,
  chopped
4 large cloves of garlic,
  chopped
1 cup chopped parsley
1 cup tomato sauce
1 cup bulgur
1/4 cup chopped fresh
  mint
3 tablespoons lemon
  juice
Salt and pepper to taste
64 bottled grape leaves

Combine lamb, onions, tomatoes, garlic, parsley, tomato sauce, bulgur, mint, lemon juice, salt and pepper in bowl; mix well with hands. Rinse grape leaves in cold water. Spoon lamb mixture onto grape leaves; roll to enclose filling. Arrange in circular manner in large saucepan. Add just enough water to cover. Simmer, covered, for 2 to 2½ hours or until done to taste. Serve hot or cold. May substitute ground beef for lamb.

Mavis Chagonjian, John I. Sabin Chapter

VEAL MARSALA

Yield:
6 servings
Utensil:
skillet

Approx Per
Serving:
Cal 379
T Fat 21 g
50% Calories
from Fat
Prot 32 g
Carbo 9 g
Fiber 1 g
Chol 148 mg
Sod 306 mg

2 pounds thinly sliced
  veal round steak
1/2 cup flour
1/2 cup butter
1 4-ounce can sliced
  mushrooms, drained
1 cup (or more) Marsala
Salt and pepper to taste

Cut veal into 2-inch strips. Pound flour into veal with meat mallet. Brown quickly in butter in skillet. Add mushrooms and enough wine to cover. Simmer, covered, for 5 to 10 minutes or until tender. Season to taste. Serve with lemon wedges. May substitute sherry for Marsala.

Susan Gregg, Sierra Pacific Chapter

VEAL PARMESAN

Yield:
4 servings
Utensil:
skillet

Approx Per Serving:
Cal 389
T Fat 25 g
57% Calories from Fat
Prot 28 g
Carbo 14 g
Fiber 1 g
Chol 149 mg
Sod 870 mg

1 pound ½-inch thick veal round steak
½ cup dry bread crumbs
¼ cup grated Parmesan cheese
⅛ teaspoon paprika
½ teaspoon salt
⅛ teaspoon pepper
1 egg, slightly beaten
⅓ cup oil
3 tablespoons water
1   8-ounce can tomato sauce
½ teaspoon oregano

Cut veal into 4 serving pieces. Pound ¼ inch thick with meat mallet. Mix bread crumbs, cheese, paprika, salt and pepper in bowl. Dip veal into egg; coat with crumb mixture. Brown on both sides in oil in large skillet for 6 minutes; reduce heat. Add water. Simmer, covered, for 30 to 40 minutes or until tender. Remove veal to serving plate. Stir tomato sauce and oregano into drippings in skillet. Cook until heated through. Serve veal and sauce over buttered spaghetti.

Shelly Brown, George S. Ladd Chapter

VEAL SCALLOPINI WITH PROSCIUTTO AND MARSALA

Yield:
4 servings
Utensil:
skillet

Approx Per Serving:
Cal 463
T Fat 34 g
67% Calories from Fat
Prot 27 g
Carbo 10 g
Fiber 5 g
Chol 215 mg
Sod 711 mg

8 thin veal scallopini
Salt and pepper to taste
2 tablespoons flour
3 tablespoons olive oil
6 tablespoons butter
½ cup Marsala
4 cups cooked spinach
4 thin slices prosciutto
2 hard-boiled eggs, sliced lengthwise
2 tablespoons chopped parsley

Pound veal thin; season with salt and pepper. Coat lightly with flour. Brown on both sides in olive oil in skillet. Melt butter in large skillet. Arrange browned veal in butter. Drizzle with wine. Simmer, covered, for 4 minutes. Simmer, uncovered, for 2 minutes longer or until slightly thickened. Spoon spinach onto 2 serving plates. Top with veal, prosciutto and egg slices. Spoon sauce over servings. Sprinkle with parsley.

Nancy Murdoch, Sierra Pacific Chapter

Poultry
and Seafood

CHICKEN AFRICAN-STYLE

Yield:
4 servings
Utensil:
skillet

Approx Per Serving:
Cal 697
T Fat 27 g
35% Calories from Fat
Prot 55 g
Carbo 56 g
Fiber 2 g
Chol 152 mg
Sod 151 mg

1 chicken, cut up, skinned
Seasoning salt and pepper to taste
Garlic powder and MSG to taste
1/4 cup corn oil
1 large onion, sliced
2 yellow chili peppers
1 green bell pepper, thinly sliced
1 tablespoon tomato paste
1/4 cup water
4 cups hot cooked rice

Rinse chicken; pat dry. Season with seasoning salt, pepper, garlic powder and MSG. Brown in hot oil in skillet; remove chicken. Add onion, peppers and tomato paste. Stir-fry for 2 minutes or until tender-crisp. Add chicken and water. Cook, covered, until chicken is tender and gravy is thickened, adding additional water if necessary. Serve over hot rice.

Girtha Sanders, Los Amigos Chapter

BAKED HAWAIIAN BARBECUED CHICKEN

Yield:
8 servings
Utensil:
baking dish

Approx Per Serving:
Cal 249
T Fat 9 g
33% Calories from Fat
Prot 27 g
Carbo 15 g
Fiber 1 g
Chol 90 mg
Sod 343 mg

8 chicken legs
8 chicken thighs
Seasoning salt and pepper to taste
Garlic powder to taste
Parsley flakes to taste
Cinnamon to taste
2 8-ounce cans sliced pineapple
1 cup barbecue sauce

Rinse chicken; pat dry. Place in large baking dish. Season with seasoning salt, pepper, garlic powder, parsley flakes and cinnamon. Bake at 400 degrees for 45 minutes or until chicken is tender. Drain pineapple, reserving juice. Arrange pineapple slices over chicken. Bake for 30 minutes. Combine reserved pineapple juice, barbecue sauce and cinnamon in bowl. Pour over chicken. Bake until sauce is heated through.

Yolanda Campbell, Los Amigos Chapter

BROWN-IN-THE-BAG CHICKEN

Yield:
4 servings
Utensil:
oven cooking bag

Approx Per
Serving:
Cal 351
T Fat 13 g
34% Calories
from Fat
Prot 50 g
Carbo 7 g
Fiber <1 g
Chol 152 mg
Sod 789 mg

1 3-pound broiler-fryer
1 tablespoon flour
1 envelope onion soup
  mix
1 envelope ranch salad
  dressing mix

Rinse chicken inside and out; pat dry. Combine flour, soup mix and salad dressing mix in bowl; mix well. Rub over chicken inside and out. Place chicken in oven cooking bag prepared using package directions. Seal and pierce holes using package directions. Place in baking pan. Bake at 350 degrees for 1 hour or until chicken is tender. Serve hot or cold.

Evelyn Mess, John I. Sabin Chapter

HERB-FRIED CHICKEN

Yield:
4 servings
Utensil:
electric skillet

Approx Per
Serving:
Cal 600
T Fat 31 g
48% Calories
from Fat
Prot 61 g
Carbo 13 g
Fiber 1 g
Chol 178 mg
Sod 1545 mg

1 3½-pound chicken,
  cut up
¼ cup flour
½ teaspoon sage
½ teaspoon thyme
½ teaspoon paprika
1 teaspoon salt
3 tablespoons oil
¾ cup chicken broth
1 10-ounce can cream
  of mushroom soup
¼ cup cooking sherry
1 4-ounce can
  mushrooms, drained

Rinse chicken; pat dry. Coat with mixture of flour, sage, thyme, paprika and salt. Preheat oil at 350 degrees in electric skillet for 3 minutes. Add chicken. Brown for 7 minutes on each side. Add ¼ cup broth; reduce temperature to 225 degrees. Simmer, covered, for 40 minutes or until chicken is tender, turning chicken once. Remove chicken to covered casserole; keep warm. Skim drippings. Increase temperature to 325 degrees. Add mixture of remaining ½ cup broth, mushroom soup and sherry. Heat just to the boiling point, stirring constantly. Add mushrooms. Cook for 5 minutes longer. Return chicken to skillet. Cook for 1 minute longer.

Linda Wright, Sierra Pacific Chapter

GRANDMA'S CHICKEN AND DUMPLINGS

Yield:
10 servings
Utensil:
stockpot

Approx Per
Serving:
Cal 357
T Fat 13 g
33% Calories
from Fat
Prot 27 g
Carbo 32 g
Fiber 2 g
Chol 94 mg
Sod 1486 mg

1 3-pound fryer, cut up
6 cups cold water
3 chicken bouillon cubes
6 peppercorns
3 whole cloves
1 10-ounce can chicken
   broth
1 10-ounce can cream
   of chicken soup
1 10-ounce can cream
   of mushroom soup

1 cup chopped celery
1½ cups chopped carrots
¼ cup chopped onion
1 cup chopped potatoes
1 cup frozen peas
1 small bay leaf
1 teaspoon seasoning salt
Feather Dumplings

Rinse chicken. Place in stockpot. Add water, 3 bouillon cubes, peppercorns and cloves. Bring to a boil; reduce heat. Simmer for 30 minutes or until chicken is tender. Let stand until cool. Remove skin and bones; cut chicken into bite-sized pieces. Strain and skim chicken broth. Combine strained broth, chicken, canned broth, chicken and mushroom soups, vegetables, bay leaf and seasoning salt in large stockpot. Simmer, covered, for 2½ hours. Remove bay leaf. Drop Feather Dumplings by teaspoonfuls into boiling soup mixture. Cook, covered, for 18 to 20 minutes or until dumplings are cooked through. Do not lift lid while cooking dumplings.

Feather Dumplings

Nutritional
information for
Feather
Dumplings is
included above.

2 cups flour
4 teaspoons baking
   powder
¼ teaspoon white or
   black pepper

1 teaspoon salt
1 egg, well beaten
2 tablespoons melted
   butter
⅔ cup milk

Sift flour, baking powder, pepper and salt together into bowl. Add egg, butter and enough milk to make stiff batter; mix well.

Dorothy Hamata, Mission Chapter

SHOYU CHICKEN

Yield:
4 servings
Utensil:
saucepan

Approx Per Serving:
Cal 363
T Fat 8 g
21% Calories from Fat
Prot 37 g
Carbo 35 g
Fiber <1 g
Chol 101 mg
Sod 4214 mg

2 pounds chicken pieces
1 cup soy sauce
1 cup water
½ cup sugar

1 teaspoon crushed garlic
1 teaspoon ginger
2 tablespoons cornstarch
¼ cup cold water

Wash chicken pieces; pat dry. Combine soy sauce, water, sugar, garlic and ginger in large saucepan. Heat until bubbly. Add chicken. Simmer for 30 minutes or until chicken is tender. Remove chicken from sauce; keep warm. Stir in mixture of cornstarch and water. Cook until thickened, stirring constantly. Add chicken. Cook for 1 minute longer. Serve over rice.

Eve Durkton, Sierra Pacific Chapter

TABASCO CREAM CHICKEN

Yield:
4 servings
Utensil:
broiler pan

Approx Per Serving:
Cal 807
T Fat 42 g
46% Calories from Fat
Prot 86 g
Carbo 21 g
Fiber 5 g
Chol 301 mg
Sod 380 mg

2   2½-pound broiler-fryers, split
¼ cup melted butter
Tabasco sauce to taste
Salt and pepper to taste
⅔ cup sour cream

1 tablespoon lemon juice
4 tomatoes, cut into halves
8 ounces cooked sweet corn

Rinse chicken; pat dry. Place on rack in broiler pan. Combine butter, Tabasco sauce, salt and pepper in small dish; mix well. Brush over chicken. Broil for 5 to 6 minutes or until brown; turn chicken. Brush with butter mixture. Broil for 3 minutes or until brown. Combine remaining butter mixture, sour cream, lemon juice and additional Tabasco sauce to taste in bowl; mix well. Spread over chicken. Arrange tomato halves around chicken; season with salt and pepper. Broil until chicken and tomatoes are tender. Arrange chicken on platter. Arrange tomato halves and corn around chicken.

Madelene Jeane Ellis, Los Amigos Chapter

HUNGARIAN CHICKEN

Yield:
4 servings
Utensil:
skillet

Approx Per Serving:
Cal 392
T Fat 18 g
41% Calories from Fat
Prot 37 g
Carbo 22 g
Fiber 2 g
Chol 114 mg
Sod 727 mg

2 pounds chicken pieces
¼ cup flour
½ cup shortening
1 onion, chopped
1 10-ounce can tomato
   soup
½ cup water

1 4-ounce can
   mushrooms, drained
2 teaspoons paprika
1 bay leaf
Salt and pepper to taste
½ cup sour cream

Rinse chicken; pat dry. Coat with flour. Brown in melted shortening in skillet; drain. Add onion, soup, ½ cup water, mushrooms, paprika, bay leaf, salt and pepper. Simmer, covered, for 1 hour. Stir in sour cream. Cook, covered, for 15 minutes. Remove bay leaf. Serve with rice or noodles.

Nutritional information does not include shortening for frying chicken.

Rusty Kamman, Mission Chapter

QUICK CHICKEN

Yield:
4 servings
Utensil:
casserole

Approx Per Serving:
Cal 496
T Fat 13 g
24% Calories from Fat
Prot 53 g
Carbo 38 g
Fiber 1 g
Chol 152 mg
Sod 305 mg

1 3-pound broiler-fryer,
   cut up
1 cup uncooked rice

3 cups water
1 envelope onion soup
   mix

Rinse chicken. Place rice in large casserole. Add water and soup mix. Arrange chicken over top. Bake at 350 degrees for 1 hour or until chicken is tender.

Grace Wolfe, Los Amigos Chapter

CHICKEN CURRY

Yield:
4 servings
Utensil:
skillet

1 3-pound chicken, cut up
Salt and pepper to taste
2 teaspoons oil
1 onion, chopped
2¹/₂ cups diluted coconut milk
¹/₂ teaspoon curry powder
¹/₂ cup undiluted coconut milk

Approx Per Serving:
Cal 454
T Fat 23 g
45% Calories from Fat
Prot 51 g
Carbo 10 g
Fiber 1 g
Chol 152 mg
Sod 309 mg

Rinse chicken; pat dry. Season with salt and pepper. Brown in oil in skillet; remove and keep warm. Sauté onion in pan drippings. Add chicken, diluted coconut milk and curry powder. Cook until liquid is almost evaporated and chicken is tender. Add undiluted coconut milk; mix well. Season with salt and pepper.

Bettina Matias, Los Amigos Chapter

QUICK CURRIED CHICKEN

Yield:
6 servings
Utensil:
baking dish

6 chicken breast filets
1 12-ounce package frozen broccoli spears
1 10-ounce can cream of chicken soup
1 cup mayonnaise
¹/₂ cup milk
1 tablespoon lemon juice
3 tablespoons (about) curry powder
1 teaspoon salt
¹/₂ teaspoon pepper
1 teaspoon garlic powder

Approx Per Serving:
Cal 476
T Fat 36 g
67% Calories from Fat
Prot 31 g
Carbo 9 g
Fiber 2 g
Chol 100 mg
Sod 1020 mg

Rinse chicken; pat dry. Place in 12-inch round baking dish. Bake at 450 degrees for 1 hour or until cooked through. Drain, reserving 1 tablespoon drippings; remove chicken. Arrange broccoli on bottom of baking dish. Arrange chicken over broccoli. Combine mayonnaise, milk, lemon juice, reserved drippings and seasonings in bowl; mix well. Pour over chicken. Bake until sauce is bubbly and broccoli is hot. Serve over rice.

Sharon L. Mossman, George S. Ladd Chapter

CRANBERRY CHICKEN

Yield:
6 servings
Utensil:
baking pan

Approx Per
Serving:
Cal 445
T Fat 22 g
45% Calories
from Fat
Prot 27 g
Carbo 34 g
Fiber 2 g
Chol 97 mg
Sod 518 mg

6 chicken breast filets
1 16-ounce can whole
  cranberry sauce
1 8-ounce bottle of
  Russian salad dressing
1 envelope onion soup mix

Rinse chicken; pat dry. Arrange in baking pan sprayed with nonstick cooking spray. Combine cranberry sauce, salad dressing and soup mix in bowl; mix well. Pour over chicken. Bake at 325 degrees for 1 hour.

Chris Campbell, John I. Sabin Chapter

CHICKEN POLONAISE

Yield:
8 servings
Utensil:
casserole

Approx Per
Serving:
Cal 493
T Fat 23 g
42% Calories
from Fat
Prot 41 g
Carbo 30 g
Fiber 2 g
Chol 163 mg
Sod 1044 mg

4 whole chicken breasts,
  split
10 ounces sharp
  Cheddar cheese, cut
  into 8 sticks
2 eggs, beaten
3/4 cup dry bread crumbs
1/4 cup margarine
2 tablespoons flour
1 chicken bouillon cube
1 cup boiling water
1/2 cup chopped onion
1/2 cup chopped green
  bell pepper
1 teaspoon salt
1/4 teaspoon pepper
2 cups cooked white rice
1 cup cooked wild rice
1 13-ounce can sliced
  mushrooms, drained

Rinse chicken; pat dry. Remove skin and bones. Flatten with meat mallet. Wrap each piece around 1 cheese stick; secure with toothpicks. Dip each roll in eggs; coat with crumbs. Brown in margarine in skillet. Remove chicken. Add flour to pan drippings; mix well. Stir in bouillon dissolved in water. Add next 4 ingredients. Cook until thickened, stirring constantly. Stir in rice and mushrooms. Pour into 9x13-inch casserole. Arrange chicken on top. Bake at 400 degrees for 30 minutes.

Brenda McCoy, John I. Sabin Chapter

JAVANESE DINNER

Yield:
12 servings
Utensil:
serving dishes

Approx Per Serving:
Cal 795
T Fat 24 g
27% Calories from Fat
Prot 28 g
Carbo 121 g
Fiber 7 g
Chol 46 mg
Sod 997 mg

3 5-ounce cans chow mein noodles
12 cups hot cooked rice
3 20-ounce cans pineapple chunks, drained
3 11-ounce cans mandarin oranges, drained
1 pint cherry tomatoes, cut into halves
1 bunch each green ouions and celery, sliced
3 whole chicken breasts, cooked, chopped
3 10-ounce cans cream of chicken soup
1 10-ounce can chicken broth
1 cup shredded coconut
1 cup blanched toasted almonds
1 8-ounce jar maraschino cherries with stems, drained

Place first 5 ingredients in separate buffet serving dishes. Combine green onions and celery. Place in serving bowl. Arrange chicken in serving dish. Dilute soup with chicken broth. Pour into gravy boat. Place coconut, almonds and cherries in separate serving bowls. Arrange all dishes on buffet in order listed. Layer ingredients in order listed on serving plates, topping with maraschino cherry.

Martha Blissitt, John I. Sabin Chapter

FIESTA CHICKEN WITH RICE

Yield:
4 servings
Utensil:
baking dish

Approx Per Serving:
Cal 616
T Fat 19 g
26% Calories from Fat
Prot 40 g
Carbo 80 g
Fiber 2 g
Chol 97 mg
Sod 1980 mg

1 16-ounce jar thick and chunky salsa
6 ounces light cream cheese, softened
1 10-ounce can enchilada sauce
2½ cups uncooked instant rice
4 chicken breast filets

Drain ½ cup salsa. Combine with cream cheese in bowl; mix well. Combine remaining salsa and enchilada sauce in bowl; mix well. Reserve ½ cup. Pour remaining enchilada sauce mixture into 7x11-inch baking dish. Stir in rice. Flatten chicken breasts between 2 pieces plastic wrap to ½-inch thickness. Spoon ¼ of the cream cheese mixture onto each; roll up. Place seam side down over rice. Drizzle remaining reserved sauce over top. Bake at 350 degrees for 45 to 60 minutes or until chicken is tender. Add a small amount of additional taco sauce to rice during baking if necessary.

Shirley Johnson, Silver State Chapter

CRISPY OVEN-FRIED MEXICAN CHICKEN

Yield:
4 servings
Utensil:
baking sheet

Approx Per
Serving:
Cal 378
T Fat 9 g
23% Calories
from Fat
Prot 46 g
Carbo 25 g
Fiber 1 g
Chol 123 mg
Sod 986 mg

1 cup mixed vegetable juice
¼ teaspoon (or more) hot sauce
1½ pounds chicken breast filets, cut into 1-inch pieces
2 ounces sharp Cheddar cheese, finely shredded

1½ cups cornflake crumbs
1 teaspoon garlic powder
½ teaspoon each salt and pepper
½ teaspoon each chili powder, paprika, oregano and cumin

Combine vegetable juice and hot sauce in shallow glass dish. Add chicken; mix well. Marinate at room temperature for 30 minutes; drain. Combine cheese, cornflake crumbs and seasonings in large plastic bag. Add chicken several pieces at a time, shaking to coat well after each addition. Place chicken on baking sheet sprayed with non-stick cooking spray. Sprinkle with any remaining cornflake crumb mixture; press crumbs into chicken. Bake in preheated 375-degree oven for 30 minutes or until chicken is tender and crisp.

Norma Harris, Silver State Chapter

GEORGE'S EASY MARSALA CHICKEN

Yield:
6 servings
Utensil:
baking dish

Approx Per
Serving:
Cal 275
T Fat 10 g
33% Calories
from Fat
Prot 28 g
Carbo 8 g
Fiber 1 g
Chol 73 mg
Sod 911 mg

1¼ cups dry Marsala wine
2 10-ounce cans golden mushroom soup

1 4-ounce can mushrooms, drained
6 chicken breasts, skinned

Combine wine, soup and mushrooms in bowl; mix well. Rinse chicken; pat dry. Arrange in 9x12-inch glass baking dish. Pour soup mixture over chicken. Bake, covered with foil, at 350 degrees for 45 minutes. Bake, uncovered, for 30 minutes or until chicken is tender. Serve with rice.

Rusty Kamman, Mission Chapter

QUICK CHICKEN AND PEPPERS

Yield:
6 servings
Utensil:
skillet

Approx Per Serving:
Cal 240
T Fat 8 g
30% Calories from Fat
Prot 28 g
Carbo 13 g
Fiber 1 g
Chol 83 mg
Sod 523 mg

3 whole chicken breasts, split
Salt and pepper to taste
2 tablespoons butter
1 teaspoon olive oil
1 onion, sliced
1 14-ounce can stewed tomatoes
2 green bell peppers, coarsely chopped
1 cup picante sauce
1 clove of garlic, minced
1/2 teaspoon oregano
1/2 teaspoon cumin
1 tablespoon cornstarch
1 tablespoon water

Bone and skin chicken breast halves. Rinse chicken; pat dry. Flatten to 1/2-inch thickness with meat mallet. Season with salt and pepper. Brown in mixture of butter and olive oil in skillet until almost tender. Pour mixture of onion, tomatoes, green peppers, picante sauce and herbs over chicken. Bring to a boil. Simmer for 15 minutes or until chicken is tender. Remove chicken with slotted spoon to platter. Stir in mixture of cornstarch and water. Cook until thickened, stirring constantly. Pour over chicken. Serve with warm tortillas and rice.

Shirley Fredenburg, George S. Ladd Chapter

HERBED CHICKEN BAKE

Yield:
6 servings
Utensil:
casserole

Approx Per Serving:
Cal 397
T Fat 16 g
39% Calories from Fat
Prot 31 g
Carbo 26 g
Fiber 1 g
Chol 97 mg
Sod 1173 mg

1 6-ounce package long grain and wild rice mix
3 large whole chicken breasts, split, boned
Salt and pepper to taste
1/4 cup butter
1 10-ounce can cream of chicken soup
3/4 cup Sauterne
1/2 cup sliced celery
1 3-ounce can sliced mushrooms, drained
2 tablespoons chopped pimento

Prepare rice mix using package directions. Rinse chicken; pat dry. Season with salt and pepper. Brown in butter in skillet over medium heat. Spoon rice into 1 1/2-quart casserole. Arrange chicken skin side up over top. Add soup to pan drippings. Stir in Sauterne gradually. Add celery, mushrooms and pimento. Bring to a boil; pour over chicken. Bake, covered, at 350 degrees for 25 minutes. Bake, uncovered, for 15 to 20 minutes longer or until tender.

Janice Bresee, De Anza Chapter

CHICKEN RICE CASSEROLE

Yield:
8 servings
Utensil:
baking dish

Approx Per Serving:
Cal 397
T Fat 10 g
25% Calories from Fat
Prot 32 g
Carbo 43 g
Fiber 1 g
Chol 73 mg
Sod 956 mg

2 cups rice
2 10-ounce cans beef bouillon
8 chicken breasts
1 envelope onion soup mix
2 10-ounce cans cream of mushroom soup
1/2 cup milk

Place rice in 9x13-inch baking dish. Pour bouillon over rice. Arrange chicken over top. Sprinkle onion soup mix over chicken. Combine soup and milk in bowl; mix well. Spoon over chicken. Bake, covered with foil, at 300 degrees for 3 hours or until tender.

Cindy Hoffman, De Anza Chapter

GRILLED CHICKEN BREASTS WITH HOT PEPPER JELLY

Yield:
4 servings
Utensil:
grill

Approx Per Serving:
Cal 218
T Fat 3 g
12% Calories from Fat
Prot 26 g
Carbo 17 g
Fiber <1 g
Chol 72 mg
Sod 69 mg

4 chicken breasts
1/3 cup hot pepper jelly
1/3 cup dry white wine

Rinse chicken breasts; pat dry. Place skin side down over hot coals on grill. Grill for 15 minutes or until chicken is brown; turn chicken. Brush with mixture of jelly and wine. Grill until brown; turn. Brush with jelly mixture. Grill until chicken is tender, dark brown and crisp, turning and brushing occasionally with jelly mixture. Heat any remaining jelly mixture. Serve with chicken.

Jim Garrotto, Sierra Pacific Chapter

MICROWAVE HAWAIIAN CHICKEN

Yield:
4 servings
Utensil:
baking dish

4 chicken breasts
1 10-ounce can cream
    of celery soup
1 8-ounce can crushed
    pineapple
1 teaspoon curry powder

Rinse chicken; pat dry. Arrange in 8x8-inch glass baking dish. Combine soup, pineapple and curry powder in medium bowl; mix well. Pour over chicken. Microwave, covered, on High for 11 minutes, turning once. Let stand for 5 minutes before serving.

Bess Birdsall, Mission Chapter

Approx Per
Serving:
Cal 236
T Fat 6 g
24% Calories
from Fat
Prot 28 g
Carbo 16 g
Fiber 1 g
Chol 80 mg
Sod 600 mg

CHICKEN DIVAN

Yield:
6 servings
Utensil:
casserole

1/2 cup butter
1/2 cup flour
4 cups milk
Salt and pepper to taste
6 chicken breast filets
1/4 cup butter
12 broccoli spears,
    cooked
2 tablespoons sour cream
3/4 cup grated Parmesan
    cheese
Paprika to taste

Melt 1/2 cup butter in saucepan. Stir in flour. Add milk gradually. Cook for 5 minutes or until slightly thickened, stirring constantly. Season with salt and pepper; set aside. Rinse chicken; pat dry. Sauté chicken in 1/4 cup butter in skillet until golden brown. Arrange broccoli in casserole. Arrange chicken over broccoli. Stir sour cream into cream sauce. Pour over chicken. Sprinkle with Parmesan cheese and paprika. Bake at 350 degrees for 20 or 25 minutes or until bubbly.

Michelle Crane, Los Amigos Chapter

Approx Per
Serving:
Cal 622
T Fat 37 g
51% Calories
from Fat
Prot 47 g
Carbo 32 g
Fiber 10 g
Chol 166 mg
Sod 598 mg

Herbed Chicken

Yield:
6 servings
Utensil:
baking pan

Approx Per Serving:
Cal 347
T Fat 19 g
53% Calories from Fat
Prot 29 g
Carbo 10 g
Fiber 1 g
Chol 112 mg
Sod 968 mg

3 large whole chicken breasts, split
1 teaspoon salt
1/4 teaspoon pepper
1/4 cup butter
1   10-ounce can cream of chicken soup
3/4 cup white Chardonnay wine
1   8-ounce can sliced water chestnuts, drained

1   3-ounce can broiled in butter sliced mushrooms
2 tablespoons chopped green bell pepper
1/4 teaspoon thyme
1 tablespoon minced dried onion
3 tablespoons butter

Rinse chicken; pat dry. Season with salt and pepper. Brown in 1/4 cup butter in skillet. Place chicken skin side up in baking pan. Add soup to pan drippings; mix well. Stir in wine gradually. Add water chestnuts, mushrooms, green pepper, thyme, onion and remaining 3 tablespoons butter; mix well. Pour over chicken. Bake, covered, at 350 degrees for 35 minutes. Bake, uncovered, for 15 minutes longer or until chicken is tender.

Rachel Arroyos, Los Amigos

Chicken and Rice

Yield:
6 servings
Utensil:
casserole

Approx Per Serving:
Cal 523
T Fat 6 g
11% Calories from Fat
Prot 34 g
Carbo 79 g
Fiber 1 g
Chol 76 mg
Sod 544 mg

3 cups uncooked rice
1   10-ounce can cream of chicken soup
1 envelope onion soup mix
6 chicken breast filets
6 soup cans water

Combine rice, soup and onion soup mix in 11x14-inch casserole; mix well. Rinse chicken; pat dry. Arrange over rice. Add water. Bake at 350 degrees for 2 to 2 1/2 hours or until chicken and rice are tender.

Mickey Williams, John I. Sabin Chapter

CHICKEN AND BROCCOLI PIE

Yield:
6 servings
Utensil:
pie plate

Approx Per
Serving:
Cal 748
T Fat 57 g
68% Calories
from Fat
Prot 38 g
Carbo 22 g
Fiber 3 g
Chol 333 mg
Sod 435 mg

4 chicken breasts,
  cooked, chopped
Flowerets of 1 large
  bunch broccoli, cooked
4 green onions, chopped
Red pepper to taste

2 cups shredded Swiss
  cheese
1 unbaked 9-inch
  deep-dish pie shell
2 cups whipping cream
4 eggs

Combine chicken, broccoli, green onions, red pepper and cheese in pie shell. Pour mixture of whipping cream and eggs over top. Bake at 350 degrees for 45 to 60 minutes or until filling is set and crust is brown.

Sharon Booker, Los Amigos Chapter

CHICKEN AND BROCCOLI CASSEROLE

Yield:
6 servings
Utensil:
baking dish

Approx Per
Serving:
Cal 587
T Fat 44 g
66% Calories
from Fat
Prot 24 g
Carbo 26 g
Fiber 4 g
Chol 82 mg
Sod 1216 mg

2 10-ounce packages
   frozen broccoli
2 cups sliced cooked
   chicken
1 cup mayonnaise
1 tablespoon lemon juice

2 10-ounce cans cream
   of chicken soup
1/2 cup shredded sharp
   Cheddar cheese
1 cup buttered bread
   crumbs

Cook broccoli using package directions; drain. Arrange in greased 7x11-inch baking dish. Arrange chicken over top. Combine mayonnaise, lemon juice and soup in bowl; mix well. Pour over chicken. Sprinkle with cheese. Top with buttered bread crumbs. Bake at 350 degrees for 25 to 30 minutes or until bubbly.

Carol Crowder, Sierra Pacific Chapter

EASY CHICKEN CASSEROLE

Yield:
6 servings
Utensil:
baking dish

*Approx Per
Serving:*
Cal 469
T Fat 34 g
*63% Calories
from Fat*
Prot 25 g
Carbo 19 g
Fiber <1 g
Chol 124 mg
Sod 760 mg

5 chicken breasts,
  cooked, chopped
1 cup sour cream
1   10-ounce can cream
  of celery soup
40 round butter crackers
1 teaspoon poppy seed
1/2 cup melted butter

Place chicken in greased 9x12-inch baking dish. Spread mixture of sour cream and soup over chicken. Layer crackers and poppy seed over top. Drizzle with butter. Bake at 350 degrees for 30 minutes or until bubbly.

Audrey F. Bogue, John I. Sabin Chapter

CHICKEN AND STUFFING CASSEROLE

Yield:
8 servings
Utensil:
baking dish

*Approx Per
Serving:*
Cal 386
T Fat 23 g
*54% Calories
from Fat*
Prot 25 g
Carbo 19 g
Fiber 1 g
Chol 83 mg
Sod 877 mg

2 cups seasoned stuffing
  mix cubes
1/2 cup melted margarine
4 cups chopped cooked
  chicken
2   10-ounce cans cream
  of celery soup
1   12-ounce can
  evaporated milk
1   8-ounce can sliced
  water chestnuts,
  drained
2 tablespoons sautéed
  chopped onion
1/2 teaspoon curry
  powder

Place half the stuffing mix in 9x13-inch baking dish. Drizzle with half the margarine. Combine chicken, soup, evaporated milk, water chestnuts, onion and curry powder in bowl; mix well. Spoon into prepared dish. Top with remaining stuffing; drizzle with remaining margarine. Bake at 325 degrees for 45 minutes or until bubbly.

Shirley Fredenburg, George S. Ladd Chapter

CHICKEN CASSEROLE SANDWICH

Yield:
6 servings
Utensil:
baking pan

Approx Per Serving:
Cal 907
T Fat 60 g
59% Calories from Fat
Prot 47 g
Carbo 45 g
Fiber 2 g
Chol 284 mg
Sod 1929 mg

4 cups chopped cooked chicken breast
1 cup chopped onion
1 cup chopped green bell pepper
1 cup chopped celery
1 cup mayonnaise
1 teaspoon salt
1 teaspoon pepper
12 sliced bread, cut into cubes
4 eggs, slightly beaten
3 cups milk
2 10-ounce cans cream of mushroom soup
1 cup shredded Cheddar cheese

Combine chicken, onion, green pepper, celery, mayonnaise, salt and pepper in bowl; mix well. Layer bread cubes and chicken mixture ½ at a time in greased 9x13-inch baking pan. Pour mixture of eggs and milk over layers. Chill, covered, overnight. Spread soup over layers. Top with cheese. Bake at 350 degrees for 1 hour.

Rosemary Reckewey, De Anza Chapter

CHICKEN ENCHILADAS

Yield:
4 servings
Utensil:
baking pan

Approx Per Serving:
Cal 267
T Fat 11 g
37% Calories from Fat
Prot 23 g
Carbo 20 g
Fiber 4 g
Chol 56 mg
Sod 352 mg

2 cloves of garlic, minced
1 tablespoon oil
1 16-ounce can tomatoes, chopped
2 tablespoons chili powder
⅛ teaspoon pepper
1½ cups chopped cooked chicken
¼ cup low-fat plain yogurt
3 tablespoons chopped green chilies
2 tablespoons finely chopped green onions
1 tablespoon chili powder
4 corn tortillas
½ cup shredded part-skim mozzarella cheese

Sauté garlic in oil in skillet for 1 minute. Add tomatoes, 2 tablespoons chili powder and pepper. Simmer for 30 minutes. Mix chicken, yogurt, chilies, green onions and 1 tablespoon chili powder in bowl. Soften tortillas in microwave using package directions. Spoon ¼ cup tomato sauce into 8-inch baking pan. Spoon chicken mixture onto tortillas; roll up. Place seam side down in prepared pan. Pour remaining sauce over tortillas. Sprinkle with cheese. Bake in preheated 350-degree oven for 30 minutes.

Kim Eads, Sierra Pacific Chapter

WHITE ENCHILADAS

Yield:
6 servings
Utensil:
baking dish

Approx Per Serving:
Cal 667
T Fat 38 g
51% Calories from Fat
Prot 36 g
Carbo 48 g
Fiber 2 g
Chol 123 mg
Sod 942 mg

2 cups sour cream
1 10-ounce can cream of chicken soup
4 chicken breasts, cooked, finely chopped
3 green chilies, chopped
1 cup shredded Cheddar cheese
12 flour tortillas
1 cup shredded Monterey Jack cheese

Combine sour cream and soup in bowl; mix well. Reserve ¹⁄₃ cup sour cream mixture. Add chicken, chilies and Cheddar cheese to remaining sour cream mixture; mix well. Soften tortillas using package directions. Fill with chicken mixture; roll up. Place seam side down in greased 9x13-inch baking dish. Spoon reserved sauce over top. Sprinkle with Monterey Jack cheese. Bake at 350 degrees for 30 to 45 minutes or until bubbly.

Eileen O'Connell, Silver State Chapter

CHICKEN FIESTA

Yield:
8 servings
Utensil:
baking dish

Approx Per Serving:
Cal 530
T Fat 30 g
50% Calories from Fat
Prot 46 g
Carbo 22 g
Fiber 2 g
Chol 139 mg
Sod 1191 mg

4 whole chicken breasts, split
6 corn tortillas
1 10-ounce can cream of chicken soup
1 10-ounce can cream of mushroom soup
1 cup milk
1 onion, finely chopped
2 4-ounce cans green chili salsa
1 pound Cheddar cheese, shredded

Rinse chicken; pat dry. Place in 9x13-inch glass baking dish. Bake at 400 degrees for 1 hour. Let stand until cool; bone and chop. Reserve ¹⁄₄ cup chicken pan juices. Cut tortillas into strips. Combine soups, milk, onion and salsa in bowl; mix well. Pour reserved pan juices into 9x13-inch glass baking dish. Alternate layers of tortilla strips, chicken, soup mixture and cheese until all ingredients are used, ending with soup mixture and cheese. Chill for 24 hours. Bake at 300 degrees for 1 to 1¹⁄₂ hours or until bubbly.

Shirley Johnson, Silver State Chapter

CHICKEN AND ALMOND RICE

Yield:
10 servings
Utensil:
baking dish

Approx Per Serving:
Cal 445
T Fat 31 g
62% Calories from Fat
Prot 17 g
Carbo 27 g
Fiber 3 g
Chol 51 mg
Sod 679 mg

3 cups chopped cooked chicken
2 cups cooked rice
2 cups chopped celery
2 10-ounce cans cream of mushroom soup
1 cup mayonnaise
2 8-ounce cans sliced water chestnuts, drained
1/4 cup chopped onion
2 tablespoons lemon juice
1/2 cup slivered almonds
1 2 1/2-ounce package potato chips, crushed

Combine chicken, rice, celery, soup, mayonnaise, water chestnuts, onion, lemon juice and almonds in bowl; mix well. Spoon into 8x12-inch glass baking dish. Chill, covered, overnight. Sprinkle potato chips over top. Bake for 1 1/4 hours or until set. May substitute 3 cups chopped cooked ham for chicken.

Winifred Raye Davis, John I. Sabin Chapter

HOT CHICKEN SALAD

Yield:
4 servings
Utensil:
baking dish

Approx Per Serving:
Cal 374
T Fat 26 g
61% Calories from Fat
Prot 24 g
Carbo 13 g
Fiber 3 g
Chol 75 mg
Sod 413 mg

2 cups chopped cooked chicken
1/3 cup chopped onion
1/2 cup chopped celery
1 4-ounce can sliced mushrooms, drained
5 1/3 ounces fresh bean sprouts
1/3 cup mayonnaise
1 teaspoon lemon juice
2 tablespoons grated Parmesan cheese
1 cup crushed potato chips
Salt and pepper to taste

Combine chicken, onion, celery, mushrooms, bean sprouts, mayonnaise and lemon juice in bowl; mix well. Spoon into 9x9-inch baking dish. Bake, covered, at 425 degrees for 30 minutes. Sprinkle mixture of Parmesan cheese, potato chips and seasonings on top. Bake for 5 minutes longer or until slightly browned.

Gretchen McDonald, John I. Sabin Chapter

ORIENTAL STIR-FRY

Yield:
4 servings
Utensil:
wok

*Approx Per
Serving:*
Cal 334
T Fat 16 g
44% Calories
from Fat
Prot 23 g
Carbo 23 g
Fiber 3 g
Chol 54 mg
Sod 616 mg

2 tablespoons oil
1/2 teaspoon minced
  fresh ginger
1 clove of garlic, minced
12 ounces boneless
  chicken breast strips
2 tablespoons oil
1 medium onion, cut
  into wedges
1 yellow bell pepper, cut
  into strips

1 cup broccoli flowerets
2 medium tomatoes, cut
  into wedges
2 tablespoons soy sauce
1 tablespoon
  Worcestershire sauce
2 tablespoons cornstarch
1 tablespoon sherry
1 teaspoon curry powder
1/2 cup water
1 bag instant rice, cooked

Heat 2 tablespoons oil in wok or skillet. Add ginger, garlic and chicken. Stir-fry until chicken is browned. Remove chicken from wok; set aside. Add remaining 2 tablespoons oil to wok. Add onion, yellow pepper and broccoli. Stir-fry for 1 minute. Add tomatoes and chicken. Combine next 5 ingredients in small bowl; mix well. Add water; mix well. Stir into chicken mixture. Cook until thickened, stirring constantly. Serve over hot cooked rice.

Bess Birdsall, Mission Chapter

TORTILLA-CHICKEN CASSEROLE

Yield:
12 servings
Utensil:
baking dish

*Approx Per
Serving:*
Cal 431
T Fat 21 g
44% Calories
from Fat
Prot 40 g
Carbo 21 g
Fiber 3 g
Chol 117 mg
Sod 799 mg

6 whole chicken breasts,
  split
1 10-ounce can cream
  of chicken soup
1 10-ounce can cream
  of mushroom soup
1 cup milk

1 medium onion, grated
1 7-ounce can chili salsa
12 corn tortillas, cut into
  1-inch pieces
1 pound sharp Cheddar
  cheese, shredded

Rinse chicken. Cook in large saucepan with water to cover until tender. Let stand until cool. Bone and chop chicken. Reserve 2 cups broth. Combine soups, milk, onion and salsa in bowl; mix well. Pour 1 cup reserved broth in bottom of large shallow baking dish. Alternate layers of tortillas, chicken, soup mixture and cheese in prepared dish until all ingredients are used, ending with soup mixture and cheese. Chill, covered, for 24 hours. Pour remaining 1 cup broth over top if mixture appears dry. Bake at 300 degrees for 1 1/2 hours or until bubbly.

Emma Rideout, Los Amigos Chapter

Chicken-Yogurt Enchilada Bake

Yield:
6 servings
Utensil:
baking dish

Approx Per Serving:
Cal 499
T Fat 26 g
47% Calories from Fat
Prot 31 g
Carbo 36 g
Fiber 5 g
Chol 102 mg
Sod 820 mg

¼ cup butter
¼ cup flour
2 cups chicken broth
1 cup plain yogurt
1 7-ounce can chopped green chilies
12 6-inch corn tortillas

2 cups chopped cooked chicken
1 small onion, chopped
2 cups shredded Monterey Jack cheese
¼ cup thinly sliced green onions

Melt butter in saucepan. Stir in flour. Cook until bubbly. Whisk in broth. Bring to a boil, stirring constantly; remove from heat. Add yogurt and chilies; mix well. Dip tortillas into water to soften; drain. Cut into 1-inch strips. Spoon ⅓ of the sauce into 9x13-inch baking dish. Arrange half the tortilla strips over sauce. Top with chicken, onion and ⅔ of the cheese. Spoon half the remaining sauce over cheese. Top with remaining tortilla strips, sauce and cheese. Bake, covered, at 400 degrees for 30 to 35 minutes or until heated through. Sprinkle green onions on top.

Norma Harris, Silver State Chapter

Tasty Cornish Hens

Yield:
6 servings
Utensil:
baking pan

Approx Per Serving:
Cal 520
T Fat 26 g
46% Calories from Fat
Prot 40 g
Carbo 30 g
Fiber 1 g
Chol 137 mg
Sod 3549 mg

3 Cornish hens, split
2 cups sour cream
¼ cup lemon juice
2 tablespoons Worcestershire sauce

2 tablespoons celery salt
1 tablespoon salt
½ teaspoon pepper
2 cups dry bread crumbs

Rinse Cornish hens; pat dry. Combine sour cream, lemon juice, Worcestershire sauce, celery salt, salt and pepper in dish; mix well. Dip each Cornish hen half into sour cream mixture. Coat with bread crumbs. Place skin side up in shallow baking pan. Bake at 350 degrees for 45 minutes or until tender.

Gloria Mercier, Los Amigos Chapter

BOUILLABAISSE

Yield:
6 servings
Utensil:
saucepan

Approx Per Serving:
Cal 406
T Fat 19 g
41% Calories from Fat
Prot 43 g
Carbo 17 g
Fiber 4 g
Chol 231 mg
Sod 520 mg

¹/₂ cup butter
2 medium onions, thinly sliced
1 clove of garlic, crushed
1 large tomato, peeled, sliced
2 bay leaves
2 6-ounce cans tomato paste

¹/₂ cup chopped parsley
8 ounces scallops
8 ounces jumbo shrimp
8 ounces halibut
8 ounces cod
8 ounces medium shrimp, cooked, peeled
1 7-ounce can crab meat

Melt butter in saucepan over medium heat; reduce heat. Add onions. Sauté for 5 minutes. Add garlic, tomato, bay leaves, tomato paste and parsley; mix well. Add scallops, jumbo shrimp, halibut, cod and enough water to cover. Bring to a boil; reduce heat. Simmer until fish flakes easily. Add cooked shrimp and crab meat. Cook for 2 minutes. Discard bay leaves. Serve with garlic bread. May substitute court bouillon for water.

Bonnie DiBenedetto, John I. Sabin Chapter

BAKED CARP WITH ONIONS

Yield:
4 servings
Utensil:
baking dish

Approx Per Serving:
Cal 476
T Fat 32 g
61% Calories from Fat
Prot 35 g
Carbo 11 g
Fiber 0 g
Chol 141 mg
Sod 769 mg

1¹/₂ pounds carp
Paprika and sage to taste
1 cup sour cream

1 teaspoon onion salt
1 3-ounce can French-fried onions

Sprinkle carp lightly with paprika and sage; place in buttered baking dish. Spread with mixture of sour cream and onion salt. Top with onions. Bake, covered, with foil, at 350 degrees for 30 minutes. Bake, uncovered, for 15 minutes longer.

Rick Combs, Silver State Chapter

CHEESY FISH STICKS AND BROCCOLI

Yield:
4 servings
Utensil:
baking pan

Approx Per Serving:
Cal 418
T Fat 20 g
43% Calories from Fat
Prot 23 g
Carbo 37 g
Fiber 3 g
Chol 145 mg
Sod 1210 mg

1   10-ounce package frozen chopped broccoli
1   10-ounce can Cheddar cheese soup
2 tablespoons milk
Seasoned salt to taste
1   16-ounce package frozen fish sticks

Cook broccoli using package directions; drain. Add soup, milk and seasoned salt. Cook on low until heated through. Arrange fish sticks in foil-lined baking pan. Bake at 425 degrees for 10 minutes. Spoon broccoli mixture over fish. Bake for 5 minutes longer. Serve with lemon wedges.

Dorothy Hamata, Mission Chapter

ORANGE ROUGHY ON SPINACH

Yield:
2 servings
Utensil:
baking dish

Approx Per Serving:
Cal 327
T Fat 13 g
34% Calories from Fat
Prot 42 g
Carbo 14 g
Fiber 4 g
Chol 101 mg
Sod 423 mg

1 large bunch spinach
2 tablespoons chopped garlic
1 tablespoon olive oil
1 tablespoon chopped fresh ginger
Juice of 1 lemon
1 small hot pepper, chopped
1/4 cup grated Parmesan cheese
2   6-ounce orange roughy filets

Blanch spinach and chop coarsely. Sauté garlic in olive oil in skillet. Add spinach, ginger, lemon juice, hot pepper and cheese; mix well. Spread in baking dish. Arrange fish on spinach mixture. Bake at 400 degrees for 12 to 15 minutes or until fish flakes easily.

Jim Garrotto, Sierra Pacific Chapter

SUMPTUOUS SALMON

Yield:
2 servings
Utensil:
broiler pan

Approx Per Serving:
Cal 461
T Fat 20 g
40% Calories from Fat
Prot 51 g
Carbo 11 g
Fiber <1 g
Chol 158 mg
Sod 608 mg

⅓ cup dry white or blush wine
⅓ cup rice vinegar
⅓ cup Worchestershire sauce
1 tablespoon hot Chinese mustard
¼ teaspoon minced garlic
½ teaspoon minced fresh ginger
½ teaspoon rosemary
1 tablespoon dill
½ teaspoon sage
2 1½ to 2-inch thick salmon steaks

Combine wine, vinegar, Worcestershire sauce, mustard, garlic, ginger, rosemary, dill and sage in jar. Shake until well mixed. Pour over salmon in container with tight-fitting lid. Marinate for 30 minutes to 2 hours, turning occasionally; drain. Place fish on rack in broiler pan. Broil for 8 minutes or until fish flakes easily. Serve over rice with steamed asparagus and tossed green salad.

Nutritional information includes the entire amount of marinade.

Rita J. Silva, Silver State Chapter

SALMON CROQUETTES

Yield:
4 servings
Utensil:
skillet

Approx Per Serving:
Cal 292
T Fat 15 g
46% Calories from Fat
Prot 24 g
Carbo 15 g
Fiber 1 g
Chol 107 mg
Sod 1141 mg

1 15-ounce can salmon, drained, flaked
1 large potato, cooked, mashed
1 egg
1 tablespoon garlic powder
1 tablespoon onion powder
1 teaspoon salt
1 tablespoon pepper
¼ cup flour
2 tablespoons oil

Combine salmon, potato, egg, garlic powder, onion powder, salt and pepper in bowl; mix well. Shape into round patties. Coat with flour. Chill until firm. Fry in oil in skillet until golden brown on both sides. Serve with tartar sauce or catsup.

Leona Hillman, Los Amigos Chapter

TUNA QUICHE

Yield:
6 servings
Utensil:
pie plate

Approx Per
Serving:
Cal 331
T Fat 19 g
51% Calories
from Fat
Prot 21 g
Carbo 20 g
Fiber 3 g
Chol 111 mg
Sod 566 mg

1 7-ounce can
water-pack tuna
1/2 cup chopped yellow
onion
1/2 cup chopped green
bell pepper
1 4-ounce jar sliced
mushrooms, drained
2 eggs
1/4 cup evaporated milk

1 unbaked 9-inch pie
shell
1 10-ounce package
frozen chopped
spinach
1/2 cup shredded
Monterey Jack cheese
1/2 cup shredded
Cheddar cheese

Combine tuna, onion, green pepper, mushrooms, eggs and evaporated milk in bowl; mix well. Spread in pie shell. Steam spinach; drain well. Spread spinach in prepared pie shell. Layer Monterey Jack cheese and Cheddar cheese over spinach. Bake at 350 degrees for 30 minutes or until brown. May substitute chicken for tuna or broccoli for spinach.

Gwendolyn White, Los Amigos Chapter

TUNA MACARONI CASSEROLE

Yield:
8 servings
Utensil:
baking dish

Approx Per
Serving:
Cal 479
T Fat 17 g
32% Calories
from Fat
Prot 35 g
Carbo 48 g
Fiber 5 g
Chol 72 mg
Sod 1184 mg

2 7-ounce packages
macaroni and cheese
dinners
2 16-ounce cans mixed
vegetables, drained
2 7-ounce cans tuna
Salt and pepper to taste
1 cup shredded Cheddar
cheese

3 ounces cream cheese,
chopped
3/4 cup milk
1/4 cup chopped onion
1/4 cup olives
1 4-ounce can sliced
mushrooms, drained
4 slices American cheese
2 tablespoons milk

Cook macaroni from dinners using package directions; drain well. Combine with vegetables, tuna, salt and pepper in bowl; mix gently. Mix cheese from dinners with shredded cheese and cream cheese in small bowl. Add to tuna mixture; mix well. Stir in 3/4 cup milk. Add onion, olives and mushrooms. Spoon into large baking dish. Top with sliced cheese. Sprinkle with 2 tablespoons milk. Bake at 350 degrees for 45 minutes or until light brown.

Yolanda Campbell, Los Amigos Chapter

TUNA CASSEROLE

Yield:
4 servings
Utensil:
baking dish

Approx Per Serving:
Cal 294
T Fat 2 g
7% Calories from Fat
Prot 30 g
Carbo 39 g
Fiber 4 g
Chol 33 mg
Sod 470 mg

1 7-ounce can tuna, drained
2 cups evaporated skim milk
4 slices bread, cubed
1 cup peas
1 cup chopped pimentos
1 cup sliced mushrooms
2 tablespoons onion flakes
1/2 teaspoon garlic powder

Combine tuna, evaporated milk and bread cubes in bowl; mix well. Add peas, pimentos, mushrooms, onion flakes and garlic powder; mix well. Spoon into baking dish. Bake at 350 degrees for 30 minutes.

Linda Lim, Los Amigos Chapter

THREE-CHEESE TUNA CASSEROLE

Yield:
6 servings
Utensil:
baking dish

Approx Per Serving:
Cal 564
T Fat 29 g
47% Calories from Fat
Prot 30 g
Carbo 45 g
Fiber 4 g
Chol 77 mg
Sod 1086 mg

8 ounces uncooked shell macaroni
1 10-ounce can cream of mushroom soup
1 cup milk
3 ounces cream cheese
1 cup shredded Cheddar cheese
1 cup shredded Monterey Jack cheese
1 10-ounce package frozen peas and carrots, thawed
1 7-ounce can water-pack tuna
1 3-ounce can French-fried onions
1/2 teaspoon salt
1/4 teaspoon pepper

Cook macaroni using package directions; drain. Combine soup, milk and cheeses in saucepan. Heat until cheeses melt. Add macaroni, peas and carrots, tuna, 1 cup onions, salt and pepper; mix well. Spoon into 2-quart baking dish. Top with remaining onions. Bake at 350 degrees for 25 minutes or until golden brown.

Ethel Hightower, Los Amigos Chapter

Tuna Noodle Casserole

| Yield: |
| 2 servings |
| Utensil: |
| baking dish |

Approx Per Serving:
Cal 686
T Fat 40 g
52% Calories from Fat
Prot 33 g
Carbo 49 g
Fiber <1 g
Chol 90 mg
Sod 1079 mg

4 ounces uncooked noodles
Salt to taste
¹/₂ 7-ounce can tuna
¹/₄ cup chopped green bell pepper
¹/₄ cup mayonnaise
¹/₂ 10-ounce can cream of celery soup
¹/₂ cup milk
¹/₂ cup shredded Cheddar cheese

Cook noodles in salted water to cover in saucepan for 8 to 10 minutes or until tender; drain. Combine tuna, green pepper, mayonnaise and salt in bowl. Add noodles; mix gently. Heat soup with milk in saucepan until mixture begins to simmer around edges. Stir in cheese until melted. Add to noodle mixture; mix well. Spoon into baking dish. Bake at 350 degrees until bubbly.

Priscilla Smith, Los Amigos Chapter

Crab Casserole

| Yield: |
| 8 servings |
| Utensil: |
| baking dish |

Approx Per Serving:
Cal 404
T Fat 26 g
57% Calories from Fat
Prot 21 g
Carbo 22 g
Fiber 1 g
Chol 180 mg
Sod 807 mg

8 slices white bread, crusts trimmed
2 6-ounce cans crab meat
¹/₂ cup mayonnaise
1 small onion, finely chopped
1 cup chopped celery
¹/₂ cup chopped green bell pepper
4 eggs
3 cups milk
1 10-ounce can cream of mushroom soup
1 cup shredded sharp Cheddar cheese

Arrange half the bread in 9x13-inch baking dish. Combine crab meat, mayonnaise, onion, celery and green pepper in bowl; mix well. Spread in prepared dish. Cut remaining bread slices into strips. Arrange over crab mixture. Beat eggs and milk in bowl. Pour gently over casserole. Chill in refrigerator overnight. Bake at 325 degrees for 15 minutes. Spread soup over top; sprinkle with cheese. Bake for 1 hour longer.

Dorothy Coats, John I. Sabin Chapter

CRAB CIOPPINO

Yield:
10 servings
Utensil:
stockpot

Approx Per Serving:
Cal 372
T Fat 11 g
26% Calories from Fat
Prot 52 g
Carbo 14 g
Fiber 3 g
Chol 238 mg
Sod 889 mg

1 cup chopped onion
1/2 cup chopped celery
3/4 cup chopped parsley
4 cloves of garlic, minced
1/3 cup olive oil
3 8-ounce cans tomato sauce
1 29-ounce can tomatoes
Salt and pepper to taste
2 pounds clams
2 crabs, cracked, cleaned
2 pounds prawns
1/2 cup Sauterne
1 1/2 pounds cod filets

Sauté onion, celery, parsley and garlic in olive oil in saucepan until light brown. Add tomato sauce, tomatoes, salt and pepper; mix well. Simmer for 3 minutes. Place clams in heavy stockpot. Pour tomato mixture over clams. Add crabs, prawns and wine. Bring to a boil. Simmer for 30 minutes. Add fish filets. Cook for 15 minutes longer. Ladle into bowls to serve. Serve with French bread and green salad. May add 8 ounces scallops if desired.

Connie Turner, Sierra Pacific Chapter

CRAB FETTUCINI WITH BASIL CREAM SAUCE

Yield:
4 servings
Utensil:
skillet

Approx Per Serving:
Cal 507
T Fat 29 g
52% Calories from Fat
Prot 13 g
Carbo 47 g
Fiber 4 g
Chol 65 mg
Sod 233 mg

8 ounces uncooked fresh linguini or fettucini
Salt to taste
3 tablespoons butter
3 tablespoons olive oil
2 tomatoes, peeled, seeded, chopped
1/2 cup finely chopped fresh basil
1 clove of garlic, chopped
1/3 cup cream
1/3 cup dry white wine
1/2 cup cooked dungeness crab meat
White pepper to taste
1/4 cup chopped parsley
1/4 cup grated fresh Parmesan cheese

Cook pasta *al dente* in salted water in saucepan; drain and keep warm. Melt butter with olive oil in heavy 12-inch skillet over medium heat. Add tomatoes, basil and garlic. Simmer until tomatoes are tender. Add cream and wine. Simmer for 10 minutes, adding additional wine if needed for desired consistency. Stir in crab meat, salt and white pepper. Cook just until heated through. Place pasta on serving platter. Spoon crab sauce over pasta. Sprinkle with parsley and cheese. Garnish with whole basil leaves. Serve with leaf lettuce salad, French bread and white wine.

Lenora Kirk, John I. Sabin Chapter

CRAB QUICHE LORRAINE

Yield:
8 servings
Utensil:
2 pie plates

Approx Per Serving:
Cal 479
T Fat 35 g
66% Calories from Fat
Prot 18 g
Carbo 22 g
Fiber 1 g
Chol 193 mg
Sod 696 mg

1/2 cup chopped ham
4 eggs
1 cup whipping cream
1/2 cup half and half
1 slice onion
1/4 teaspoon nutmeg
1/2 teaspoon salt
White pepper to taste
1 7-ounce can crab meat
1 cup chopped Swiss cheese
2 unbaked 9-inch pie shells

Combine ham, eggs, cream, half and half, onion, nutmeg, salt and white pepper in blender container; process for just 10 seconds. Sprinkle crab meat and cheese in pie shells. Pour egg mixture into prepared pie shells. Bake at 350 degrees for 20 minutes.

Evelyn Mess, John I. Sabin Chapter

SHELLFISH CASSEROLE

Yield:
8 servings
Utensil:
baking dish

Approx Per Serving:
Cal 280
T Fat 14 g
46% Calories from Fat
Prot 32 g
Carbo 5 g
Fiber <1 g
Chol 182 mg
Sod 783 mg

1 pound fresh crab meat
8 ounces fresh lobster meat
1 10-ounce can cream of mushroom soup
2 tablespoons flour
1/2 cup milk
Worcestershire sauce or cooking sherry to taste
Turmeric, salt and pepper to taste
1 pound fresh shrimp, peeled
8 ounces sharp Cheddar cheese, shredded

Flake crab meat and lobster meat with fork; combine in lightly greased baking dish. Heat soup in saucepan. Stir in mixture of flour and milk. Add Worcestershire sauce, turmeric, salt, pepper and shrimp. Simmer for 3 minutes, stirring constantly. Spoon into baking dish; stir lightly to mix well with crab and lobster. Top with cheese. Bake at 375 degrees until bubbly and light brown.

Joyce M. Allen, Los Amigos Chapter

SHRIMP ACAPULCO

Yield:
1 serving
Utensil:
skillet

Approx Per Serving:
Cal 546
T Fat 26 g
43% Calories from Fat
Prot 57 g
Carbo 9 g
Fiber 1 g
Chol 582 mg
Sod 795 mg

12 jumbo shrimp
Cayenne pepper to taste
2 tablespoons butter
1 clove of garlic, minced
2 green onions, chopped
1 teaspoon chopped chives
1½ teaspoons brandy
¼ cup dry white wine
1 lemon
Salt and pepper to taste

Sprinkle shrimp with cayenne pepper. Sauté shrimp in butter in skillet for 3 minutes or until pink. Add garlic, green onions, chives, brandy and white wine. Squeeze juice of lemon over top; season with salt and pepper. Simmer for 5 minutes longer. Serve with French bread for dipping in sauce.

Ursula Mensey, Los Amigos Chapter

SHRIMP SAUTÉED IN GARLIC AND WINE

Yield:
2 servings
Utensil:
skillet

Approx Per Serving:
Cal 576
T Fat 41 g
66% Calories from Fat
Prot 39 g
Carbo 8 g
Fiber 1 g
Chol 385 mg
Sod 507 mg

1 pound large (16 to 20-count) shrimp
2 tablespoons flour
¼ cup olive oil
1 clove of garlic, sliced
1 tablespoon chopped green onions
Salt and cayenne pepper to taste
¼ cup dry white wine
2 tablespoons fresh lemon juice
2 tablespoons butter
2 tablespoons chopped parsley

Peel and devein shrimp; coat with flour. Heat 12-inch skillet over medium heat. Add olive oil and shrimp. Cook until brown on 1 side. Turn shrimp. Add garlic, green onions, salt and cayenne pepper. Cook until brown on second side. Add wine and lemon juice, stirring to deglaze skillet. Cook until liquid is reduced to desired consistency, swirling to prevent sticking. Stir in butter; remove from heat immediately. Sprinkle with parsley. Serve with garlic toast, green onion pasta and tossed green salad.

Aundrea De Cou, Los Amigos Chapter

SHRIMP SCAMPI

Yield:
3 servings
Utensil:
broiler pan

Approx Per Serving:
Cal 564
T Fat 33 g
53% Calories from Fat
Prot 48 g
Carbo 6 g
Fiber 1 g
Chol 516 mg
Sod 811 mg

30 medium shrimp
1 cup sliced mushrooms
6 green onions, sliced
6 cloves of garlic, minced
1/2 cup melted butter
1 tablespoon Worcestershire sauce
Hot pepper sauce to taste
1/2 cup dry sherry

Peel and devein shrimp; place in broiler pan. Top with mushrooms, green onions and garlic. Combine butter, Worcestershire sauce and pepper sauce in bowl; mix well. Pour over shrimp. Broil for 8 to 10 minutes or until shrimp are pink. Drizzle with wine.

Theresa Henry, Los Amigos Chapter

SHRIMP AND EGGPLANT

Yield:
4 servings
Utensil:
saucepan

Approx Per Serving:
Cal 146
T Fat 1 g
3% Calories from Fat
Prot 9 g
Carbo 31 g
Fiber 6 g
Chol 44 mg
Sod 1661 mg

2 eggplant
2   16-ounce cans stewed tomatoes
1 ounce mushrooms
1/4 cup chopped onion
1 tablespoon Worcestershire sauce
1 teaspoon garlic salt
1 teaspoon seasoned salt
1 teaspoon pepper
4 ounces peeled shrimp
1 tablespoon chopped parsley

Peel and chop eggplant. Combine with water to cover, tomatoes, mushrooms, onion, Worcestershire sauce, garlic salt, seasoned salt and pepper in heavy saucepan. Bring to a boil; reduce heat. Simmer, covered, for 1 hour or until tender. Add shrimp and parsley. Simmer until shrimp are tender and mixture is of desired consistency. May serve with rice.

Charlotte Bocage, Los Amigos Chapter

SHRIMP-STUFFED PEPPERS

Yield:
4 servings
Utensil:
baking dish

Approx Per
Serving:
Cal 428
T Fat 15 g
32% Calories
from Fat
Prot 30 g
Carbo 41 g
Fiber 1 g
Chol 199 mg
Sod 881 mg

1 envelope duck sauce
   mix
1   7-ounce package Far
   East rice mix
4 large green bell
   peppers

1 pound baby shrimp,
   cooked
Crushed red pepper to
   taste
1 cup shredded
   mozzarella cheese

Prepare duck sauce and rice using package directions. Cut off tops of green peppers and discard seed. Parboil green peppers until tender; drain well. Combine shrimp, rice, red pepper and duck sauce in bowl; mix well. Spoon into green peppers. Place in baking dish; sprinkle with cheese. Bake at 375 degrees for 10 to 15 minutes or until cheese is light brown.

Rose Acard, Los Amigos Chapter

BATTER FOR SHRIMP

Yield:
4 servings
Utensil:
bowl

Approx Per
Serving:
Cal 116
T Fat <1 g
2% Calories
from Fat
Prot 3 g
Carbo 24 g
Fiber 1 g
Chol 0 mg
Sod 432 mg

1 cup flour
1 cup water
1/2 teaspoon salt

2 teaspoons baking
   powder

Combine flour, water, salt and baking powder in bowl; mix until smooth. Let stand for several minutes. Use to coat shrimp for frying.

Marian Babcock, John I. Sabin Chapter

Vegetables
and Side Dishes

BARBECUE BEANS

Yield:
6 servings
Utensil:
baking dish

Approx Per
Serving:
Cal 275
T Fat 9 g
28% Calories
from Fat
Prot 14 g
Carbo 37 g
Fiber 15 g
Chol 24 mg
Sod 1018 mg

1½ cups dried large
lima beans
4 cups boiling water
1½ teaspoons salt
1 onion, chopped
1 clove of garlic, minced
2 tablespoons butter
2 tablespoons molasses

1 8-ounce can tomato
sauce
1 teaspoon
Worcestershire sauce
1 teaspoon chili powder
¾ cup shredded
American cheese

Sort and rinse beans. Combine beans and boiling water in saucepan. Boil for 2 minutes; remove from heat. Let stand, covered, for 1 hour. Add salt. Simmer for 1 to 1½ hours or until tender. Sauté onion and garlic in butter in skillet until tender. Add molasses, tomato sauce, Worcestershire sauce and chili powder. Drain beans; add to sauce. Pour into shallow 6x10-inch baking dish. Sprinkle with cheese. Bake, covered, at 350 degrees for 45 minutes. Bake, uncovered, for 15 minutes longer.

Florence Schomburg, Mission Chapter

JEAN'S BEANS

Yield:
8 servings
Utensil:
cast-iron skillet

Approx Per
Serving:
Cal 316
T Fat 8 g
21% Calories
from Fat
Prot 13 g
Carbo 52 g
Fiber 11 g
Chol 21 mg
Sod 836 mg

12 slices bacon
1 large onion, chopped
1 53-ounce can pork
and beans

⅓ cup packed brown
sugar
2 tablespoons mustard

Fry bacon in large cast-iron skillet until crisp; drain, reserving bacon drippings. Sauté onion in reserved bacon drippings in skillet until light brown. Bring beans to a rolling boil in skillet. Crumble bacon into beans. Add onions, brown sugar and mustard. Cook for 10 minutes; reduce heat. Simmer for 30 minutes longer. Adjust seasonings.

Nick Trisch, John I. Sabin Chapter

FRIED BEAN PATTIES

Yield:
4 servings
Utensil:
heavy skillet

**Approx Per
Serving:**
*Cal 308
T Fat 20 g
56% Calories
from Fat
Prot 10 g
Carbo 24 g
Fiber 11 g
Chol 53 mg
Sod 20 mg*

2 cups drained cooked
  pinto beans
1 egg

¹/₄ cup sesame seed
¹/₄ cup olive oil

Mash beans with fork. Add egg; mix well. Shape into patties; coat with sesame seed. Heat olive oil in skillet over medium heat. Add bean patties. Fry until brown on both sides. Serve with taco sauce, chili sauce or Tabasco sauce.

Clara Catley, Los Amigos Chapter

GREEN BEAN BAKE

Yield:
6 servings
Utensil:
baking dish

**Approx Per
Serving:**
*Cal 165
T Fat 11 g
56% Calories
from Fat
Prot 4 g
Carbo 15 g
Fiber 3 g
Chol 3 mg
Sod 545 mg*

1 10-ounce can cream
  of mushroom soup
¹/₂ cup milk
1 teaspoon soy sauce
Pepper to taste

2 9-ounce packages
  frozen cut green
  beans, cooked
1 2.8-ounce can
  French-fried onions

Combine soup, milk, soy sauce and pepper in 1¹/₂-quart baking dish; mix well. Drain beans well; add to soup mixture. Add half the onions; mix well. Bake at 350 degrees for 25 minutes or until bubbly. Mix gently. Top with remaining onions. Bake for 5 minutes longer.

Debbie Smith, George S. Ladd Chapter

Cheesy Green Bean Casserole

Yield:
10 servings
Utensil:
baking dish

Approx Per Serving:
Cal 135
T Fat 8 g
52% Calories from Fat
Prot 5 g
Carbo 12 g
Fiber 3 g
Chol 12 mg
Sod 718 mg

3 16-ounce cans cut green beans, drained
1 8-ounce can sliced water chestnuts
1 10-ounce can cream of mushroom soup
1 4-ounce can chopped mushrooms, drained
2 tablespoons margarine
1 cup shredded Cheddar cheese
Salt and lemon pepper to taste

Combine green beans, water chestnuts, soup and mushrooms in bowl; mix well. Pour into 8-inch square baking dish. Dot with margarine. Sprinkle with cheese and seasonings. Bake at 350 degrees for 45 minutes.

Ruth P. Bambas, John I. Sabin Chapter

Louisiana Red Beans

Yield:
20 servings
Utensil:
slow cooker

Approx Per Serving:
Cal 78
T Fat <1 g
2% Calories from Fat
Prot 5 g
Carbo 14 g
Fiber 5 g
Chol 0 mg
Sod 11 mg

1 pound dried red beans
2 smoked ham hocks
3 cloves of garlic, minced
1 small jalapeño pepper, chopped
1/2 green bell pepper, chopped
1/2 red bell pepper, chopped
3 stalks celery, chopped
2 bay leaves
Cayenne and black pepper to taste

Sort beans; rinse well. Soak in water to cover overnight. Drain. Combine beans, ham hocks, garlic, jalapeño pepper, green and red peppers, celery, bay leaves and peppers in slow cooker. Add water to 1 inch from top of cooker. Cook on High until mixture comes to a boil; reduce to Medium. Cook for 4 to 6 hours to overnight, stirring occasionally. Serve over hot cooked rice as accompaniment with meat dish.

Nutritional information does not include ham hocks.

Joseph E. Favre, Los Amigos Chapter

RED BEAN TOSS

Yield: *6 servings* *Utensil:* *baking dish*

Approx Per *Serving:* *Cal 338* *T Fat 24 g* *62 % Calories* *from Fat* *Prot 9 g* *Carbo 23 g* *Fiber 7 g* *Chol 29 mg* *Sod 1006 mg*

1   16-ounce can kidney beans
1 cup thinly sliced celery
1/3 cup chopped sweet pickles
1/4 cup chopped onion
1/2 teaspoon Worcestershire sauce
4 ounces American cheese, chopped
1/2 teaspoon chili powder
1/2 teaspoon salt
1/2 cup mayonnaise
1 cup coarsely crushed corn chips

Drain beans. Combine with celery, pickles, onion, Worcestershire sauce and cheese in bowl; mix well. Blend chili powder and salt with mayonnaise in small bowl. Add to bean mixture; toss lightly. Spoon into 1-quart baking dish. Sprinkle with corn chips. Bake at 450 degrees for 10 minutes. May be prepared except for corn chips and refrigerated overnight before baking. May be served hot or cold.

Velda Wheeler, John I. Sabin Chapter

SANTA MARIA-STYLE BEANS

Yield: *8 servings* *Utensil:* *saucepan*

Approx Per *Serving:* *Cal 282* *T Fat 7 g* *21% Calories* *from Fat* *Prot 20 g* *Carbo 37 g* *Fiber 13 g* *Chol 22 mg* *Sod 741 mg*

1 pound dried poquitos beans
2 teaspoons salt
1/2 teaspoon pepper
4 ounces bacon, chopped
8 ounces ground beef
1 small onion, chopped
2 cloves of garlic, minced
1/2 envelope chili seasoning mix
1/2 teaspoon oregano
1 cup tomato juice

Sort beans; rinse well. Place in large saucepan. Add water to cover generously. Bring to a boil. Add salt and pepper. Simmer for 2 to 3 hours or until tender. Sauté bacon, ground beef, onion, garlic, seasoning mix and oregano in skillet. Add to beans. Stir in tomato juice. Simmer for 1 hour. May substitute small red beans or pink beans for poquitos beans.

Jim Garrotto, Sierra Pacific Chapter

Vegetables

BAKED BROCCOLI AND CHEESE

Yield:
4 servings
Utensil:
baking dish

Approx Per Serving:
Cal 247
T Fat 15 g
53% Calories from Fat
Prot 18 g
Carbo 12 g
Fiber 3 g
Chol 142 mg
Sod 476 mg

4 cups chopped fresh broccoli
2 eggs, beaten
1 cup low-fat cottage cheese
2 teaspoons minced onion
1/2 teaspoon Worcestershire sauce
Pepper to taste
1/4 cup shredded Cheddar cheese
1/4 cup fresh bread crumbs
1/4 cup shredded Cheddar cheese
2 tablespoons butter

Cook broccoli in a small amount of boiling water in saucepan for 7 minutes; drain. Place in greased 2-quart baking dish. Combine eggs, cottage, cheese, onion, Worcestershire sauce, pepper and 1/4 cup cheese in bowl; mix well. Spoon over broccoli. Top with bread crumbs and 1/4 cup cheese. Dot with butter. Bake at 350 degrees for 25 to 30 minutes or until bubbly.

Yvette Henry, Mission Chapter

BROCCOLI AND CHEESE CASSEROLE

Yield:
20 servings
Utensil:
slow cooker

Approx Per Serving:
Cal 199
T Fat 12 g
55% Calories from Fat
Prot 7 g
Carbo 16 g
Fiber 1 g
Chol 15 mg
Sod 559 mg

1 large onion, chopped
1/2 cup margarine
2   10-ounce cans cream of mushroom soup
1   16-ounce jar Cheez Whiz
4 cups cooked rice
2   10-ounce packages frozen cut broccoli, thawed

Sauté onion in margarine in skillet until tender. Add soup and Cheez Whiz; mix well. Mix in rice and broccoli. Pour into slow cooker. Cook on Low for 2 to 4 hours or longer or on High for shorter cooking time and keep warm for serving on Low. May use instant rice. This recipe is good for potlucks and family gatherings.

Dorothy Hunsicker, Mission Chapter

STIR-FRY BROCCOLI AND ALMONDS

Yield:
4 servings
Utensil:
skillet

Approx Per Serving:
Cal 98
T Fat 8 g
68% Calories from Fat
Prot 3 g
Carbo 5 g
Fiber 3 g
Chol 0 mg
Sod 85 mg

1 10-ounce package frozen chopped broccoli
2 tablespoons margarine
2 green onions, thinly sliced
2 tablespoons slivered almonds
Juice of 1/2 lemon

Rinse broccoli under running water; drain on paper towels. Melt margarine in large skillet over high heat. Add drained broccoli, green onions and almonds. Stir-fry until broccoli is tender-crisp. Squeeze lemon juice over top just before serving.

Dorothy Hamata, Mission Chapter

BROCCOLI WITH WILD RICE

Yield:
6 servings
Utensil:
baking dish

Approx Per Serving:
Cal 315
T Fat 11 g
30% Calories from Fat
Prot 12 g
Carbo 46 g
Fiber 4 g
Chol 22 mg
Sod 1120 mg

1 pound fresh broccoli
8 ounces fresh mushrooms, sliced
1 7-ounce package long grain and wild rice mix
1/2 teaspoon salt
1 envelope sour cream sauce mix
2 cups milk
1 tablespoon melted butter
3/4 cup bread crumbs
1 teaspoon paprika

Separate broccoli into flowerets. Cook broccoli and mushrooms in a small amount of water in saucepan for 10 minutes; drain. Prepare rice mix using package directions. Blend salt and sour cream mix with milk in bowl. Stir into rice mixture. Fold in broccoli mixture. Spoon into baking dish. Mix butter, crumbs and paprika in small bowl. Sprinkle over rice mixture. Bake at 350 degrees for 20 to 25 minutes or until golden brown.

Debbie Carlin, Los Amigos Chapter

Broccoli and Corn Casserole

Yield:
10 servings
Utensil:
baking dish

1 20-ounce package frozen chopped broccoli, thawed
4 eggs, beaten
2 16-ounce cans cream-style corn

½ cup melted margarine
12 butter crackers, crushed
1 cup shredded Cheddar cheese

Approx Per Serving:
Cal 258
T Fat 17 g
54% Calories from Fat
Prot 9 g
Carbo 23 g
Fiber 4 g
Chol 97 mg
Sod 513 mg

Combine broccoli, eggs, corn, margarine and half the cracker crumbs in bowl; mix well. Pour into 9x13-inch baking dish. Top with cheese. Sprinkle with remaining cracker crumbs. Bake at 350 degrees for 1½ hours.

Henrietta Lange, Mission Chapter

Corn Custard

Yield:
8 servings
Utensil:
casserole

1 16-ounce can cream-style corn
1 16-ounce can whole kernel corn
1 egg, beaten

½ to 1 cup milk
Salt and pepper to taste
1 cup crushed butter crackers

Approx Per Serving:
Cal 157
T Fat 6 g
28% Calories from Fat
Prot 5 g
Carbo 28 g
Fiber 2 g
Chol 31 mg
Sod 432 mg

Combine cream-style and whole kernel corn in bowl. Beat egg with milk, salt and pepper. Add to corn mixture. Add cracker crumbs; mix well with fork. Pour into well buttered 2-quart casserole. Bake at 350 degrees for 35 to 60 minutes or until knife inserted in center comes out clean.

Arliss Summers, Mission Chapter

FLUFFY CORN PUDDING

Yield:
8 servings
Utensil:
baking dish

Approx Per Serving:
Cal 224
T Fat 18 g
70% Calories from Fat
Prot 5 g
Carbo 13 g
Fiber 2 g
Chol 155 mg
Sod 255 mg

1 small onion, minced
¼ cup butter
1 16-ounce can cream-style corn

1 cup light cream
Salt and freshly ground pepper to taste
4 eggs, separated

Sauté onion in butter in skillet until tender; do not brown. Combine with corn, cream, salt and pepper in bowl; mix well. Beat egg yolks lightly; stir into corn mixture. Beat egg whites until frothy. Add pinch of salt. Beat until stiff peaks form. Fold into corn mixture. Pour into buttered baking dish. Bake at 325 degrees for 40 minutes. Increase temperature to 400 degrees. Bake for 5 minutes longer. May add 1 cup cheese cracker crumbs and chopped green chilies to taste.

Jim O'Toole, Los Amigos Chapter

SCALLOPED CORN

Yield:
12 servings
Utensil:
baking pan

Approx Per Serving:
Cal 317
T Fat 9 g
25% Calories from Fat
Prot 10 g
Carbo 53 g
Fiber 5 g
Chol 45 mg
Sod 712 mg

1 12-ounce can evaporated milk
2 eggs
1 onion, chopped
2 cups bread crumbs
3 16-ounce cans cream-style corn

2 16-ounce cans whole kernel corn, drained
½ green bell pepper, chopped
Salt and pepper to taste
1½ cups bread crumbs
¼ cup melted margarine

Process evaporated milk, eggs and onion in blender until well mixed. Combine with 2 cups bread crumbs, cream-style corn, whole kernel corn, green pepper, salt and pepper in bowl; mix well. Pour into greased 9x13-inch baking pan. Bake, covered, at 350 degrees for 30 minutes. Toss 1½ cups bread crumbs with melted margarine; sprinkle over top. Bake, uncovered, for 30 minutes longer. May mix crumbled crisp-fried bacon with corn mixture.

Dorothy Garrotto, Sierra Pacific Chapter

EGGPLANT AND TOMATO CASSEROLE

Yield:
6 servings
Utensil:
baking dish

Approx Per Serving:
Cal 41
T Fat <1 g
7% Calories from Fat
Prot 2 g
Carbo 9 g
Fiber 4 g
Chol 0 mg
Sod 306 mg

1 eggplant, peeled, cubed
2 stalks celery, chopped
1 green bell pepper, chopped
6 large mushrooms, chopped
1/2 red onion, chopped
1   14-ounce can peeled tomatoes, chopped
1/2 teaspoon oregano
1 teaspoon lite salt
1/4 teaspoon pepper

Parboil eggplant, celery, green pepper, mushrooms and onion; drain. Pour into baking dish. Add tomatoes and seasonings; mix well. Bake at 350 degrees for 1 hour. Serve with baked chicken or fish.

Ruth Keirn, John I. Sabin Chapter

CHEESY EGGPLANT CASSEROLE

Yield:
6 servings
Utensil:
baking dish

Approx Per Serving:
Cal 108
T Fat 8 g
62% Calories from Fat
Prot 6 g
Carbo 5 g
Fiber 2 g
Chol 82 mg
Sod 354 mg

1 eggplant, peeled
1/2 cup water
1/2 teaspoon seasoned salt
1/2 onion, chopped
1 tablespoon margarine
2 eggs, beaten
1/2 cup shredded Cheddar cheese
1/2 teaspoon seasoned salt
Freshly ground pepper to taste
Tabasco sauce to taste
2 tablespoons grated Parmesan cheese
Paprika to taste

Slice eggplant 1/2 inch thick; cut into cubes. Combine eggplant, water and 1/2 teaspoon seasoned salt in saucepan. Simmer, covered, until tender; drain. Sauté onion in margarine in skillet. Combine eggplant, sautéed onion, eggs, Cheddar cheese, remaining 1/2 teaspoon seasoned salt, pepper and Tabasco sauce in bowl; mix well. Pour into buttered 9-inch square baking dish. Sprinkle Parmesan cheese and paprika over top. Bake at 350 degrees for 30 minutes or until knife inserted in center comes out clean.

Linda Wright, Sierra Pacific Chapter

MUSHROOM CASSEROLE

Yield:
8 servings
Utensil:
baking dish

Approx Per
Serving:
Cal 459
T Fat 38 g
72% Calories
from Fat
Prot 9 g
Carbo 23 g
Fiber 2 g
Chol 122 mg
Sod 943 mg

1 pound fresh
    mushrooms, sliced
1/4 cup butter
8 slices white bread
1/2 cup butter, softened
1/2 cup chopped onion
1/2 cup chopped celery
1/2 cup chopped green
    bell pepper
1/2 cup mayonnaise
3/4 teaspoon salt
1/4 teaspoon pepper
2 eggs, slightly beaten
1 1/2 cups milk
1 10-ounce can cream
    of mushroom soup
1/2 cup shredded
    Cheddar cheese

Sauté mushrooms in 1/4 cup butter in skillet until almost dry. Spread bread slices with softened butter. Cut 6 slices into 1-inch squares. Combine mushrooms with onion, celery, green pepper, mayonnaise, salt and pepper in bowl; mix well. Layer bread squares and mushroom mixture 1/2 at a time in greased shallow baking dish. Beat eggs with milk; pour over layers. Chill, covered, for 1 hour or longer. Spread soup over top. Cut remaining 2 bread slices into squares; sprinkle over soup. Bake at 350 degrees for 40 to 50 minutes. Top with cheese. Bake for 10 minutes longer.

Barbara Jarrett, Los Amigos Chapter

AU GRATIN POTATOES

Yield:
10 servings
Utensil:
casserole

Approx Per
Serving:
Cal 300
T Fat 16 g
46% Calories
from Fat
Prot 11 g
Carbo 29 g
Fiber 2 g
Chol 49 mg
Sod 438 mg

8 large potatoes
1/4 cup finely chopped
    onion
1/4 cup butter
1/4 cup flour
4 cups milk
1 teaspoon salt
1/4 teaspoon hot pepper
    sauce
1/4 teaspoon marjoram
2 cups shredded
    Cheddar cheese

Cook unpeeled potatoes in water to cover in saucepan until tender; drain, peel and cube. Sauté onion in butter in saucepan. Add flour; mix well. Remove from heat. Stir in milk gradually. Cook over medium heat until thickened, stirring constantly. Add seasonings and cheese; stir until cheese melts. Mix in potatoes. Pour into casserole. Bake at 350 degrees for 25 minutes. Garnish with sprinkle of paprika and minced parsley.

Anne Marie Frame, Los Amigos Chapter

POTATO CASSEROLE

Yield:
8 servings
Utensil:
casserole

6 potatoes, boiled
1/4 cup melted butter
1/3 cup chopped green
   onions
1 teaspoon salt
1/4 teaspoon pepper

2 cups sour cream
2 cups shredded
   Cheddar cheese
2 tablespoons melted
   butter

*Approx Per
Serving:
Cal 404
T Fat 30 g
66% Calories
from Fat
Prot 11 g
Carbo 24 g
Fiber 2 g
Chol 79 mg
Sod 550 mg*

Peel and grate potatoes. Combine with 1/4 cup butter, green onions, salt, pepper, sour cream and cheese in bowl; mix well. Pour into large casserole. Drizzle 2 tablespoons melted butter over top. Bake at 350 degrees for 25 to 30 minutes or until bubbly.

Anna Lewis, Los Amigos Chapter

FABULOUS POTATOES

Yield:
10 servings
Utensil:
baking pan

2 12-ounce packages
   frozen Southern-style
   hashed brown potatoes
1 teaspoon salt
1 10-ounce can cream
   of chicken soup

1 cup shredded Cheddar
   cheese
1/2 cup sour cream
2 cups crushed
   cornflakes
1/2 cup melted butter

*Approx Per
Serving:
Cal 379
T Fat 25 g
58% Calories
from Fat
Prot 7 g
Carbo 34 g
Fiber 2 g
Chol 44 mg
Sod 781 mg*

Combine potatoes, salt, soup, cheese and sour cream in bowl; mix well. Pour into greased 9x13-inch baking pan. Mix cornflakes with melted butter in bowl. Sprinkle over potato mixture. Bake at 350 degrees for 45 minutes.

Nita Lorenzo, John I. Sabin Chapter

HASHED BROWN CASSEROLE

Yield:
10 servings
Utensil:
baking pan

Approx Per Serving:
Cal 439
T Fat 27 g
54% Calories from Fat
Prot 10 g
Carbo 42 g
Fiber 2 g
Chol 43 mg
Sod 605 mg

1 32-ounce package frozen hashed brown potatoes
1 cup sour cream
1½ cups shredded sharp Cheddar cheese
1 10-ounce can cream of chicken soup
1 small onion, chopped
⅛ teaspoon salt
2 cups crushed cornflakes
¼ cup melted butter

Place hashed brown potatoes in greased 9x13-inch baking pan. Combine sour cream, cheese, soup, onion and salt in bowl; mix well. Spread over potatoes. Sprinkle cornflakes over sour cream mixture. Drizzle butter over top. Bake at 350 degrees for 45 minutes.

Evelyn Mess, John I. Sabin Chapter

CHEESY POTATOES

Yield:
10 servings
Utensil:
baking dish

Approx Per Serving:
Cal 322
T Fat 19 g
52% Calories from Fat
Prot 6 g
Carbo 34 g
Fiber 2 g
Chol 50 mg
Sod 158 mg

12 medium potatoes, peeled, cubed
½ cup butter
1 cup sour cream
Salt to taste
3 ounces cream cheese
½ cup shredded Cheddar cheese

Cook potatoes in boiling water in saucepan for 30 minutes or until tender; drain. Combine with butter, sour cream, salt and cream cheese in mixer bowl. Beat until very smooth. Pour into greased baking dish. Sprinkle with Cheddar cheese. Bake at 325 degrees for 20 minutes.

Shari R. Ruddy, Sierra Chapter

CHEDDARY SCALLOPED POTATOES

Yield:
4 servings
Utensil:
skillet

Approx Per
Serving:
Cal 493
T Fat 19 g
34% Calories
from Fat
Prot 8 g
Carbo 74 g
Fiber 5 g
Chol 3 mg
Sod 2065 mg

1 small onion, sliced
2 tablespoons margarine
1 10-ounce can broccoli
   cheese soup
¹/₃ cup milk
¹/₈ teaspoon pepper
4 medium potatoes,
   cooked, sliced

Sauté onion in margarine in skillet over medium heat until tender. Add soup, milk and pepper; mix well. Add potatoes; mix gently. Simmer, covered, for 5 minutes.

Shelly Brown, George S. Ladd Chapter

SOUR CREAM POTATOES

Yield:
8 servings
Utensil:
skillet

Approx Per
Serving:
Cal 179
T Fat 11 g
51% Calories
from Fat
Prot 3 g
Carbo 20 g
Fiber 2 g
Chol 24 mg
Sod 56 mg

5 potatoes, peeled,
   thinly sliced
1 large onion, thinly
   sliced into rings
3 tablespoons melted
   butter
1 cup sour cream

Layer potatoes and onion in 9-inch skillet. Add water to just cover. Simmer for 10 minutes or until almost tender; drain. Stir in butter and sour cream. Cook, covered, over low heat for 10 minutes or until tender. Do not add salt until potatoes are served.

Mary T. Twomey, DeAnza Chapter

ZESTY SPINACH

Yield:
4 servings
Utensil:
skillet

Approx Per Serving:
Cal 105
T Fat 7 g
55% Calories from Fat
Prot 6 g
Carbo 7 g
Fiber 6 g
Chol 33 mg
Sod 235 mg

2 slices bacon
1/4 cup chopped onion
2 tablespoons red wine vinegar

1/2 teaspoon prepared horseradish
11/2 pounds fresh spinach
Salt and pepper to taste

Fry bacon in skillet until crisp; drain and crumble. Add onion to bacon drippings in skillet. Sauté for 3 minutes. Add vinegar and horseradish. Cook until liquid is reduced. Add whole spinach leaves; toss to coat. Add salt and pepper. Sauté until spinach is limp and glistening. Add crumbled bacon.

Jim Moore, George S. Ladd Chapter

SPINACH AND BROCCOLI CASSEROLE

Yield:
6 servings
Utensil:
baking dish

Approx Per Serving:
Cal 132
T Fat 7 g
47% Calories from Fat
Prot 8 g
Carbo 10 g
Fiber 3 g
Chol 22 mg
Sod 545 mg

1 10-ounce package frozen chopped spinach
1 10-ounce package frozen chopped broccoli

1/4 cup minced onion
1 10-ounce can cream of potato soup
1 teaspoon minced garlic
1 cup shredded Cheddar cheese

Thaw vegetables; drain and squeeze dry. Combine with onion, soup, garlic and cheese in bowl; mix well. Pour into 11/2-quart baking dish. Bake at 350 degrees for 25 to 35 minutes or until bubbly.

Marilyn Ferrucci, George S. Ladd Chapter

SQUASH CASSEROLE

Yield:
6 servings
Utensil:
baking dish

Approx Per
Serving:
Cal 186
T Fat 9 g
40% Calories
from Fat
Prot 5 g
Carbo 24 g
Fiber 3 g
Chol 12 mg
Sod 541 mg

2 pounds yellow squash, sliced
1 onion, minced
Salt and pepper to taste
1 10-ounce can cream of mushroom soup
1 cup fine dry bread crumbs
2 tablespoons butter

Cook squash and onion in a small amount of water in saucepan until tender; drain. Season with salt and pepper. Alternate layers of squash, undiluted soup and crumbs in greased baking dish, dotting each layer with butter. Bake at 350 degrees for 30 minutes.

Lucille Turner, Los Amigos Chapter

SWEET POTATO SOUFFLÉ

Yield:
8 servings
Utensil:
baking dish

Approx Per
Serving:
Cal 558
T Fat 23 g
37% Calories
from Fat
Prot 4 g
Carbo 86 g
Fiber 3 g
Chol 4 mg
Sod 377 mg

1 29-ounce can sweet potatoes, drained
6 tablespoons margarine, softened
1½ cups sugar
1 cup milk
½ teaspoon cinnamon
¼ teaspoon nutmeg
½ cup packed brown sugar
6 tablespoons margarine
¾ cup crushed cornflakes
½ cup chopped pecans

Combine sweet potatoes, softened margarine, sugar, milk, cinnamon and nutmeg in mixer bowl; beat until smooth and fluffy. Pour into greased 8-inch square baking dish. Bake at 300 degrees for 20 to 30 minutes. Heat brown sugar and 6 tablespoons margarine in saucepan until melted, stirring frequently; remove from heat. Add cornflakes and pecans; mix until crumbly. Sprinkle over sweet potato mixture. Bake for 15 minutes longer or until soufflé is firm and topping is crunchy.

Corabell C. Peterson, DeAnza Chapter

SWEET POTATOES WITH TEQUILA AND LIME

Yield:
10 servings
Utensil:
skillet

Approx Per Serving:
Cal 469
T Fat 28 g
55% Calories from Fat
Prot 3 g
Carbo 50 g
Fiber 5 g
Chol 75 mg
Sod 256 mg

1½ cups butter
¼ cup sugar
4 pounds sweet potatoes, peeled, shredded
2 tablespoons lime juice
¼ cup tequila
Salt and pepper to taste

Melt butter with sugar in large skillet. Add sweet potatoes. Cook for 15 minutes or until potatoes caramelize, stirring frequently. Stir in lime juice and tequila. Season with salt and pepper. Garnish with lime wedges.

Lynn Fox-Norris, Silver State Chapter

ZUCCHINI CASSEROLE

Yield:
8 servings
Utensil:
casserole

Approx Per Serving:
Cal 195
T Fat 15 g
69% Calories from Fat
Prot 7 g
Carbo 8 g
Fiber 1 g
Chol 91 mg
Sod 1025 mg

1½ pound zucchini, sliced
1 large onion, chopped
¼ cup butter
1 cup shredded sharp Cheddar cheese
1 teaspoon MSG
1 teaspoon salt
½ teaspoon pepper
2 eggs, beaten
1½ cups soft bread crumbs
2 tablespoons melted butter

Cook zucchini in a small amount of water in saucepan until tender-crisp; drain. Sauté onion in ¼ cup butter in skillet until golden. Add zucchini; mix well. Stir in cheese, MSG, salt and pepper. Let stand until cool. Add eggs; mix lightly. Pour into buttered 1½-quart casserole. Toss crumbs with melted butter; sprinkle over zucchini mixture. Bake at 350 degrees for 30 to 45 minutes or until knife inserted in center comes out clean.

Marjorie Hermance, John I. Sabin Chapter

ZUCCHINI AND RICE CASSEROLE

Yield:
6 servings
Utensil:
casserole

Approx Per Serving:
Cal 224
T Fat 13 g
51% Calories from Fat
Prot 8 g
Carbo 20 g
Fiber 2 g
Chol 37 mg
Sod 976 mg

³/₄ cup shredded sharp
   Cheddar cheese
1¹/₂ pounds zucchini,
   sliced
¹/₂ cup long grain rice
1 10-ounce can cream
   of mushroom soup
1 soup can water
1 4-ounce can sliced
   mushrooms
1 teaspoon salt
¹/₄ teaspoon pepper
2 slices bacon

Reserve ¹/₄ cup cheese. Alternate layers of zucchini, cheese and rice in buttered 2-quart casserole, ending with zucchini. Combine soup, water, mushrooms, salt and pepper in saucepan. Heat until well mixed, stirring occasionally. Pour over layers. Top with reserved cheese. Cut bacon into 1-inch pieces. Arrange over top. Bake, covered, at 350 degrees for 30 minutes. Bake, uncovered, for 30 minutes longer.

Cindy Willyard, Sierra Pacific Chapter

CALIFORNIA VEGETABLE MEDLEY

Yield:
8 servings
Utensil:
casserole

Approx Per Serving:
Cal 192
T Fat 14 g
65% Calories from Fat
Prot 4 g
Carbo 13 g
Fiber 2 g
Chol 31 mg
Sod 434 mg

1 16-ounce package
   frozen carrots,
   cauliflower and
   broccoli, thawed
1 large onion, chopped
1 cup sliced mushrooms
3 tablespoons butter
1 10-ounce can cream
   of chicken soup
1 cup sour cream
1¹/₂ cups seasoned
   croutons
1 tablespoons melted
   butter

Sauté thawed vegetables, onion and mushrooms in 3 tablespoons butter in skillet for 3 minutes. Add soup and sour cream; mix well. Stir in 1 cup croutons. Pour into buttered 1¹/₂-quart casserole. Sauté remaining ¹/₂ cup croutons in 1 tablespoon butter until coated. Sprinkle over vegetable mixture. Bake at 350 degrees for 30 minutes.

Carol Crowder, Sierra Pacific Chapter

Swiss Vegetable Medley

Yield:
6 servings
Utensil:
casserole

Approx Per Serving:
Cal 282
T Fat 19 g
59% Calories from Fat
Prot 9 g
Carbo 20 g
Fiber 4 g
Chol 26 mg
Sod 619 mg

1 16-ounce package frozen mixed vegetables
1 10-ounce can cream of mushroom soup
1/3 cup sour cream
1/2 cup shredded Cheddar cheese
1/4 teaspoon pepper
1 4-ounce jar chopped pimento, drained
1 2.8-ounce can French-fried onions
1/2 cup shredded Cheddar cheese

Combine vegetables, soup, sour cream, 1/2 cup cheese, pepper, pimento and half the onions in bowl; mix well. Pour into shallow 1-quart casserole. Bake, covered, at 350 degrees for 30 minutes or until vegetables are tender. Sprinkle remaining onions and 1/2 cup cheese in diagonal rows over top. Bake, uncovered, for 5 minutes longer or until golden brown. May microwave, covered, on High for 8 to 10 minutes, top with onions and cheese and microwave, uncovered, for 1 minute longer.

Leone Burke, Mission Chapter

Broccoli and Cheese Pie

Yield:
6 servings
Utensil:
pie plate

Approx Per Serving:
Cal 255
T Fat 16 g
55% Calories from Fat
Prot 19 g
Carbo 10 g
Fiber 2 g
Chol 212 mg
Sod 1095 mg

3/4 cup uncooked salad macaroni, cooked
1 egg yolk, beaten
1 tablespoon minced chives
1 1/2 cups shredded Cheddar cheese
1 10-ounce package frozen chopped broccoli, cooked
4 eggs, beaten
1 egg white, beaten
1 cup cream-style cottage cheese
1 tablespoon snipped chives
1 teaspoon salt
Paprika to taste

Combine macaroni with mixture of egg yolk and 1 tablespoon chives; mix well. Press over bottom and side of greased 9-inch pie plate with back of spoon. Bake at 375 degrees for 10 minutes. Cool for 10 minutes. Increase temperature to 450 degrees. Layer cheese and drained broccoli in prepared pie plate. Combine remaining ingredients in bowl; mix well. Pour over layers. Sprinkle with paprika. Bake for 15 minutes. Reduce temperature to 300 degrees. Bake for 30 minutes or until set. Let stand for 10 minutes before serving.

Carol Sloane, Sierra Pacific Chapter

CHILI EGG PUFF

Yield:
12 servings
Utensil:
baking pan

10 eggs
1/2 cup flour
1 teaspoon baking
  powder
1/2 teaspoon salt
2 cups cottage cheese

4 cups shredded
  Monterey Jack cheese
1/2 cup melted margarine
2 4-ounce cans chopped
  green chilies

Approx Per
Serving:
Cal 335
T Fat 25 g
68% Calories
from Fat
Prot 20 g
Carbo 7 g
Fiber <1 g
Chol 217 mg
Sod 741 mg

Beat eggs in bowl until light and lemon-colored. Add flour, baking powder, salt, cottage cheese, Monterey Jack cheese and margarine; beat until well blended. Stir in chilies. Pour into buttered 9x13-inch baking pan. Bake at 350 degrees for 35 minutes or until brown and firm in center. May also cut into small squares and serve warm or cold as appetizer.

Helen Benavidez, Los Amigos Chapter

CHILIES RELLENOS WITH MARINARA SAUCE

Yield:
8 servings
Utensil:
baking dish

1 pound soft tofu
1 1/2 cups shredded
  Monterey Jack cheese
2 7-ounce cans whole
  green chilies
6 egg whites
2 eggs
2/3 cup skim milk

1 cup flour
1 teaspoon baking
  powder
1 1/4 cups shredded
  Cheddar cheese
1/2 cup sliced black olives
1 16-ounce can
  marinara sauce

Approx Per
Serving:
Cal 359
T Fat 21 g
51% Calories
from Fat
Prot 22 g
Carbo 24 g
Fiber 2 g
Chol 92 mg
Sod 1123 mg

Rinse tofu; mash coarsely with fork. Drain in colander for 10 minutes or longer. Mix tofu with Monterey Jack cheese in bowl. Cut lengthwise slit in each chili; discard seed. Stuff with tofu mixture; arrange chilies in lightly oiled 3-quart baking dish. Beat egg whites and eggs in mixer bowl at high speed until thick and foamy. Add milk, flour and baking powder; beat until smooth. Fold in half the Cheddar cheese. Pour over chilies. Top with remaining Cheddar cheese. Bake, uncovered, at 375 degrees for 25 to 30 minutes or until golden brown. Sprinkle chilies rellenos with olives. Serve with hot marinara sauce.

Joanne Rossi, John I. Sabin Chapter

GREEN CHILI AND CHEESE PIE

Yield:
6 servings
Utensil:
pie plate

1 unbaked 9-inch pie
  shell
1 cup shredded Cheddar
  cheese
½ cup shredded
  Monterey Jack cheese
1 7-ounce can whole
   green chilies
3 eggs, slightly beaten
1 cup whipping cream
¼ teaspoon salt
⅛ teaspoon cumin

**Approx Per
Serving:**
Cal 446
T Fat 37 g
*73% Calories
from Fat*
Prot 13 g
Carbo 17 g
Fiber 1 g
Chol 189 mg
Sod 724 mg

Prick pie shell with fork. Bake at 400 degrees for 12 minutes. Reduce temperature to 325 degrees. Reserve a small amount of Cheddar cheese for topping. Sprinkle Monterey Jack and remaining Cheddar cheese into pie shell. Seed chilies; arrange over cheeses. Beat eggs with whipping cream, salt and cumin. Pour over chilies. Sprinkle with reserved Cheddar cheese. Bake at 325 degrees until golden brown and set in center.

Brenda McCoy, John I. Sabin Chapter

KID'S ENCHILADAS

Yield:
12 servings
Utensil:
baking dish

1 cup cottage cheese
2 cups shredded
  Cheddar cheese
2 cups shredded
  Monterey Jack cheese
1 bunch green onions,
  chopped
1 dozen corn tortillas
1 12-ounce can
   enchilada sauce

**Approx Per
Serving:**
Cal 267
T Fat 15 g
*50% Calories
from Fat*
Prot 15 g
Carbo 20 g
Fiber 3 g
Chol 40 mg
Sod 645 mg

Combine cottage cheese, 1 cup Cheddar cheese and 1 cup Monterey Jack cheese in bowl; mix well. Mix in green onions. Spoon onto tortillas; roll each to enclose filling. Arrange in 9x13-inch baking dish. Spoon enchilada sauce over tortillas. Sprinkle with remaining Cheddar and Monterey Jack cheeses. Bake at 350 degrees for 15 minutes or until cheese melts.

Cathy McFarland, John I. Sabin Chapter

NEVADA OMELET

<table>
<tr><td>

Yield:
2 servings
Utensil:
skillet

</td><td>

1 small avocado, mashed
1 tablespoon mayonnaise
3 eggs, beaten
1 tablespoon water
1/8 teaspoon salt
Pepper to taste
1/2 4-ounce can chopped
   green chillies, drained,
   rinsed

</td><td>

1 tablespoon butter
1 8-inch flour tortilla
1/2 cup shredded
   Monterey Jack cheese
1/4 cup sour cream
Hot Tomato Sauce

</td></tr>
</table>

Approx Per
Serving:
Cal 658
T Fat 54 g
72% Calories
from Fat
Prot 21 g
Carbo 26 g
Fiber 9 g
Chol 378 mg
Sod 1241 mg

Blend avocado with mayonnaise in bowl; set aside. Beat eggs with water, 1/8 teaspoon salt and pepper in bowl. Stir in chilies. Heat butter in 8-inch skillet over medium heat. Add egg mixture, tilting skillet to spread evenly. Lift edges as eggs set to allow uncooked eggs to flow underneath. Cook until set. Place tortilla on serving plate. Spread with avocado mixture. Sprinkle with half the cheese. Invert omelet onto tortilla; roll tortilla and omelet as for jelly roll. Top with remaining cheese and sour cream. Garnish with additional cilantro. Serve with Hot Tomato Sauce.

Hot Tomato Sauce

Nutritional
information for
Hot Tomato
Sauce is
included above.

1 medium tomato,
  peeled, cut up
1/2 4-ounce can
  chopped green chilies,
  drained, rinsed
1/2 small onion, cut up
	1 tablespoon cilantro
	1 tablespoon olive oil
	Cayenne pepper to taste
	1 small clove of garlic
	1/4 teaspoon salt
	Pepper to taste

Combine tomato, green chilies, onion, cilantro, olive oil, cayenne pepper, garlic, 1/4 teaspoon salt and pepper in blender container; process until almost smooth. Pour into saucepan. Bring to a boil; reduce heat. Cook for 5 minutes or until slightly thickened, stirring constantly. Keep warm.

Pat Norris, John I. Sabin Chapter

SOUTH OF THE BORDER CASSEROLE

Yield:
6 servings
Utensil:
casserole

Approx Per Serving:
Cal 513
T Fat 33 g
57% Calories from Fat
Prot 20 g
Carbo 36 g
Fiber 7 g
Chol 36 mg
Sod 1637 mg

½ small onion, chopped
2 tablespoons margarine
3 cups corn chips
1 cup chopped Velveeta cheese
1   16-ounce can chili without beans
1   16-ounce can kidney beans, drained
1   12-ounce can whole kernel corn
1 cup chopped Velveeta cheese
1 cup corn chips

Sauté onion in margarine in skillet until golden. Add 3 cups corn chips, 1 cup cheese, chili, beans and corn; mix well. Spoon into greased casserole. Sprinkle remaining 1 cup cheese in center of casserole and remaining 1 cup corn chips around edge. Bake at 350 degrees for 20 minutes.

Barbara Moser, John I. Sabin Chapter

FIVE-CHEESE MUSHROOM QUICHE

Yield:
6 servings
Utensil:
pie plate

Approx Per Serving:
Cal 568
T Fat 44 g
70% Calories from Fat
Prot 23 g
Carbo 21 g
Fiber 1 g
Chol 274 mg
Sod 830 mg

1   8-count package crescent rolls
½ cup each shredded Muenster, Cheddar, Swiss and mozzarella cheese
2 cups sliced mushrooms
1 bunch green onions, chopped
½ cup butter
1 teaspoon basil
1 teaspoon thyme
Salt, pepper and garlic salt to taste
5 eggs
1 cup cottage cheese
1 cup half and half

Spray pie plate with nonstick cooking spray. Line with crescent roll dough, sealing edges. Mix Muenster, Cheddar, Swiss and mozzarella cheeses in bowl. Reserve ½ cup cheese mixture for topping. Sprinkle remaining cheese mixture into prepared pie plate. Sauté mushrooms and green onions in butter in skillet until tender. Add seasonings. Spoon over cheeses. Combine next 3 ingredients in blender container. Process until smooth. Pour over layers. Top with reserved cheese mixture. Bake at 325 degrees for 50 minutes or until set.

Bonnie Boelens, John I. Sabin Chapter

CRUSTLESS QUICHE

Yield:	
6 servings	
Utensil:	
pie plate	

4 eggs
1 cup cottage cheese
1 cup sour cream
1/2 cup grated Parmesan
   cheese
1/4 cup flour

1 teaspoon onion powder
1/4 teaspoon salt
4 drops of Tabasco sauce
2 cups shredded
   Cheddar cheese

Approx Per Serving:
Cal 372
T Fat 28 g
68% Calories from Fat
Prot 22 g
Carbo 8 g
Fiber <1 g
Chol 209 mg
Sod 658 mg

Combine eggs, cottage cheese, sour cream, Parmesan cheese, flour, onion powder, salt and Tabasco sauce in food processor. Process until blended; pour into bowl. Add Cheddar cheese; stir until well mixed. Pour into greased deep pie plate. Bake at 350 degrees for 45 minutes or until set. May add your choice of additional ingredients such as sautéed mushrooms, zucchini or ham.

Bonna Auffhammer, Sierra Pacific Chapter

EASY QUICHE

Yield:
4 servings
Utensil:
baking dish

2 cups baking mix
1/2 cup half and half
1   16-ounce package
   frozen chopped
   broccoli
1 onion, chopped

Pepper to taste
8 ounces Swiss cheese,
   sliced
6 ounces ham, chopped
3 eggs, beaten
1 1/2 cups half and half

Approx Per Serving:
Cal 814
T Fat 45 g
50% Calories from Fat
Prot 43 g
Carbo 59 g
Fiber 4 g
Chol 280 mg
Sod 1635 mg

Combine baking mix and 1/2 cup half and half in bowl; mix well. Roll on lightly floured surface; fit into 8-inch square baking dish. Cook broccoli using package directions; drain well. Layer broccoli, onion, pepper, 3/4 of the cheese and ham in prepared pan. Beat eggs with 1 1/2 cups half and half. Pour over layers. Top with remaining cheese. Bake at 425 degrees for 15 minutes. Reduce temperature to 300 degrees. Bake for 45 minutes longer.

Mary Buehler, John I. Sabin Chapter

FANCY FETTUCINI ALFREDO

Yield:
6 servings
Utensil:
saucepan

Approx Per Serving:
Cal 552
T Fat 42 g
68% Calories from Fat
Prot 12 g
Carbo 32 g
Fiber 2 g
Chol 133 mg
Sod 404 mg

½ cup butter
1½ cups whipping cream
2 tablespoons sherry or port
1 cup grated Parmesan cheese
1 tablespoon flour
¼ cup minced fresh parsley
1 8-ounce package fettucini, cooked

Melt butter in saucepan. Cool. Add cream gradually, whisking constantly until well blended. Whisk in sherry, cheese, flour and parsley. Cook over low heat until thickened, whisking constantly; do not boil. Pour over hot cooked fettucini; toss with large salad spoons until coated. Serve immediately.

John Sobol, Sierra Pacific Chapter

MACARONI AND CHEESE

Yield:
20 servings
Utensil:
baking pan

Approx Per Serving:
Cal 265
T Fat 17 g
58% Calories from Fat
Prot 11 g
Carbo 17 g
Fiber 1 g
Chol 50 mg
Sod 262 mg

1 12-ounce package macaroni
½ cup butter
1½ pounds Colby cheese, shredded
2 tablespoons sugar
Salt and pepper to taste
1 12-ounce can evaporated milk

Cook macaroni using package directions; drain. Add butter to hot macaroni; mix until butter melts and macaroni is coated. Alternate layers of macaroni and cheese in greased baking pan, sprinkling each layer with sugar, salt and pepper and ending with cheese. Pour evaporated milk over layers. Bake at 350 degrees for 30 minutes or until brown. May substitute Cheddar cheese for Colby cheese.

Marsha Byrd, Los Amigos Chapter

MEATLESS MANICOTTI

Yield:
12 servings
Utensil:
baking pan

1 pound ricotta cheese
¼ cup grated Parmesan
  cheese
¼ cup grated Romano
  cheese
1 egg, beaten

½ bunch parsley,
  chopped
4 cups shredded
  mozzarella cheese
24 manicotti shells
Mushroom-Tomato Sauce

Approx Per
Serving:
Cal 376
T Fat 17 g
41% Calories
from Fat
Prot 19 g
Carbo 36 g
Fiber 4 g
Chol 69 mg
Sod 258 mg

Combine ricotta, Parmesan and Romano cheeses, egg, parsley and half the mozzarella cheese in bowl; mix well. Chill, covered, in refrigerator. Cook manicotti using package directions; do not overcook. Drain and rinse. Stuff manicotti with cheese mixture. Cover bottom of baking pan with layer of Mushroom-Tomato Sauce. Arrange stuffed manicotti in single layer in pan. Ladle remaining sauce over top. Sprinkle with remaining mozzarella cheese. Bake at 350 degrees for 45 minutes to 1 hour or until bubbly.

Mushroom-Tomato Sauce

Nutritional
information for
Mushroom-
Tomato Sauce
is included
above.

1 large onion, chopped
6 large cloves of garlic,
  chopped
8 ounces fresh
  mushrooms, sliced
½ bunch parsley,
  chopped

Basil, rosemary, oregano
  and thyme to taste
2 tablespoons olive oil
1 12-ounce can tomato
  paste
1 tablespoon sugar

Sauté onion, garlic, mushrooms, parsley, basil, rosemary, oregano and thyme in olive oil in skillet until mushrooms are tender. Blend tomato paste with 3 tomato paste cans water and sugar in saucepan. Add sautéed vegetables. Simmer for 1 hour or longer, stirring occasionally.

Gina Chapman, Los Amigos Chapter

NOODLES AMANDINE

Yield:
8 servings
Utensil:
casserole

Approx Per Serving:
Cal 628
T Fat 42 g
59% Calories from Fat
Prot 17 g
Carbo 49 g
Fiber 2 g
Chol 95 mg
Sod 877 mg

1 cup slivered blanched almonds
3 tablespoons butter
⅓ cup melted butter
3 tablespoons flour
1⅓ cups light cream
1⅓ cups milk
2 teaspoons salt
Freshly ground white pepper to taste
1 16-ounce package noodles
1 cup shredded American cheese

Sauté almonds in 3 tablespoons butter in skillet over low heat until golden brown. Blend melted butter and flour in saucepan over low heat. Stir in cream and milk gradually. Cook until thickened, stirring constantly. Add salt and pepper. Cook noodles using package directions. Combine sauce, noodles and half the almonds in large bowl; toss to mix. Pour into casserole. Mix remaining almonds with American cheese. Sprinkle over noodles. Bake at 350 degrees for 20 minutes.

Beverly Adams, Los Amigos Chapter

MEXICAN LASAGNA

Yield:
6 servings
Utensil:
casserole

Approx Per Serving:
Cal 454
T Fat 33 g
62% Calories from Fat
Prot 16 g
Carbo 30 g
Fiber 6 g
Chol 65 mg
Sod 691 mg

¼ cup chopped onion
1 tablespoon vegetable oil
1 28-ounce can tomatoes, chopped
2 2-ounce cans sliced black olives, drained
½ 4-ounce can chopped green chilies
Salt to taste
9 corn tortillas
1½ cups sour cream
2 cups shredded Cheddar cheese

Sauté onion in oil in skillet over medium-high heat for 5 minutes or just until onion begins to brown. Add undrained tomatoes, olives and chilies. Simmer, uncovered, for 10 minutes. Add salt. Cut tortillas into strips. Layer tortilla strips, sauce, sour cream and cheese ⅓ at a time in 2-quart casserole. Bake at 350 degrees for 35 minutes or until bubbly.

Betty J. Van Roggen, John I. Sabin Chapter

WHITE SAUCE WITH PASTA

Yield:
4 servings
Utensil:
skillet

Approx Per
Serving:
Cal 676
T Fat 34 g
46% Calories
from Fat
Prot 23 g
Carbo 69 g
Fiber 5 g
Chol 146 mg
Sod 597 mg

1 egg yolk
½ cup whipping cream
4 slices bacon, chopped
1 12-ounce package
   pasta
¼ cup butter

1 cup freshly grated
   Parmesan cheese
⅓ cup chopped fresh
   parsley
2 large fresh tomatoes,
   sliced

Beat egg yolk with whipping cream in small bowl; set aside. Fry bacon in small skillet until crisp; drain and set aside. Cook pasta using package directions; drain but do not rinse. Melt butter in large skillet. Add pasta. Add cream mixture and cheese alternately, tossing constantly. Add bacon; toss to mix. Pour onto large platter. Sprinkle with parsley; arrange tomato slices around pasta.

Linda Colon, John I. Sabin Chapter

PINEAPPLE CASSEROLE

Yield:
10 servings
Utensil:
baking dish

Approx Per
Serving:
Cal 248
T Fat 16 g
54% Calories
from Fat
Prot 4 g
Carbo 26 g
Fiber 1 g
Chol 37 mg
Sod 233 mg

½ cup sugar
3 tablespoons flour
½ cup melted butter
3 tablespoons pineapple
   juice
1 cup shredded Cheddar
   cheese

1 20-ounce can
   pineapple tidbits,
   drained
1 cup butter cracker
   crumbs

Combine sugar and flour in bowl. Blend in butter and pineapple juice. Add cheese and pineapple; mix well. Pour into greased 9-inch square baking dish. Sprinkle crumbs on top. Bake at 350 degrees for 20 to 30 minutes or until golden brown.

Jo Bailey, John I. Sabin Chapter

CALIFORNIA RICE CASSEROLE

Yield:
10 servings
Utensil:
baking dish

Approx Per Serving:
Cal 355
T Fat 23 g
58% Calories from Fat
Prot 12 g
Carbo 26 g
Fiber 1 g
Chol 60 mg
Sod 637 mg

1 cup chopped onion
1/4 cup butter
4 cups freshly cooked rice
2 cups sour cream
1 cup cream-style cottage cheese
1 large bay leaf, crumbled
1/2 teaspoon salt
1/8 teaspoon pepper
1   12-ounce can green chilies
2 cups shredded sharp Cheddar cheese

Sauté onion in butter in skillet until tender. Combine sautéed onion with hot rice, sour cream, cottage cheese, bay leaf, salt and pepper in bowl; mix well. Drain, seed and chop green chilies. Alternate rice mixture, green chilies and cheese 1/2 at a time in greased 8x12-inch baking dish. Bake, uncovered, at 375 degrees for 25 minutes. Garnish with chopped parsley.

Helen Berta, DeAnza Chapter

CHEDDAR AND RICE CASSEROLE

Yield:
6 servings
Utensil:
baking dish

Approx Per Serving:
Cal 350
T Fat 21 g
53% Calories from Fat
Prot 13 g
Carbo 28 g
Fiber <1 g
Chol 57 mg
Sod 390 mg

1 cup rice
2 cups shredded Cheddar cheese
1 cup sour cream
1   4-ounce can chopped green chilies
Salt to taste

Cook rice using package directions. Let stand until cool. Combine with cheese, sour cream, green chilies and salt in bowl; mix well. Spoon into greased 1 1/2-quart baking dish. Bake at 350 degrees for 30 minutes.

Lucille Turner, Los Amigos Chapter

CHINESE RICE

Yield:
6 servings
Utensil:
skillet

Approx Per Serving:
Cal 344
T Fat 17 g
43% Calories from Fat
Prot 8 g
Carbo 43 g
Fiber 3 g
Chol 0 mg
Sod 758 mg

³/₄ cup chopped celery
1 small green pepper, chopped
¹/₂ cup chopped green onions
1   8-ounce can sliced water chestnuts, drained
1   2-ounce can sliced mushrooms, drained

¹/₄ cup vegetable oil
4 cups cooked rice
1 teaspoon salt
Pepper to taste
³/₄ cup coarsely ground peanuts
1¹/₂ to 2 tablespoons soy sauce

Sauté vegetables in oil in skillet over low heat for 5 minutes or until tender-crisp. Add rice, salt and pepper. Heat to serving temperature. Stir in peanuts and soy sauce. May add chopped cooked chicken or ham and serve as entrée.

Evelyn Mess, John I. Sabin Chapter

DIRTY RICE WITH SAUSAGE

Yield:
10 servings
Utensil:
slow cooker

Approx Per Serving:
Cal 243
T Fat 10 g
38% Calories from Fat
Prot 9 g
Carbo 28 g
Fiber 2 g
Chol 23 mg
Sod 387 mg

1 large eggplant, peeled, chopped
1 bunch green onions
8 ounces bacon
2 or 3 green peppers, chopped
1 pound hot link or smoked sausage, sliced

6 cups cooked instant rice
1¹/₂ tablespoons crab boil
Old Bay seasoning, oregano, garlic powder, salt and pepper to taste

Cook eggplant in water in saucepan until tender; drain and mash. Chop bulbs and stems of green onions separately. Fry bacon in skillet until crisp; drain on paper towel, reserving drippings. Sauté green onion bulbs and green peppers in reserved drippings in skillet. Add sausage and mashed eggplant. Cook until heated through. Add rice, crab boil and seasonings; mix well. Pour into slow cooker. Cook on Low for 2 hours. Stir in crumbled bacon and green onion stems. Cook for 30 minutes longer.

Brenda McCoy and Terry Bailey, John I. Sabin Chapter

GRANDMA MABEN'S RICE

Yield:
4 servings
Utensil:
skillet

Approx Per Serving:
Cal 199
T Fat 5 g
22% Calories from Fat
Prot 6 g
Carbo 33 g
Fiber 2 g
Chol 8 mg
Sod 157 mg

6 slices bacon, chopped
½ cup chopped green bell pepper
¼ cup chopped green onions
1 8-ounce can sliced water chestnuts, drained
2 cups cooked rice

Cook bacon and green pepper in skillet until bacon is crisp and green pepper is tender. Add green onions, water chestnuts and rice; mix well. Heat to serving temperature.

Karen Maben, John I. Sabin Chapter

MOZZARELLA RICE

Yield:
6 servings
Utensil:
casserole

Approx Per Serving:
Cal 471
T Fat 31 g
61% Calories from Fat
Prot 19 g
Carbo 26 g
Fiber <1 g
Chol 93 mg
Sod 558 mg

1 7-ounce can chopped green chilies
2 cups sour cream
3 cups cooked long grain rice, cooled
1 pound mozzarella cheese, shredded

Combine green chilies and sour cream in bowl; mix well. Layer rice, sour cream mixture and cheese ½ at a time in greased 3-quart casserole. Bake at 350 degrees for 40 to 45 minutes or until bubbly.

Deborah Colyer, John I. Sabin Chapter

SAVORY BAKED RICE

Yield:
6 servings
Utensil:
casserole

Approx Per
Serving:
Cal 209
T Fat 10 g
44% Calories
from Fat
Prot 3 g
Carbo 27 g
Fiber 1 g
Chol 0 mg
Sod 304 mg

1 cup uncooked long
  grain rice
1/3 cup melted margarine
2 cups water

1 envelope onion soup
  mix
1 4-ounce can
  mushroom pieces

Combine uncooked rice, margarine, water, soup mix and undrained mushrooms in greased 2-quart casserole. Bake, covered, at 350 degrees for 1 hour. Stir before serving.

Marian Babcock, John I. Sabin Chapter

SPANISH RICE

Yield:
4 servings
Utensil:
baking dish

Approx Per
Serving:
Cal 338
T Fat 23 g
60% Calories
from Fat
Prot 10 g
Carbo 25 g
Fiber 3 g
Chol 27 mg
Sod 729 mg

6 tablespoons uncooked
  rice
4 slices American
  cheese, chopped
1/4 cup oil

1 cup boiling water
1 28-ounce can
  tomatoes, cut up
1 small onion, cut up
Salt and pepper to taste

Layer rice, cheese and oil in 2 1/2-quart baking dish. Add boiling water, undrained tomatoes, onion, salt and pepper; mix well. Bake, covered, at 350 degrees for 1 1/4 hours.

Carol Holmes, John I. Sabin Chapter

Breads

WORLD'S GREATEST BISCUITS

Yield:
6 servings
Utensil:
baking sheet

Approx Per Serving:
Cal 179
T Fat 11 g
54% Calories from Fat
Prot 3 g
Carbo 17 g
Fiber 1 g
Chol 14 mg
Sod 244 mg

1 cup self-rising flour
2 tablespoons shortening
³/₄ cup sour cream
¹/₄ cup milk

Combine flour and shortening in bowl; mix until crumbly. Beat sour cream with milk until smooth. Pour into flour mixture. Stir with 1 finger until mixed; do not use conventional method. Shape dough into large biscuits with floured hands; place on baking sheet. Bake at 450 degrees for 10 to 12 minutes or just until baked not browned. Turn on broiler. Broil until browned to taste; watch carefully.

Mary E. Martin, DeAnza Chapter

CAKE MIX COFFEE CAKE

Yield:
12 servings
Utensil:
bundt pan

Approx Per Serving:
Cal 539
T Fat 30 g
49% Calories from Fat
Prot 6 g
Carbo 64 g
Fiber 1 g
Chol 88 mg
Sod 381 mg

1 2-layer package white cake mix
¹/₂ cup oil
4 eggs
1 6-ounce package vanilla instant pudding mix
2 cups sour cream
³/₄ cup sugar
1 teaspoon cinnamon
1 teaspoon baking cocoa
1 cup chopped pecans

Combine cake mix, oil, eggs, pudding mix and sour cream in bowl; mix with fork until smooth. Mix sugar, cinnamon, cocoa and pecans in small bowl. Layer batter and pecan mixture ¹/₂ at a time in greased bundt pan. Cut through with knife. Bake at 350 degrees for 1 hour or until cake tests done. Invert onto serving plate.

Connie Pincus, John I. Sabin Chapter

Orange-Glazed Biscuit Coffee Cake

Yield:
15 servings
Utensil:
bundt pan

Approx Per Serving:
Cal 251
T Fat 13 g
48% Calories from Fat
Prot 3 g
Carbo 30 g
Fiber 1 g
Chol 27 mg
Sod 576 mg

30 canned biscuits
3/4 cup butter

3/4 cup sugar
Grated rind of 1 orange

Arrange biscuits on edge in greased bundt pan. Melt butter in saucepan. Add sugar and orange rind. Cook until sugar dissolves. Pour over biscuits. Bake at 400 degrees for 20 minutes. Invert onto serving plate.

Rusty Kamman, Mission Chapter

Cajun Corn Bread

Yield:
15 servings
Utensil:
baking pan

Approx Per Serving:
Cal 187
T Fat 8 g
40% Calories from Fat
Prot 5 g
Carbo 23 g
Fiber 1 g
Chol 28 mg
Sod 399 mg

2 cups corn bread mix
3/4 cup milk
1 cup chopped onion
1 cup chopped green bell pepper
Salt and pepper to taste
1 16-ounce can cream-style corn

5 slices crisp-fried bacon, crumbled
3 tablespoons bacon drippings
2 tablespoons sugar
1 cup shredded Cheddar cheese

Combine corn bread mix, milk, onion, green pepper, salt, pepper, corn, bacon, bacon drippings and sugar in bowl; mix well. Pour half the batter into greased 9x13-inch baking pan. Sprinkle with cheese. Add remaining batter. Bake at 350 degrees for 45 minutes or until golden brown.

Ursula Mensey, Los Amigos Chapter

Eye-Opener Jalapeño Corn Bread

Yield:
15 servings
Utensil:
baking pan

Approx Per Serving:
Cal 175
T Fat 8 g
40% Calories from Fat
Prot 6 g
Carbo 21 g
Fiber 2 g
Chol 39 mg
Sod 292 mg

1 cup cornmeal
1 cup buttermilk
1 cup flour
3 tablespoons sugar
1/2 teaspoon baking soda
1 teaspoon baking powder
1/4 cup corn oil

2 eggs
1 cup cream-style corn
1   4-ounce can chopped jalapeño peppers
1 cup shredded Cheddar cheese
1/4 cup shredded Monterey Jack cheese

Combine cornmeal and buttermilk in bowl; mix well. Let stand for 30 minutes. Add flour, sugar, baking soda, baking powder, corn oil, eggs and corn; mix well. Stir in peppers and cheeses. Pour into greased 9x13-inch baking pan. Bake at 375 degrees for 30 minutes.

Karolyn Tillisch Aznoe, John I. Sabin Chapter

Banana Bread

Yield:
12 servings
Utensil:
loaf pan

Approx Per Serving:
Cal 271
T Fat 12 g
56% Calories from Fat
Prot 4 g
Carbo 39 g
Fiber 1 g
Chol 36 mg
Sod 170 mg

1 cup sugar
1/2 cup shortening
2 cups sifted flour
1 teaspoon baking soda
1/2 teaspoon salt

2 eggs, beaten
3 large bananas, mashed
1/3 cup finely chopped pecans

Cream sugar and shortening in mixer bowl until light and fluffy. Add flour, baking soda, salt, eggs and bananas; mix well. Stir in pecans. Pour into greased 5x9-inch loaf pan. Bake at 350 degrees for 40 minutes or until loaf tests done. Cool on wire rack. Remove to wire rack to cool.

Mildred L. De Jardins, Los Amigos Chapter

BRAZILCOT BREAD

Yield:
12 servings
Utensil:
loaf pan

Approx Per Serving:
Cal 391
T Fat 17 g
37% Calories from Fat
Prot 7 g
Carbo 57 g
Fiber 5 g
Chol 36 mg
Sod 318 mg

1 cup dried apricot halves
1/3 cup sugar
1 cup boiling water
1 3/4 cups pastry flour
1 cup whole wheat flour
1 teaspoon salt
1/2 teaspoon baking soda
1 tablespoon baking powder
2 eggs, beaten, at room temperature
1 cup packed light brown sugar
1 cup sliced Brazil nuts

Cut each apricot half into 3 pieces; place in bowl. Dissolve sugar in boiling water. Add to apricots. Let stand until cool. Sift dry ingredients into large bowl. Beat eggs until very light. Mix with brown sugar. Add eggs and apricot mixtures to dry ingredients; mix well but do not beat. Stir in nuts. Pour into greased 5x9-inch loaf pan. Bake at 325 degrees for 1 hour. Cool on wire rack. Wrap tightly. Store for 24 hours before serving.

Hettie Coonradt, DeAnza Chapter

COCONUT BREAD

Yield:
24 servings
Utensil:
loaf pans

Approx Per Serving:
Cal 321
T Fat 17 g
46% Calories from Fat
Prot 4 g
Carbo 41 g
Fiber 2 g
Chol 39 mg
Sod 101 mg

4 eggs, beaten
2 cups sugar
1 cup oil
2 teaspoons coconut extract
3 cups flour
1/2 teaspoon baking powder
1/2 teaspoon salt
1/2 teaspoon baking soda
1 cup buttermilk
2 cups coconut
1 cup chopped pecans
1 cup sugar
1/2 cup water
2 tablespoons butter
1 teaspoon coconut extract

Beat eggs with 2 cups sugar, oil and 2 teaspoons coconut extract in bowl. Add sifted dry ingredients alternately with buttermilk, mixing well after each addition. Fold in coconut and pecans. Pour into 2 greased and floured 4x8-inch loaf pans. Bake at 325 degrees for 1 hour or until loaves test done. Combine 1 cup sugar, 1/2 cup water and butter in saucepan. Cook for 5 minutes. Stir in 1 teaspoon coconut extract. Pour over hot loaves. Let stand for 30 to 45 minutes. Remove to wire rack to cool completely.

Martha Blissitt, John I. Sabin Chapter

Pecan Bread with Variations

Yield:
12 servings
Utensil:
loaf pan

3 cups baking mix
1/2 cup sugar
1/3 cup flour

1 egg
1 cup milk
1 1/2 cups chopped pecans

Combine baking mix, sugar, flour, egg and milk in bowl; beat with spoon until well mixed. Stir in pecans. Pour into greased 5x9-inch loaf pan. Bake at 350 degrees for 55 to 60 minutes or until loaf tests done. Cool in pan for several minutes. Remove to wire rack to cool completely. **Banana Pecan Bread Variation:** Increase sugar to 2/3 cup, decrease milk to 1/2 cup, add 1 cup mashed bananas and decrease pecans to 3/4 cup. **Orange Pecan Bread Variation:** Increase sugar to 2/3 cup, substitute orange juice for milk, add 1 tablespoon grated orange rind and decrease pecans to 3/4 cup. **Gumdrop Pecan Bread Variation:** Stir 1 cup cut up gumdrops into batter with pecans. Omit black gumdrops.

Shelly Brown, George S. Ladd Chapter

Approx Per Serving:
Cal 299
T Fat 16 g
47% Calories from Fat
Prot 5 g
Carbo 36 g
Fiber 1 g
Chol 21 mg
Sod 412 mg

Peanut Butter Bread

Yield:
12 servings
Utensil:
loaf pan

2 cups flour
1 tablespoon baking
  powder
1 1/4 teaspoons salt
1/3 cup sugar

1 cup peanut butter
2 eggs, beaten
1/2 cup evaporated milk
1/2 cup water

Sift dry ingredients into bowl. Cut in peanut butter until crumbly. Beat eggs with evaporated milk and water in bowl. Add to peanut butter mixture; mix until moistened. Pour into greased 4x8-inch loaf pan. Bake at 350 degrees for 1 hour or until loaf tests done.

Sharon Regley, Los Amigos Chapter

Approx Per Serving:
Cal 253
T Fat 13 g
45% Calories from Fat
Prot 10 g
Carbo 26 g
Fiber 2 g
Chol 39 mg
Sod 414 mg

PINEAPPLE DATE BREAD

Yield:
12 servings
Utensil:
loaf pan

Approx Per Serving:
Cal 275
T Fat 7 g
22% Calories from Fat
Prot 4 g
Carbo 50 g
Fiber 2 g
Chol 18 mg
Sod 209 mg

1 egg, beaten
1/3 cup milk
1   9-ounce can crushed pineapple
1 cup chopped dates
1/3 cup oil

3 cups sifted flour
4 teaspoons baking powder
3/4 cup sugar
1/2 teaspoon salt

Beat egg with milk, undrained pineapple, dates and oil in bowl. Sift in dry ingredients; mix until moistened. Batter will be thick. Pour into greased 5x9-inch loaf pan. Bake at 350 degrees for 1 hour and 10 minutes or until loaf tests done. Cool on wire rack.

Yvette Henry, Mission Chapter

PUMPKIN BREAD

Yield:
36 servings
Utensil:
loaf pans

Approx Per Serving:
Cal 175
T Fat 7 g
35% Calories from Fat
Prot 2 g
Carbo 27 g
Fiber 1 g
Chol 24 mg
Sod 182 mg

3 cups sugar
1 cup oil
4 eggs, beaten
1   16-ounce can pumpkin
3 1/2 cups flour
2 teaspoons baking soda
2 teaspoons salt

1 teaspoon baking powder
1 teaspoon nutmeg
1 teaspoon allspice
1 teaspoon cinnamon
1/2 teaspoon cloves
2/3 cup water

Blend sugar and oil in large bowl. Add eggs and pumpkin; mix well. Add sifted dry ingredients alternately with water, mixing well after each addition. Pour into 3 greased and floured 5x9-inch loaf pans. Bake at 350 degrees for 1 hour or until loaves test done. Cool in pans for 10 minutes. Remove to wire rack to cool completely.

Ursula Mensey, Los Amigos Chapter

TEXAS BEER BREAD

Yield:
12 servings
Utensil:
loaf pan

Approx Per Serving:
Cal 157
T Fat 1 g
5% Calories from Fat
Prot 4 g
Carbo 32 g
Fiber 1 g
Chol 18 mg
Sod 344 mg

3 cups self-rising flour
1/2 cup sugar
1   12-ounce can lite beer
1 egg, beaten
1 tablespoon water

Combine flour, sugar and beer in bowl; mix well. Let stand for 10 minutes. Pour into 5x9-inch loaf pan sprayed with nonstick cooking spray and rubbed with butter. Beat egg with water in bowl; pour over loaf. Bake at 350 degrees for 40 minutes.

Janie Yanez, John I. Sabin Chapter

ZUCCHINI BREAD

Yield:
24 servings
Utensil:
loaf pans

Approx Per Serving:
Cal 290
T Fat 16 g
48% Calories from Fat
Prot 4 g
Carbo 35 g
Fiber 1 g
Chol 36 mg
Sod 205 mg

4 cups coarsely
  shredded zucchini
3 cups flour
1 1/2 teaspoons salt
1 1/2 teaspoons baking
  soda
1/2 teaspoon baking
  powder
1 tablespoon cinnamon
2 1/2 cups sugar
1 1/4 cups vegetable oil
4 eggs, beaten
4 teaspoons vanilla
  extract
1 cup chopped pecans

Grease two 5x9-inch loaf pans generously on bottoms only. Combine zucchini, flour, salt, baking soda, baking powder, cinnamon, sugar, oil, eggs and vanilla in large mixer bowl. Beat at low speed for 1 minute, scraping side of bowl constantly. Beat at medium speed for 1 minute. Stir in pecans. Pour into prepared pans. Bake at 325 degrees for 50 to 60 minutes or until loaves test done. Cool in pans for 10 minutes. Remove to wire rack to cool completely.

Carol Holmes, John I. Sabin Chapter

CHOCOLATE ZUCCHINI BREAD

Yield:
40 servings
Utensil:
loaf pans

Approx Per Serving:
Cal 182
T Fat 9 g
42% Calories from Fat
Prot 3 g
Carbo 25 g
Fiber 1 g
Chol 21 mg
Sod 122 mg

3 cups sugar
1 cup vegetable oil
4 eggs
2 teaspoons vanilla extract
3 cups flour
1 teaspoon baking soda

1½ teaspoons baking powder
1½ teaspoons salt
½ cup baking cocoa
3 cups grated zucchini
1 cup coconut
1 cup chopped walnuts

Combine sugar, oil, eggs and vanilla in large bowl; mix well. Add flour, baking soda, baking powder, salt and cocoa; mix well. Stir in zucchini, coconut and walnuts. Pour into 4 greased and floured medium loaf pans. Bake at 350 degrees for 1½ hours or until loaves test done.

Robin Cuthbert, John I. Sabin Chapter

FRESH APPLE MUFFINS

Yield:
16 servings
Utensil:
muffin pans

Approx Per Serving:
Cal 272
T Fat 13 g
40% Calories from Fat
Prot 4 g
Carbo 39 g
Fiber 2 g
Chol 27 mg
Sod 247 mg

4 cups chopped apples
1 cup sugar
2 eggs, beaten
½ cup vegetable oil
2 teaspoons vanilla extract

2 cups flour
2 teaspoons baking soda
2 teaspoons cinnamon
1 teaspoon salt
1 cup raisins
1 cup broken walnuts

Mix apples and sugar in large bowl; set aside. Beat eggs with oil and vanilla in bowl. Mix flour, baking soda, cinnamon and salt in small bowl; mix with fork. Add egg mixture to apple mixture; mix well. Sprinkle flour mixture over apple mixture; mix well. Batter is very stiff. Mix in raisins and walnuts. Spoon into greased muffin cups. Bake at 325 degrees for 25 minutes or until muffins test done. Serve warm.

Janie Yanez, John I. Sabin Chapter

JELLY CORN BREAD MUFFINS

Yield:
12 servings
Utensil:
muffin pans

1 cup yellow cornmeal
1 cup flour
3 tablespoons sugar
1 teaspoon salt
2 teaspoons baking
  powder

1 egg, beaten
1 cup milk
3 tablespoons melted
  butter
¹/₄ cup favorite jelly

Approx Per Serving:
Cal 153
T Fat 4 g
25% Calories from Fat
Prot 3 g
Carbo 25 g
Fiber 1 g
Chol 28 mg
Sod 273 mg

Combine cornmeal, flour, sugar, salt and baking powder in bowl. Beat egg with milk and butter in bowl. Add to cornmeal mixture; mix just until moistened. Spoon half the batter into greased muffin cups. Add 1 teaspoon jelly to each cup. Top with remaining batter. Bake at 425 degrees for 25 minutes or until golden brown.

Carolyn Allen, Los Amigos Chapter

EILEEN'S CORNMEAL MUFFINS

Yield:
12 servings
Utensil:
muffin pans

1 cup flour
1 cup cornmeal
1 egg, beaten
¹/₂ cup honey

1 tablespoon baking
  powder
¹/₂ teaspoon salt
1 cup low-fat milk

Approx Per Serving:
Cal 141
T Fat 1 g
7% Calories from Fat
Prot 3 g
Carbo 30 g
Fiber 1 g
Chol 20 mg
Sod 188 mg

Combine flour, cornmeal, egg, honey, baking powder, salt and milk in bowl. Beat with spoon for 40 to 50 strokes. Spoon into muffin cups sprayed with nonstick cooking spray. Bake at 350 degrees for 20 to 25 minutes or until golden brown.

Edna A. Bodle, John I. Sabin Chapter

Sourdough Muffins

<table>
<tr><td>

Yield:
12 servings
Utensil:
muffin pans

</td></tr>
</table>

2 cups unbleached flour
1/2 cup whole wheat flour
3/4 teaspoon baking soda
1 cup Sourdough Starter
1/2 cup peanut oil

1/2 cup milk
2 tablespoons brown
  sugar
1 egg

Combine unbleached flour and whole wheat flour in bowl. Make well in center. Add baking soda, Sourdough Starter, peanut oil, milk, brown sugar and egg; stir until mixed. Batter will be lumpy. Spoon into muffin cups sprayed with nonstick cooking spray. Bake at 400 degrees for 20 to 25 minutes or until golden brown.

<table>
<tr><td>

Approx Per
Serving:
Cal 212
T Fat 10 g
44% Calories
from Fat
Prot 4 g
Carbo 26 g
Fiber 1 g
Chol 19 mg
Sod 63 mg

</td></tr>
</table>

Sourdough Starter

<table>
<tr><td>

Nutritional
information for
1 cup
Sourdough
Starter is
included above.

</td></tr>
</table>

1 envelope dry yeast
2 1/2 cups 110 to 115-
  degree water

2 cups all-purpose flour
1 tablespoon sugar

Dissolve yeast in warm water in 1-quart jar. Add flour and sugar; mix until smooth. Cover jar with cheesecloth. Let stand at room temperature for 5 to 10 days, stirring 2 or 3 times daily. Remove desired amount of Starter as needed. Replenish with equal parts flour and water. Store, covered with cheesecloth, in refrigerator; do not cover tightly with metal lid. Starter may be used for many other recipes and will last for years.

Jim and Holly Tompson, John I. Sabin Chapter

HOT APPLE FRITTERS

Yield: 12 servings *Utensil:* deep fryer	

3 large apples
2 egg yolks, beaten
2/3 cup beer
2 tablespoons melted butter
1 cup sifted flour
1/2 teaspoon salt
2 tablespoons sugar
2 egg whites
Oil for deep frying

Approx Per Serving:
Cal 110
T Fat 3 g
26% Calories from Fat
Prot 2 g
Carbo 18 g
Fiber 2 g
Chol 41 mg
Sod 116 mg

Remove and discard apple cores; cut each apple crosswise into 4 slices. Beat egg yolks in bowl until light. Add beer and butter; blend well. Sift flour, salt and sugar together. Sift into egg yolk mixture; mix well. Beat egg whites in mixer bowl until stiff but not dry. Fold gently into batter. Dip apple slices into batter. Deep-fry several at a time at 370 degrees for 5 minutes or until golden brown; drain well.

Nutritional information does not include oil for deep frying.

Marian Babcock, John I. Sabin Chapter

FLOUR TORTILLAS

Yield: 12 servings *Utensil:* griddle

3 cups flour
1 1/2 teaspoons baking powder
1/2 teaspoon salt
1/4 cup corn oil
1 cup (about) warm water

Combine flour, baking powder and salt in bowl. Add oil. Add enough warm water gradually to make of desired consistency. Knead dough until well mixed. Shape into balls slightly larger than golf balls. Roll to desired thickness. Bake on hot griddle until cooked through, turning once. May prepare dough in food processor.

Approx Per Serving:
Cal 155
T Fat 5 g
29% Calories from Fat
Prot 3 g
Carbo 24 g
Fiber 1 g
Chol 0 mg
Sod 131 mg

Helen Benavidez, Los Amigos Chapter

BAKED FRENCH TOAST

Yield:
12 servings
Utensil:
baking pan

Approx Per
Serving:
Cal 178
T Fat 8 g
40% Calories
from Fat
Prot 8 g
Carbo 18 g
Fiber <1 g
Chol 150 mg
Sod 366 mg

1 10-ounce loaf Italian
   bread
8 eggs, beaten
3 cups milk
4 teaspoons sugar
3/4 teaspoon salt
1 tablespoon vanilla
   extract
2 tablespoons margarine

Slice bread 1 inch thick. Arrange slices in greased 9x13-inch baking pan. Beat eggs with milk, sugar, salt and vanilla. Pour over bread. Dot with margarine. Chill, tightly covered, for 4 to 36 hours. Bake, uncovered, at 350 degrees for 45 to 50 minutes or until puffed and golden brown. Let stand for 5 minutes before serving. Serve with syrup, sour cream or sprinkle of confectioners' sugar. May be served cold.

Paula Sherman, John I. Sabin Chapter

PORTUGUESE SWEET BREAD

Yield:
20 servings
Utensil:
baking pans

Approx Per
Serving:
Cal 171
T Fat 4 g
21% Calories
from Fat
Prot 4 g
Carbo 29 g
Fiber 1 g
Chol 50 mg
Sod 140 mg

1 envelope dry yeast
1/4 cup warm water
1/2 cup milk
1/4 cup butter
1 teaspoon salt
3 eggs
1 egg yolk
3/4 cup sugar
4 to 4 1/2 cups flour

Dissolve yeast in water in large bowl. Heat milk, butter and salt in saucepan over low heat just until butter melts. Beat eggs, egg yolk and sugar in mixer bowl until thick and light-colored. Stir in milk mixture. Stir into yeast mixture. Add 3 cups flour. Beat with wooden spoon until well mixed. Stir in enough remaining flour to make soft dough that will form ball. Knead on lightly floured surface for 8 to 10 minutes or until smooth and elastic. Place in greased bowl, turning to grease surface. Let rise, covered, for 1 1/2 hours or until doubled in bulk. Shape into 2 balls. Press each into greased 8-inch baking pans to cover bottoms of pans. Let rise, covered, for 1 hour or until doubled in bulk. Bake at 350 degrees for 25 to 30 minutes or until golden brown.

Shelly Brown, George S. Ladd Chapter

BUTTERMILK ROLLS

Yield:
48 servings
Utensil:
baking pan

Approx Per Serving:
Cal 113
T Fat 3 g
27% Calories from Fat
Prot 3 g
Carbo 18 g
Fiber 1 g
Chol 3 mg
Sod 161 mg

2 envelopes dry yeast
1/2 cup warm water
2 cups buttermilk
5 tablespoons sugar
1 tablespoon (scant) salt
1/2 teaspoon baking soda
1/2 cup shortening
1/4 cup butter
6 to 8 cups flour

Dissolve yeast in warm water. Heat buttermilk in saucepan. Add sugar, salt, baking soda, shortening and butter; stir until shortening and butter melt. Cool to lukewarm. Combine with yeast in large bowl. Add enough flour to make medium dough. Knead on floured surface until smooth and elastic. Place in greased bowl, turning to coat surface. Let rise, covered, until doubled in bulk. Shape into rolls; place close together in greased baking pan. Let rise until doubled in bulk. Bake at 375 degrees for 20 minutes. Brush with butter if desired.

Evelyn Gist, Los Amigos Chapter

FRESH YEAST ROLLS

Yield:
12 servings
Utensil:
baking pan

Approx Per Serving:
Cal 155
T Fat 3 g
18% Calories from Fat
Prot 4 g
Carbo 27 g
Fiber 1 g
Chol 3 mg
Sod 143 mg

1 cake yeast
1/4 cup warm water
1 cup milk, scalded
3/4 teaspoon salt
2 tablespoons sugar
2 tablespoons (or more) shortening
3 cups (about) flour

Dissolve yeast in warm water. Combine milk, salt, sugar and shortening in large bowl. Let stand until cooled to lukewarm. Add yeast and enough flour to make soft dough; mix well. Knead on floured surface until smooth and elastic. Place in greased bowl, turning to coat surface. Shape as desired; place in greased baking pan. Let rise until doubled in bulk. Bake at 425 degrees for 15 to 20 minutes or until golden brown. May increase shortening for more tender rolls or add 1 egg for richer rolls.

Juanita Stockstill, Los Amigo Chapter

EASY PULL-APART SWEET ROLLS

Yield:
20 servings
Utensil:
tube pan

1 3-pound package frozen dinner rolls
1 cup chopped pecans
1 3-ounce package butterscotch pudding and pie filling mix
Cinnamon to taste
1/2 cup melted margarine
1/2 cup packed brown sugar

Approx Per Serving:
Cal 325
T Fat 13 g
37% Calories from Fat
Prot 5 g
Carbo 45 g
Fiber 2 g
Chol <1 mg
Sod 456 mg

Arrange half the rolls in greased tube or bundt pan. Mix pecans, dry pudding mix and cinnamon in small bowl. Sprinkle half the mixture over rolls. Add layers of remaining rolls and pecan mixture. Blend margarine with brown sugar in bowl. Pour over layers. Cover with foil and towel. Let stand in draft-free place overnight. Bake at 350 degrees for 35 to 40 minutes or until golden brown. Invert onto serving plate immediately. Do not use instant pudding mix.

Alice Milovich, Silver State Chapter

BACON AND CHEESE FRENCH LOAF

Yield:
12 servings
Utensil:
baking sheet

1 16-ounce loaf French bread
1/2 cup butter, softened
1 small onion, finely chopped
1 tablespoon poppy seed
1 to 3 tablespoons prepared mustard
8 ounces Swiss cheese, sliced
4 slices bacon, chopped

Approx Per Serving:
Cal 265
T Fat 16 g
53% Calories from Fat
Prot 10 g
Carbo 21 g
Fiber 1 g
Chol 40 mg
Sod 416 mg

Cut bread into halves horizontally. Combine butter, onion, poppy seed and mustard in bowl; mix well. Spread on cut surfaces. Place cut surfaces together; cut into slices to but not through bottom. Place cheese slices between bread slices. Top with bacon; place on baking sheet. Bake at 400 degrees for 20 minutes or until bacon is crisp and cheese is melted. May substitute Monterey Jack cheese for Swiss cheese.

Robin Cuthbert, John I. Sabin Chapter

KILLER GARLIC BREAD

Yield:
15 servings
Utensil:
baking sheet

2 16-ounce loaves
  sweet sourdough
  bread
1 cup melted butter
1 tablespoon (or more)
  garlic purée

¹/₂ cup grated Romano
  cheese
¹/₂ cup grated Parmesan
  cheese
Parsley flakes to taste

**Approx Per
Serving:**
Cal 296
T Fat 16 g
*48% Calories
from Fat*
Prot 9 g
Carbo 31 g
Fiber <1 g
Chol 38 mg
Sod 558 mg

Slice bread into halves horizontally; place on baking sheet. Toast lightly under broiler at 425 degrees. Combine butter and garlic purée in bowl; mix well. Brush over bread. Sprinkle with cheeses and parsley. Toast until cheeses are light brown. Cut into 2-inch slices and serve immediately or freeze in freezer bag for another meal.

Bruce Buehler, John I. Sabin Chapter

PARSLEY CHEESE BREAD

Yield:
15 servings
Utensil:
baking sheet

1 16-ounce loaf French
  bread
2 to 3 cups shredded
  sharp Cheddar cheese
¹/₂ cup finely chopped
  parsley

1 tablespoon (about)
  Worcestershire sauce
¹/₂ cup (or more)
  mayonnaise
Garlic powder, salt and
  pepper to taste

**Approx Per
Serving:**
Cal 231
T Fat 15 g
*57% Calories
from Fat*
Prot 9 g
Carbo 16 g
Fiber 1 g
Chol 28 mg
Sod 371 mg

Cut bread into slices to but not through bottom. Combine Cheddar cheese, parsley, Worcestershire sauce, mayonnaise, garlic powder, salt and pepper in bowl; mix well. Spread slices with cheese mixture. Wrap loaf tightly in foil; place on baking sheet. Bake at 450 degrees until cheese melts and bubbles.

Dyane Jordan, John I. Sabin Chapter

Desserts

BEST APPLE DUMPLINGS

Yield:
10 servings
Utensil:
baking dish

Approx Per Serving:
Cal 658
T Fat 31 g
42% Calories from Fat
Prot 5 g
Carbo 93 g
Fiber 3 g
Chol 37 mg
Sod 322 mg

8 ounces cream cheese, softened
2 cups flour
1 teaspoon butter flavoring
1 cup margarine
10 tart apples, peeled, cored
2¹/₂ cups sugar
2 teaspoons (or more) cinnamon
¹/₄ cup butter
3 tablespoons cinnamon red hot candies
4 cups water

Mix first 3 ingredients in bowl. Cut in margarine until crumbly. Shape into ball. Roll to less than ¹/₈-inch thickness on floured surface. Cut into 10 squares. Place 1 apple on each. Spoon mixture of ¹/₂ cup sugar and 1¹/₂ teaspoons cinnamon into each apple. Bring opposite points of dough to center over apple; moisten and seal. Place in 9x13-inch baking dish. Bring 2 cups sugar, ¹/₂ teaspoon cinnamon, butter, candies and water to a boil in saucepan. Cook for 3 minutes, stirring occasionally. Pour over dumplings. Bake at 425 degrees for 40 to 45 minutes or until apples are tender and crust is brown. Serve with syrup. Garnish with whipped cream.

Georgina Boyles, Silver State Chapter

BANANA SPLIT DESSERT

Yield:
15 servings
Utensil:
baking dish

Approx Per Serving:
Cal 531
T Fat 31 g
51% Calories from Fat
Prot 3 g
Carbo 64 g
Fiber 2 g
Chol 73 mg
Sod 204 mg

1 cup graham cracker crumbs
¹/₃ cup melted butter
1 cup butter, softened
2 eggs, beaten
1 1-pound box confectioners' sugar
2 teaspoons vanilla extract
4 bananas, sliced
1 16-ounce can crushed pineapple
1 cup chopped pecans
16 ounces whipped topping

Combine graham cracker crumbs and ¹/₃ cup melted butter in bowl; mix well. Press into 9x13-inch baking dish. Combine 1 cup butter, eggs, confectioners' sugar and vanilla in mixer bowl. Beat for 5 minutes. Layer confectioners' sugar mixture, bananas, crushed pineapple, pecans and whipped topping over graham cracker crust. Garnish with additional pecans. Chill in refrigerator until serving time.

Tina Nemeth, Silver State Chapter

CHEESECAKE

Yield:
12 servings
Utensil:
springform pan

**Approx Per
Serving:**
*Cal 329
T Fat 24 g
64% Calories
from Fat
Prot 5 g
Carbo 25 g
Fiber <1 g
Chol 94 mg
Sod 206 mg*

¼ cup melted butter
16 graham crackers,
  crushed
2 tablespoons sugar
2 eggs, beaten
½ cup sugar
¼ teaspoon vanilla extract

¼ teaspoon cinnamon
12 ounces cream cheese,
  softened
2 cups sour cream
¼ teaspoon vanilla
  extract
5 tablespoons sugar

Combine butter, graham cracker crumbs and 2 table-spoons sugar in bowl; mix well. Press onto bottom and up sides of greased 9-inch springform pan. Bake at 375 degrees for 5 minutes. Cool to room temperature. Beat eggs and ½ cup sugar in mixer bowl until light and fluffy. Add ¼ teaspoon vanilla, cinnamon and cream cheese; mix well. Spoon onto cooled crust. Bake at 350 degrees for 20 minutes. Cool to room temperature. Combine sour cream, remaining ¼ teaspoon vanilla and 5 tablespoons sugar in bowl; mix well. Pour over cooled filling. Bake at 350 degrees for 5 minutes. Cool in pan for several minutes. Remove sides of springform pan. Chill until serving time.

Stella Williams, Los Amigos Chapter

KATHY'S CHEESECAKE

Yield:
12 servings
Utensil:
springform pan

**Approx Per
Serving:**
*Cal 727
T Fat 53 g
65% Calories
from Fat
Prot 13 g
Carbo 51 g
Fiber 1 g
Chol 176 mg
Sod 611 mg*

1 tablespoon margarine,
  softened
1 1-pound box graham
  cracker crumbs
48 ounces cream cheese,
  softened

1 cup sugar
2 eggs, beaten
2 cups sour cream
1 teaspoon vanilla extract
¼ teaspoon almond
  extract

Grease sides and bottom of 8-inch springform pan with margarine; sprinkle sides with graham cracker crumbs and layer remaining crumbs on bottom. Combine cream cheese, sugar, eggs, sour cream, vanilla and almond ex-tract in mixer bowl; beat well. Spoon into springform pan. Bake at 300 degrees for 1 hour. Turn off oven heat. Let cheesecake stand in oven for 30 minutes longer. Remove to wire rack to cool. Remove sides of springform pan. Chill in refrigerator until firm.

Kathy Nichols, George S. Ladd Chapter

RICOTTA CHEESECAKE

Yield:
12 servings
Utensil:
springform pan

Approx Per
Serving:
Cal 643
T Fat 27 g
37% Calories
from Fat
Prot 9 g
Carbo 94 g
Fiber 2 g
Chol 97 mg
Sod 391 mg

1 1-pound package
   graham cracker crumbs
¹/₃ cup ricotta cheese
16 ounces cream cheese,
   softened
³/₄ cup sugar
¹/₄ teaspoon cinnamon
1 teaspoon vanilla extract
1 tablespoon lemon juice

2 egg yolks, beaten
2 egg whites, stiffly
   beaten
2 cups sour cream
¹/₂ cup sugar
1 tablespoon vanilla
   extract
Raspberry Sauce

Prepare graham cracker crust using package directions, substituting brown sugar for sugar. Press onto bottom and up sides of 8-inch springform pan. Bake at 375 degrees for 8 minutes. Cool to room temperature. Press ricotta cheese through sieve. Combine ricotta cheese, cream cheese, ³/₄ cup sugar, cinnamon, 1 teaspoon vanilla, lemon juice and egg yolks in mixer bowl; beat well. Fold in stiffly beaten egg whites. Spoon onto cooled crust. Bake at 300 degrees for 45 minutes. Cool on wire rack for 45 minutes. Combine sour cream, ¹/₂ cup sugar and 1 tablespoon vanilla in bowl. Spoon onto cooled cheesecake. Bake at 300 degrees for 10 minutes. Cool on wire rack to room temperature. Remove sides of springform pan. Chill in refrigerator for several hours before serving. Serve with Raspberry Sauce.

Raspberry Sauce

Nutritional
information for
Raspberry
Sauce is
included above.

2 cups red current jelly
1 10-ounce package
   frozen raspberries

1 tablespoon cornstarch

Combine jelly and raspberries in saucepan; mix well. Simmer until raspberries have thawed, stirring occasionally. Add cornstarch; mix well. Cook until thickened, stirring frequently.

Vincent J. Capitani, John I. Sabin Chapter

TASTY CHEESECAKE

Yield:
12 servings
Utensil:
springform pan

Approx Per Serving:
Cal 563
T Fat 39 g
61% Calories from Fat
Prot 9 g
Carbo 47 g
Fiber 1 g
Chol 171 mg
Sod 383 mg

¹/₃ cup confectioners' sugar
1¹/₂ cups graham cracker crumbs
¹/₂ cup butter, melted
24 ounces cream cheese, softened
1 cup sugar
1 teaspoon (or more) vanilla extract
4 eggs, beaten
2 cups sour cream
1 21-ounce can blueberry pie filling

Combine confectioners' sugar, graham cracker crumbs and butter in bowl; mix well. Press onto bottom and up sides of greased springform pan. Combine cream cheese, sugar, vanilla and eggs in mixer bowl; beat well. Spoon onto graham cracker crust. Bake at 350 degrees for 50 minutes. Top with sour cream. Bake for 5 minutes longer. Remove to wire rack to cool. Remove sides of springform pan. Top with pie filling. Chill overnight in refrigerator before serving. May substitute cherry or strawberry pie filling for blueberry.

Juanita Stockstill, Los Amigos Chapter

CHOCOLATE DELIGHT

Yield:
15 servings
Utensil:
baking dish

Approx Per Serving:
Cal 533
T Fat 36 g
59% Calories from Fat
Prot 7 g
Carbo 49 g
Fiber 1 g
Chol 40 mg
Sod 335 mg

2 cups flour
1 cup margarine
1 cup chopped pecans
16 ounces cream cheese, softened
2 cups confectioners' sugar
12 ounces whipped topping
1 6-ounce package chocolate instant pudding mix
3 cups milk

Combine flour and margarine in bowl. Cut in margarine until crumbly. Add pecans; mix well. Press into greased 9x13-inch baking dish. Bake at 350 degrees for 25 minutes. Cool to room temperature. Combine cream cheese, confectioners' sugar and 2 cups whipped topping in bowl; mix well. Prepare pudding with milk using package directions. Layer cream cheese mixture, pudding and remaining whipped topping over cooled crust. Garnish with grated chocolate bar. Chill overnight before serving.

Janie Yanez, John I. Sabin Chapter

APPLE COBBLER

Yield:
6 servings
Utensil:
baking dish

Approx Per Serving:
Cal 486
T Fat 9 g
17% Calories from Fat
Prot 3 g
Carbo 100 g
Fiber 3 g
Chol 25 mg
Sod 333 mg

¹/₄ cup butter
1 cup flour
1 cup sugar
3 teaspoons baking powder
¹/₄ teaspoon salt
³/₄ cup milk
6 cups sliced apples
1 cup sugar
1 teaspoon cinnamon

Melt butter at 350 degrees in 9x13-inch baking dish. Combine flour, 1 cup sugar, baking powder, salt and milk in bowl. Pour over melted butter. Combine apples, 1 cup sugar and cinnamon in bowl; toss to mix. Pour on top of batter. Do not mix. Bake at 350 degrees for 1 hour. May use 6 cups any favorite sliced fruit.

Doris Hanson, John I. Sabin Chapter

EASY PEACH COBBLER

Yield:
10 servings
Utensil:
baking dish

Approx Per Serving:
Cal 487
T Fat 25 g
46% Calories from Fat
Prot 4 g
Carbo 64 g
Fiber 2 g
Chol 0 mg
Sod 427 mg

2 16-ounce cans sliced cling peaches
1 2-layer package yellow cake mix
¹/₂ cup margarine
1¹/₂ cups chopped pecans

Pour undrained peaches into greased 9x13-inch baking dish. Sprinkle with cake mix; dot with margarine. Sprinkle with pecans. Bake at 350 degrees for 45 minutes or until golden brown.

Diane Perkins, Mission Chapter

TASTY PEACH COBBLER

Yield:
10 servings
Utensil:
baking dish

Approx Per
Serving:
Cal 189
T Fat 5 g
25% Calories
from Fat
Prot 2 g
Carbo 35 g
Fiber 1 g
Chol 15 mg
Sod 168 mg

1/4 cup butter
1 cup sugar
3/4 cup flour
3/4 cup milk
1/4 teaspoon salt

2 teaspoons baking
  powder
1   16-ounce can sliced
  peaches, drained

Melt butter at 350 degrees in 9x13-inch baking dish. Combine sugar, flour, milk, salt and baking powder in bowl. Pour over melted butter. Do not stir. Top with peaches. Bake at 350 degrees for 40 minutes or until brown. Almond extract may be added to flour mixture.

Lorraine Robinson, John I. Sabin Chapter

DATE NUT ROLL

Yield:
12 servings
Utensil:
waxed paper

Approx Per
Serving:
Cal 536
T Fat 13 g
20% Calories
from Fat
Prot 5 g
Carbo 110 g
Fiber 6 g
Chol 14 mg
Sod 172 mg

1   1½-pound package
  marshmallows
1   1½-pound package
  pitted dates
8 ounces graham cracker
  crumbs

1 cup chopped pecans
1 cup maraschino cherry
  quarters
1/2 cup whipping cream

Cut large marshmallows into quarters. Cut dates into eights. Combine marshmallows, dates, graham cracker crumbs, pecans, cherries and cream in bowl; mix well. Cut one 20-inch piece of waxed paper. Shape mixture into roll at end of waxed paper. Roll waxed paper to enclose mixture. Chill in refrigerator for 24 hours. Cut into 1/2-inch slices. Garnish with whipped cream.

Arliss Summers, Mission Chapter

DATE TORTE

Yield:
6 servings
Utensil:
baking pan

Approx Per Serving:
Cal 397
T Fat 11 g
25% Calories from Fat
Prot 5 g
Carbo 73 g
Fiber 4 g
Chol 46 mg
Sod 361 mg

1 cup chopped dates
1 teaspoon baking soda
1 cup sugar
2 tablespoons butter
½ teaspoon salt
1 cup boiling water
1 egg, beaten
1 cup flour
½ cup ground walnuts

Combine dates, baking soda, sugar, butter and salt in bowl; mix well. Pour in boiling water. Let stand for 15 minutes. Add egg, flour and walnuts; mix well. Pour into greased 8-inch square baking pan. Bake at 350 degrees for 30 minutes. Cool to room temperature. Cut into squares. Garnish with whipped cream.

Annie L. Modlin, John I. Sabin Chapter

EASY FUDGY PUDDING CAKE

Yield:
6 servings
Utensil:
baking pan

Approx Per Serving:
Cal 400
T Fat 10 g
21% Calories from Fat
Prot 9 g
Carbo 74 g
Fiber 2 g
Chol 23 mg
Sod 380 mg

1 cup baking mix
¼ cup baking cocoa
¾ cup chocolate syrup
1 teaspoon vanilla extract
1 14-ounce can sweetened condensed milk
½ cup hot water

Combine baking mix, cocoa, ¼ cup chocolate syrup, vanilla and 1 cup condensed milk in bowl; mix well. Spoon into greased 8-inch square baking pan. Combine remaining condensed milk and ½ cup syrup with hot water in bowl; mix well. Pour over cake mixture. Do not stir. Bake at 375 degrees for 25 to 30 minutes or until center is set and cake pulls away from sides of pan. Let stand on wire rack for 15 minutes. Spoon into serving dishes. Spoon pudding from bottom of pan over top. Serve warm. Garnish with whipped cream. Refrigerate leftovers.

Leone Burke, Mission Chapter

ORANGE ICEBOX CAKE

Yield:
12 servings
Utensil:
double boiler

Approx Per Serving:
Cal 248
T Fat 11 g
38% Calories from Fat
Prot 5 g
Carbo 34 g
Fiber <1 g
Chol 159 mg
Sod 143 mg

1 tablespoons (heaping) cornstarch
1/2 cup sugar
3 egg yolks, beaten
1 1/2 cups orange juice
Grated rind of 1 orange

3 egg whites, stiffly beaten
1   16-ounce sponge cake
1 cup whipping cream, whipped

Combine cornstarch, sugar and egg yolks in top of double boiler; mix well. Add orange juice and rind; mix well. Cook over hot water until thickened, stirring constantly. Cool to room temperature. Fold in stiffly beaten egg whites. Cut sponge cake into 4 layers. Spread orange juice mixture between layers and over top and side of cake. Chill in refrigerator for 24 hours before serving. Cover cake with unsweetened whipped cream.

Joan Church, De Anza Chapter

WALNUT GRAHAM CRACKER ICEBOX CAKE

Yield:
9 servings
Utensil:
baking dish

Approx Per Serving:
Cal 408
T Fat 22 g
47% Calories from Fat
Prot 5 g
Carbo 52 g
Fiber 1 g
Chol 51 mg
Sod 263 mg

1/2 cup melted butter
1 cup packed brown sugar
1 egg, beaten

8 ounces graham crackers, crushed
1 cup broken walnuts
1 teaspoon vanilla extract

Combine butter, brown sugar and egg in saucepan. Bring to a full rolling boil, stirring frequently. Boil for 1 minute, stirring constantly. Pour over graham cracker crumbs in bowl. Add walnuts and vanilla; mix well. Press into greased, shallow 8-inch square baking dish, packing with back of spoon dipped in hot water. Top with thick butter icing of your choice. Chill in refrigerator.

Donna Palmer, Los Amigos Chapter

LEMON CREAM DREAM DESSERT

Yield:
12 servings
Utensil:
baking dish

Approx Per Serving:
Cal 413
T Fat 26 g
54% Calories from Fat
Prot 5 g
Carbo 43 g
Fiber 1 g
Chol 50 mg
Sod 275 mg

1 cup flour
½ cup melted butter
1 cup finely chopped pecans
8 ounces cream cheese, softened
1 cup confectioners' sugar
1½ cups whipped topping
2 4-ounce packages lemon instant pudding mix
3 cups milk

Combine flour and butter in bowl; mix well. Stir in pecans. Press into greased 9x13-inch baking dish. Bake at 350 degrees for 20 minutes or until light brown. Cool to room temperature. Combine cream cheese and confectioners' sugar in bowl; mix well. Fold in whipped topping. Spread over cooled crust. Prepare lemon pudding with milk using package directions. Spread over cream cheese layer. Garnish with additional chopped pecans. Chill until serving time.

Helen H. Maple, John I. Sabin Chapter

RITZY LEMON DESSERT

Yield:
15 servings
Utensil:
baking dish

Approx Per Serving:
Cal 312
T Fat 19 g
52% Calories from Fat
Prot 3 g
Carbo 36 g
Fiber <1 g
Chol 9 mg
Sod 232 mg

60 butter crackers, crushed
¼ cup confectioners' sugar
½ cup melted margarine
1 6-ounce can frozen pink lemonade, thawed
1 14-ounce can sweetened condensed milk
14 ounces whipped topping

Combine cracker crumbs and confectioners' sugar in bowl; mix well. Stir in melted margarine. Press half the mixture into greased 9x13-inch baking dish. Combine lemonade and condensed milk in bowl; mix well. Fold in whipped topping. Spread over crumb layer; sprinkle with remaining crumbs. Chill in refrigerator.

Karolyn Tillisch Aznoe, John I. Sabin Chapter

ORANGE DELIGHT

Yield:
8 servings
Utensil:
dessert dishes

Approx Per Serving:
Cal 125
T Fat 3 g
22% Calories from Fat
Prot 9 g
Carbo 16 g
Fiber 1 g
Chol 5 mg
Sod 280 mg

2 cups low-fat, small curd cottage cheese
2 cups juice-packed crushed pineapple, drained
2 3-ounce packages sugar-free orange gelatin
2 cups low-calorie whipped topping

Combine cottage cheese, crushed pineapple, orange gelatin and whipped topping in bowl; fold gently until mixed. Chill, covered, in refrigerator until serving time. Spoon into 8 dessert dishes. Garnish with fresh strawberries and mint.

Bess Birdsall, Mission Chapter

KAHLUA PEACHES

Yield:
15 servings
Utensil:
baking dish

Approx Per Serving:
Cal 149
T Fat <1 g
1% Calories from Fat
Prot 1 g
Carbo 36 g
Fiber 1 g
Chol 0 mg
Sod 12 mg

2 29-ounce cans peach halves
1/2 cup Kahlua
1/2 cup packed brown sugar
1/4 cup tarragon vinegar
3 sticks of cinnamon
4 1-inch slices of orange
Rind of 1 lemon

Drain peaches, reserving 1/2 cup liquid. Combine peach liquid, Kahlua, brown sugar, vinegar, cinnamon sticks, orange slices and lemon rind in saucepan. Simmer for 5 minutes, stirring frequently. Spoon peaches into 9x13-inch baking dish. Pour syrup over peaches. Chill, covered, in refrigerator. May keep for 7 to 10 days.

Karolyn Tillisch Aznoe, John I. Sabin Chapter

PEAR BETTY

Yield:
6 servings
Utensil:
pie plate

Approx Per Serving:
Cal 358
T Fat 16 g
39% Calories from Fat
Prot 2 g
Carbo 54 g
Fiber 4 g
Chol 41 mg
Sod 131 mg

4 cups unpeeled pear slices
¼ cup orange juice
¾ cup sugar
½ teaspoon cinnamon
¼ teaspoon nutmeg
¾ cup flour
½ cup butter

Place pear slices in greased 9-inch pie plate; drizzle with orange juice. Combine sugar, cinnamon, nutmeg and flour in bowl; mix well. Cut in butter until crumbly. Sprinkle over pears. Bake at 375 degrees for 40 minutes.

Betty Eckels, John I. Sabin Chapter

PINEAPPLE DELIGHT

Yield:
15 servings
Utensil:
baking dish

Approx Per Serving:
Cal 239
T Fat 9 g
32% Calories from Fat
Prot 4 g
Carbo 39 g
Fiber 2 g
Chol 4 mg
Sod 245 mg

1 16-ounce angel food cake
1 16-ounce can crushed pineapple
1 cup chopped pecans
2 cups milk
1 6-ounce package vanilla instant pudding mix
¼ cup whipped topping
1 3-ounce can coconut

Break cake into bite-sized pieces; place in 9x13-inch baking dish. Pour pineapple over cake; sprinkle with pecans. Combine milk and pudding mix in bowl; stir until thickened. Fold in whipped topping. Spread over layers; sprinkle with coconut. Chill in refrigerator.

Alice Clark, John I. Sabin Chapter

PINK LADY

Yield:
15 servings
Utensil:
baking dish

Approx Per
Serving:
Cal 151
T Fat 4 g
23% Calories
from Fat
Prot 3 g
Carbo 28 g
Fiber 1 g
Chol 0 mg
Sod 176 mg

1   3-ounce package
   strawberry gelatin
1 cup boiling water
1   16-ounce package
   frozen strawberries

8 ounces whipped
   topping
1   16-ounce angel food
   cake

Dissolve gelatin in boiling water in bowl. Add frozen strawberries, stirring until thawed. Chill in refrigerator until partially set. Fold in whipped topping. Break cake into bite-sized pieces; place in 9x13-inch baking dish. Pour gelatin mixture over cake. Chill until set.

Hilda Syhre, Los Amigos Chapter

LEMON PUFF PUDDING

Yield:
6 servings
Utensil:
baking dish

Approx Per
Serving:
Cal 278
T Fat 11 g
34% Calories
from Fat
Prot 6 g
Carbo 41 g
Fiber <1 g
Chol 130 mg
Sod 193 mg

3 tablespoons butter,
   softened
1 cup sugar
1/4 cup flour
3 egg yolks, beaten
1/4 cup lemon juice

2 teaspoons grated
   lemon rind
1 1/2 cups milk
3 egg whites
1/4 teaspoon salt

Combine butter, 1/2 cup sugar and flour in bowl; mix well. Add egg yolks, lemon juice, lemon rind and milk; mix well. Beat egg whites with salt until soft peaks form. Add remaining 1/2 cup sugar gradually, beating until stiff peaks form. Fold into mixture. Pour into buttered 1 1/2-quart baking dish. Place dish in shallow pan. Fill pan with boiling water to 1-inch depth. Bake at 325 degrees for 1 hour. Garnish with whipped cream.

Bess Birdsall, Mission Chapter

POOR MAN'S PUDDING

Yield:
6 serving
Utensil:
baking pan

Approx Per Serving:
Cal 459
T Fat 6 g
11% Calories from Fat
Prot 4 g
Carbo 100 g
Fiber 1 g
Chol 49 mg
Sod 166 mg

1½ cups hot water
1½ cups packed brown sugar
2 tablespoons butter
1 cup flour
½ cup sugar
1½ teaspoons baking powder
½ cup milk
1 teaspoon vanilla extract
1 egg, beaten

Combine hot water, brown sugar and butter in saucepan. Bring to a boil, stirring frequently. Pour into greased 8-inch square baking pan. Combine flour, sugar and baking powder in mixer bowl. Add milk, vanilla and egg; beat well. Pour over hot liquid in baking pan. Bake at 350 degrees for 30 minutes.

Yvette Henry, Mission Chapter

PUMPKIN DESSERT

Yield:
15 servings
Utensil:
baking dish

Approx Per Serving:
Cal 399
T Fat 17 g
38% Calories from Fat
Prot 7 g
Carbo 56 g
Fiber 1 g
Chol 106 mg
Sod 448 mg

6 eggs, beaten
1 29-ounce can pumpkin
1½ cups sugar
1 teaspoon salt
1 teaspoon ginger
2 teaspoons cinnamon
½ teaspoon cloves
2 cups milk
½ cup butter
1 2-layer package yellow cake mix
1 cup chopped walnuts

Combine eggs, pumpkin, sugar, salt, ginger, cinnamon, cloves and milk in bowl; mix well. Pour into 9x13-inch baking dish. Combine butter and cake mix in bowl. Cut in butter until crumbly. Spread over pumpkin mixture; sprinkle with walnuts. Bake at 350 degrees for 50 to 60 minutes or until brown. May be served warm or cold. Garnish with whipped cream.

Robin Cuthbert, John I. Sabin Chapter

Cakes

APPLE CAKE

Yield:
15 servings
Utensil:
cake pan

*Approx Per
Serving:*
Cal 460
T Fat 21 g
*40% Calories
from Fat*
Prot 5 g
Carbo 67 g
Fiber 2 g
Chol 51 mg
Sod 192 mg

2 eggs
1/2 cup oil
1 cup sugar
1 cup packed brown
  sugar
2 cups flour
2 teaspoons baking soda
2 teaspoons cinnamon

1/2 teaspoon nutmeg
Ground cloves and salt
  to taste
4 cups chopped apples
1 cup chopped walnuts
1 recipe Cream Cheese
  Frosting (page 233)

Combine eggs, oil, sugar and brown sugar in mixer bowl; mix until smooth. Add flour, baking soda, cinnamon, nutmeg, cloves and salt; mix well. Stir in apples and walnuts. Spoon into greased 9x13-inch cake pan. Bake at 350 degrees for 35 to 45 minutes or until cake tests done. Cool on wire rack. Spread with Cream Cheese Frosting.

Jan Moore, John I. Sabin Chapter

FRESH APPLE CAKE

Yield:
15 servings
Utensil:
cake pan

*Approx Per
Serving:*
Cal 300
T Fat 12 g
*36% Calories
from Fat*
Prot 5 g
Carbo 45 g
Fiber 1 g
Chol 28 mg
Sod 262 mg

4 cups chopped apples
2 cups sugar
1/2 cup oil
1 cup chopped walnuts
2 eggs, beaten

2 teaspoons vanilla extract
2 cups flour
2 teaspoons baking soda
2 teaspoons cinnamon
1 teaspoon salt

Mix apples and sugar in large bowl. Add oil, walnuts, eggs and vanilla; mix well. Sift in flour, baking soda, cinnamon and salt; mix well. Spoon into ungreased 9x13-inch cake pan. Bake at 350 degrees for 45 to 60 minutes or until cake tests done.

Lori Welch, John I. Sabin Chapter

APPLESAUCE CAKE

Yield:
16 servings
Utensil:
tube pan

Approx Per Serving:
Cal 250
T Fat 9 g
32% Calories from Fat
Prot 4 g
Carbo 40 g
Fiber 2 g
Chol 28 mg
Sod 185 mg

¹/₄ cup shortening
1 cup sugar
2 eggs
1¹/₂ cups applesauce
¹/₂ cup milk
1 cup raisins
1 cup chopped walnuts
2 cups flour
2 teaspoons baking soda
3 tablespoons baking cocoa
1 tablespoon cornstarch
¹/₂ teaspoon cinnamon
¹/₂ teaspoon salt

Cream shortening and sugar in mixer bowl until light and fluffy. Add eggs, applesauce, milk, raisins and walnuts; mix with spoon. Stir in flour, baking soda, cocoa, cornstarch, cinnamon and salt. Spoon into tube pan sprayed with nonstick cooking spray. Bake at 350 degrees for 1 hour. Remove to wire rack to cool.

Charlene Kennedy, Sierra Pacific Chapter

APPLE-RAISIN CUPCAKES

Yield:
12 servings
Utensil:
muffin pan

Approx Per Serving:
Cal 196
T Fat 4 g
18% Calories from Fat
Prot 2 g
Carbo 41 g
Fiber 2 g
Chol 0 mg
Sod 116 mg

¹/₄ cup margarine, softened
²/₃ cup sugar
1 teaspoon vanilla extract
1¹/₂ teaspoons (or more) cinnamon
1 cup flour
1 teaspoon baking soda
1¹/₂ cups dark raisins
1¹/₂ cups grated unpeeled Granny Smith apples

Cream margarine and sugar in mixer bowl until light and fluffy. Beat in vanilla and cinnamon. Sift in flour and baking soda; mix until consistency of coarse cornmeal. Stir in raisins and apples gradually. Spoon into 12 muffin cups sprayed with nonstick cooking spray. Bake at 350 degrees for 25 minutes. Cool in pan for 5 minutes. Remove to wire rack to cool completely.

Dorothy Hunsicker, Mission Chapter

ARMENIAN CAKE

Yield:
9 servings
Utensil:
cake pan

Approx Per Serving:
Cal 527
T Fat 21 g
35% Calories from Fat
Prot 5 g
Carbo 82 g
Fiber 1 g
Chol 63 mg
Sod 226 mg

2 cups packed brown sugar
2 cups flour, sifted
1/2 cup butter
1 egg, beaten
1 teaspoon nutmeg
1 cup sour cream
1 teaspoon baking soda
1/2 cup chopped pecans
Cinnamon to taste

Combine brown sugar, flour and butter in bowl; mix until crumbly. Spread half the mixture in greased 9x9-inch cake pan. Add egg, nutmeg and mixture of sour cream and baking soda to remaining crumb mixture; mix well. Spread in prepared pan. Sprinkle with pecans and cinnamon. Bake at 350 degrees for 40 minutes. Do not open oven door for first 30 minutes of baking time. Cool cake on wire rack.

Helen H. Maple, John I. Sabin Chapter

FRANKLIN'S AVOCADO SPICE CAKE

Yield:
12 servings
Utensil:
loaf pan

Approx Per Serving:
Cal 341
T Fat 16 g
41% Calories from Fat
Prot 4 g
Carbo 48 g
Fiber 3 g
Chol 36 mg
Sod 179 mg

1/2 cup shortening
1 3/4 cups sugar
2 eggs
1 1/2 cups flour
1/2 teaspoon salt
1 teaspoon baking soda
1/2 teaspoon nutmeg
1/2 teaspoon cinnamon
1/2 teaspoon cardamom
1/3 cup buttermilk
1 cup mashed avocado
1/2 cup currants
1/2 cup chopped pecans

Cream shortening and sugar in mixer bowl until light and fluffy. Add eggs; mix well. Sift flour, salt, baking soda and spices together. Add to creamed mixture alternately with buttermilk, mixing well after each addition. Add avocado, currants and pecans; mix well. Pour into greased and floured 4x8-inch loaf pan. Bake at 375 degrees for 1 1/4 hours. Remove to wire rack to cool.

Sharon Negley, Los Amigos Chapter

BLACK FOREST CHERRY CAKE

Yield:
15 servings
Utensil:
cake pan

Approx Per Serving:
Cal 204
T Fat 4 g
16% Calories
from Fat
Prot 3 g
Carbo 41 g
Fiber 1 g
Chol 28 mg
Sod 231 mg

1 2-layer package
   chocolate cake mix
1 21-ounce can cherry
   pie filling

2 eggs
1 teaspoon almond
   extract
¹⁄₃ cup flour

Combine cake mix, pie filling, eggs, almond extract and flour in mixer bowl; mix well. Spoon into greased 9x13-inch cake pan. Bake at 350 degrees for 35 to 40 minutes or until cake tests done. Cool on wire rack.

Velda Wheeler, John I. Sabin Chapter

EASY BUNDT CAKE

Yield:
16 servings
Utensil:
bundt pan

Approx Per Serving:
Cal 361
T Fat 21 g
50% Calories
from Fat
Prot 4 g
Carbo 42 g
Fiber <1 g
Chol 60 mg
Sod 270 mg

1 2-layer package
   yellow cake mix
1 4-ounce package
   vanilla instant
   pudding mix
4 eggs
1 cup sour cream

¹⁄₂ cup water
¹⁄₂ cup oil
4 ounces German's
   chocolate, grated
¹⁄₂ cup chocolate chips
¹⁄₂ cup chopped pecans

Combine cake mix, pudding mix, eggs, sour cream, water and oil in large mixer bowl; mix well. Add grated chocolate, chocolate chips and pecans. Beat for 4 minutes. Spoon into greased and floured bundt pan. Bake at 350 degrees for 55 minutes or until knife inserted in center comes out clean. Cool in pan for 10 minutes. Invert onto serving plate to cool completely. Garnish with confectioners' sugar.

Linda Desjardins, John I. Sabin Chapter

BUNDT CAKE

Yield:
16 servings
Utensil:
bundt pan

Approx Per Serving:
Cal 345
T Fat 14 g
37% Calories from Fat
Prot 4 g
Carbo 49 g
Fiber <1 g
Chol 67 mg
Sod 372 mg

6 to 8 pecan halves
1 2-layer package
    yellow cake mix
4 eggs
1 cup sour cream
3 to 4 tablespoons butter
1 package coconut-pecan
    frosting mix

Arrange pecan halves ridged side down in flutes of greased and floured bundt pan. Combine cake mix, eggs and sour cream in mixer bowl. Beat for 2 to 3 minutes or until smooth. Spoon 1/3 of the cake batter into prepared pan. Melt butter in saucepan over low heat; remove from heat. Stir in frosting mix. Layer frosting mixture and remaining cake batter 1/2 at a time in bundt pan. Bake at 350 degrees for 35 to 40 minutes or until cake tests done. Cool in pan for 10 minutes. Invert onto plate to cool completely. Garnish with confectioners' sugar.

Gwen Cameron, Los Amigos Chapter

CARROT CAKE

Yield:
15 servings
Utensil:
cake pan

Approx Per Serving:
Cal 826
T Fat 47 g
51% Calories from Fat
Prot 6 g
Carbo 99 g
Fiber 4 g
Chol 105 mg
Sod 388 mg

1¼ cups all-purpose flour
1¼ cups whole wheat
    flour
2 teaspoons baking soda
2 teaspoons baking
    powder
2 teaspoons cinnamon
½ teaspoon salt
1½ cups oil
1 cup sugar
1 cup packed brown sugar
4 eggs
¼ cup wheat germ
2 cups grated carrots
1 cup crushed pineapple
1 cup chopped dates
½ cup coconut
1 cup chopped pecans
1 recipe Carrot Cake
    Frosting (page 233)

Sift all-purpose flour, whole wheat flour, baking soda, baking powder, cinnamon and salt together. Beat oil, sugar, brown sugar and eggs in mixer bowl until thick. Add wheat germ and dry ingredients gradually, mixing well after each addition. Stir in mixture of carrots, pineapple, dates, coconut and pecans. Spoon into greased 9x13-inch cake pan. Bake at 350 degrees for 40 to 45 minutes or until cake tests done. Cool on wire rack. Frost with Carrot Cake Frosting. May top with additional pecans if desired.

Bonnie Boelens, John I. Sabin Chapter

Easy Carrot Cake

Yield:
15 servings
Utensil:
cake pan

Approx Per Serving:
Cal 391
T Fat 21 g
48% Calories from Fat
Prot 5 g
Carbo 47 g
Fiber 1 g
Chol 57 mg
Sod 152 mg

4 eggs
1 cup oil
1 cup sugar
2 8-ounce jars junior baby food carrots
1 cup packed brown sugar
2 cups flour
2 teaspoons baking soda
2 teaspoons cinnamon
1 cup chopped walnuts

Combine eggs, oil, sugar, carrots, brown sugar, flour, baking soda, cinnamon and walnuts in mixer bowl; mix until smooth. Spoon into greased 9x13-inch cake pan. Bake at 300 degrees for 50 minutes. Cool on wire rack. Frost with cream cheese frosting.

Jim Moore, George S. Ladd Chapter

Fourteen-Karat Cake

Yield:
15 servings
Utensil:
cake pan

Approx Per Serving:
Cal 565
T Fat 35 g
54% Calories from Fat
Prot 5 g
Carbo 62 g
Fiber 1 g
Chol 65 mg
Sod 348 mg

2 cups flour
2 teaspoons baking powder
1¹/₂ teaspoons baking soda
2 teaspoons cinnamon
1 teaspoon salt
2 cups sugar
1¹/₂ cups oil
4 eggs
1 cup grated carrots
1 8-ounce can crushed pineapple, drained
1 cup chopped pecans
¹/₄ cup margarine, softened
4 ounces cream cheese, softened
¹/₂ 1-pound package confectioners' sugar
1¹/₂ teaspoons vanilla extract

Sift flour with baking powder, baking soda, cinnamon and salt. Beat sugar and oil in mixer bowl until thick. Beat in eggs. Add dry ingredients; mix well. Stir in carrots, pineapple and pecans. Spoon into greased and floured 9x13-inch cake pan. Bake at 350 degrees for 40 to 50 minutes or until cake tests done. Cool on wire rack. Cream margarine and cream cheese in mixer bowl until light. Add confectioners' sugar and vanilla; mix well. Spread over cake.

Elinor Sheets, John I. Sabin Chapter

CHOCOLATE ANGEL FOOD CAKE

Yield:
16 servings
Utensil:
tube pan

Approx Per Serving:
Cal 110
T Fat <1 g
2% Calories from Fat
Prot 3 g
Carbo 24 g
Fiber <1 g
Chol 0 mg
Sod 99 mg

¹/₄ cup baking cocoa, sifted
1 package angel food cake mix

¹/₄ teaspoon chocolate flavoring

Combine cocoa with flour packet from cake mix in bowl. Prepare cake mix using package directions. Fold in chocolate flavoring. Spoon into ungreased tube pan. Bake using package directions. Cool in pan. Remove to serving plate. May add 1 teaspoon cream of tartar for lighter consistency.

Marian Babcock, John I. Sabin Chapter

CHOCOLATE BROWNIE CAKE

Yield:
15 servings
Utensil:
cake pan

Approx Per Serving:
Cal 539
T Fat 25 g
40% Calories from Fat
Prot 5 g
Carbo 79 g
Fiber 2 g
Chol 29 mg
Sod 290 mg

2 cups sugar
2 cups flour
1 cup margarine
1 cup water
¹/₄ cup baking cocoa
¹/₂ cup buttermilk
2 eggs
1 teaspoon baking soda

1 teaspoon vanilla extract
¹/₂ cup margarine
¹/₄ cup baking cocoa
1 tablespoon buttermilk
1 1-pound package confectioners' sugar
1 teaspoon vanilla extract
1 cup chopped walnuts

Mix sugar and flour in large bowl. Bring 1 cup margarine, water and ¹/₄ cup cocoa to a boil in saucepan over medium heat, stirring to mix well. Pour over flour mixture; mix well. Add ¹/₂ cup buttermilk, eggs, baking soda and 1 teaspoon vanilla; mix well. Spoon into greased and floured 9x13-inch cake pan. Bake at 400 degrees for 20 minutes. Combine ¹/₂ cup margarine, ¹/₄ cup cocoa and 1 tablespoon buttermilk in saucepan. Heat just to the boiling point, stirring to mix well; remove from heat. Stir in confectioners' sugar, 1 teaspoon vanilla and walnuts. Pour over hot cake. Chill in refrigerator.

Norma Kotoulas, Los Amigos Chapter

CHOCOLATE CHERRY CAKE

Yield:
15 servings
Utensil:
cake pan

Approx Per Serving:
Cal 247
T Fat 8 g
29% Calories from Fat
Prot 2 g
Carbo 43 g
Fiber 1 g
Chol 14 mg
Sod 226 mg

1 2-layer package chocolate cake mix
1/3 cup oil
1 21-ounce can cherry pie filling

1 egg
1/2 cup confectioners' sugar
2 1/2 teaspoons water

Combine cake mix, oil, pie filling and egg in mixer bowl; mix until smooth. Spoon into 9x13-inch cake pan. Bake at 350 degrees for 30 to 40 minutes or until cake tests done. Cool on wire rack. Blend confectioners' sugar and water in bowl. Drizzle over cake.

Eve Durkton, Sierra Pacific Chapter

EASY CHOCOLATE CAKE

Yield:
15 servings
Utensil:
cake pan

Approx Per Serving:
Cal 198
T Fat 5 g
22% Calories from Fat
Prot 4 g
Carbo 35 g
Fiber 0 g
Chol 33 mg
Sod 254 mg

1 2-layer package white cake mix
1 4-ounce package chocolate pudding mix

2 eggs
2 cups milk

Combine cake mix, pudding mix, eggs and milk in mixer bowl. Beat at medium speed for 2 minutes. Spoon into greased and floured 9x13-inch cake pan. Bake at 350 degrees for 40 minutes. Cool on wire rack. May spread with coconut-pecan frosting. May bake three 8-inch layers for 35 to 40 minutes or two 9-inch layers for 30 to 35 minutes if preferred.

Marian Babcock, John I. Sabin Chapter

EIGHTEEN-MINUTE CHOCOLATE CAKE

Yield:
24 servings
Utensil:
cake pan

Approx Per Serving:
Cal 339
T Fat 16 g
40% Calories from Fat
Prot 3 g
Carbo 49 g
Fiber 1 g
Chol 18 mg
Sod 220 mg

2 cups flour
2 cups sugar
³/₄ teaspoon baking soda
¹/₂ teaspoon salt
1 cup margarine
¹/₄ cup baking cocoa
1 cup hot water
¹/₂ cup buttermilk
2 eggs, beaten

1 teaspoon vanilla extract
¹/₂ cup melted margarine
¹/₃ cup buttermilk
¹/₄ cup baking cocoa
1 1-pound package confectioners' sugar
1 teaspoon vanilla extract
1 cup chopped pecans

Sift first 4 ingredients into bowl. Melt 1 cup margarine in saucepan. Stir in ¹/₄ cup cocoa and hot water. Bring to a boil. Add to sifted dry ingredients; mix well. Add ¹/₂ cup buttermilk, eggs and 1 teaspoon vanilla; mix well. Spoon into greased 10x15-inch cake pan. Bake at 400 degrees for 18 minutes. Mix ¹/₂ cup margarine, ¹/₃ cup buttermilk, ¹/₄ cup cocoa, confectioners' sugar, 1 teaspoon vanilla and pecans in bowl. Spoon over hot cake. Let stand until cool.

Lois McNeil, John I. Sabin Chapter

MISSISSIPPI FUDGE CAKE

Yield:
15 servings
Utensil:
cake pan

Approx Per Serving:
Cal 577
T Fat 25 g
38% Calories from Fat
Prot 6 g
Carbo 87 g
Fiber 2 g
Chol 58 mg
Sod 210 mg

1 cup margarine
¹/₃ cup baking cocoa
4 eggs, slightly beaten
2 cups sugar
1¹/₂ cups flour
2 teaspoons vanilla extract
1¹/₂ cups chopped walnuts

Salt to taste
1 7-ounce jar marshmallow creme
¹/₄ cup margarine
¹/₃ cup baking cocoa
¹/₃ cup milk
1 teaspoon vanilla extract
1 1-pound package confectioners' sugar

Melt 1 cup margarine with ¹/₃ cup cocoa in saucepan, stirring to mix well. Cool to room temperature. Beat in eggs. Add sugar, flour, 2 teaspoons vanilla, walnuts and salt; mix well. Spoon into 9x13-inch cake pan which has been greased on the bottom only. Bake at 375 degrees for 25 minutes. Spread immediately with marshmallow creme. Combine ¹/₄ cup margarine, ¹/₃ cup cocoa, milk and 1 teaspoon vanilla in saucepan. Cook until bubbly, stirring to mix well. Stir in confectioners' sugar. Spread over cooled marshmallow layer. Let stand for 2 hours before serving.

Brenda Albury, John I. Sabin Chapter

Mississippi Mud Cake

Yield:
15 servings
Utensil:
cake pan

Approx Per Serving:
Cal 635
T Fat 31 g
42% Calories from Fat
Prot 5 g
Carbo 89 g
Fiber 3 g
Chol 59 mg
Sod 252 mg

1 cup margarine, softened
2 cups sugar
4 eggs
1 teaspoon vanilla extract
1½ cups sifted flour
¼ cup baking cocoa
1 3-ounce can flaked coconut
1½ cups chopped pecans
1 7-ounce jar marshmallow creme
½ cup margarine, softened
⅓ cup baking cocoa
½ cup evaporated milk
1 1-pound package confectioners' sugar
1 teaspoon vanilla extract

Cream 1 cup margarine and sugar in mixer bowl until light and fluffy. Beat in eggs and 1 teaspoon vanilla. Add flour and ¼ cup cocoa; mix well. Stir in coconut and pecans. Spoon into greased and floured 9x13-inch cake pan. Bake at 350 degrees for 35 to 40 minutes or until cake tests done. Spread hot cake with marshmallow creme. Combine ½ cup margarine, ⅓ cup cocoa, evaporated milk, confectioners' sugar and 1 teaspoon vanilla extract in mixer bowl; mix until smooth. Spread over cooled marshmallow creme. Let stand until cool.

Ruth Flores, Sierra Pacific Chapter

Nebraska Chocolate Cake

Yield:
16 servings
Utensil:
cake pan

Approx Per Serving:
Cal 308
T Fat 12 g
33% Calories from Fat
Prot 4 g
Carbo 50 g
Fiber 2 g
Chol 28 mg
Sod 219 mg

2 cups flour
2 cups sugar
1 teaspoon baking soda
½ teaspoon baking powder
¾ cup baking cocoa
1 teaspoon salt
¾ cup water
¾ cup milk
½ cup shortening
2 eggs
¼ cup oil
1 teaspoon vanilla extract
Marshmallow Frosting without Marshmallows (page 234)

Mix flour, sugar, baking soda, baking powder, cocoa and salt in large mixer bowl. Add water, milk, shortening, eggs, oil and vanilla. Mix at low speed for 30 seconds, scraping bowl constantly. Beat at high speed for 3 minutes, scraping bowl occasionally. Spoon into greased 9x13-inch cake pan. Bake at 350 degrees for 40 to 45 minutes or until cake tests done. Cool on wire rack. Frost with Marshmallow Frosting without Marshmallows. May bake in two 9-inch layers or three 8-inch layers for 30 to 35 minutes if preferred.

June A. Schelb, Mission Chapter

SECRET CHOCOLATE SENSATION CAKE

Yield:
16 servings
Utensil:
2 cake pans

Approx Per Serving:
Cal 248
T Fat 15 g
53% Calories from Fat
Prot 2 g
Carbo 28 g
Fiber 0 g
Chol 48 mg
Sod 301 mg

1 2-layer package pudding-recipe chocolate cake mix
1 cup mayonnaise
1 cup water
3 eggs

Combine cake mix, mayonnaise, water and eggs in mixer bowl. Mix at low speed for 30 seconds. Beat at medium speed for 2 minutes. Spoon into 2 greased and floured 9-inch cake pans. Bake at 350 degrees for 30 to 35 minutes or until layers pull away from sides of pans. Cool in pans for 10 minutes. Remove to wire rack to cool completely. Fill and frost as desired. May substitute other flavors of pudding-recipe cake mix for chocolate.

Pamela Allen, Los Amigos Chapter

COTTON PICKING CAKE

Yield:
16 servings
Utensil:
3 cake pans

Approx Per Serving:
Cal 378
T Fat 20 g
47% Calories from Fat
Prot 4 g
Carbo 48 g
Fiber 1 g
Chol 53 mg
Sod 267 mg

1 2-layer package butter-recipe yellow cake mix
1/2 cup oil
4 eggs
1 11-ounce can mandarin oranges
1 cup chopped pecans
1 4-ounce package vanilla instant pudding mix
1 16-ounce can crushed pineapple
9 ounces whipped topping

Combine cake mix, oil, eggs and undrained oranges in mixer bowl; mix until smooth. Stir in pecans. Spoon into 3 greased and floured 8-inch cake pans. Bake at 350 degrees for 30 minutes. Cool in pans for 10 minutes. Remove to wire rack to cool completely. Combine pudding mix and undrained pineapple in bowl; mix well. Fold in whipped topping. Spread between layers and over top and side of cake. Store in airtight container in refrigerator.

Carol Crowder, Sierra Pacific Chapter

DAFFODIL CAKE

Yield:
16 servings
Utensil:
tube pan

Approx Per Serving:
Cal 139
T Fat 2 g
14% Calories from Fat
Prot 4 g
Carbo 26 g
Fiber <1 g
Chol 80 mg
Sod 75 mg

6 egg yolks
12 egg whites (1½ cups)
1½ teaspoons cream of tartar
¼ teaspoon salt
¾ cup sugar
½ teaspoon almond extract
1½ teaspoons vanilla extract
1 cup cake flour
¾ cup plus 2 tablespoons sugar

Beat egg yolks in small mixer bowl until thick and lemon-colored. Beat egg whites with cream of tartar and salt in mixer bowl until frothy. Beat in ¾ cup sugar 2 tablespoons at a time, beating constantly until stiff peaks form. Fold in flavorings. Mix flour and ¾ cup plus 2 tablespoons sugar in bowl. Sprinkle ¼ at a time over egg whites, folding in gently. Fold half the egg white mixture into egg yolks. Alternate remaining egg white mixture and egg yolk mixture in ungreased tube pan until both batters are used. Cut through batters gently to swirl. Bake at 375 degrees for 40 minutes. Invert onto funnel; let stand until cool. Remove to serving plate.

Ruth Flores, Sierra Pacific Chapter

APPLESAUCE FRUITCAKES

Yield:
48 servings
Utensil:
4 loaf pans

Approx Per Serving:
Cal 211
T Fat 8 g
34% Calories from Fat
Prot 2 g
Carbo 35 g
Fiber 1 g
Chol 0 mg
Sod 93 mg

4 cups flour
2 tablespoons cornstarch
4 tablespoons baking cocoa
4 teaspoons baking soda
2 cups sugar
½ teaspoon cinnamon
½ teaspoon nutmeg
½ teaspoon allspice
½ teaspoon cloves
½ teaspoon salt
4 cups applesauce
1 cup oil
1 cup raisins
1 cup currants
1 pound mixed candied fruit
2 cups chopped pecans

Sift flour, cornstarch, cocoa, baking soda, sugar, cinnamon, nutmeg, allspice, cloves and salt into large bowl. Add applesauce and oil; mix well. Stir in raisins, currants, candied fruit and pecans; mix gently. Spoon into 4 lightly greased loaf pans. Bake at 350 degrees for 1 hour and 10 minutes. Remove to wire rack to cool. Wrap in cloth soaked with brandy or rum. Freeze, wrapped in plastic wrap, until ready to serve.

Val King, John I. Sabin Chapter

Festive No-Bake Fruitcake

Yield:
20 servings
Utensil:
tube pan

Approx Per Serving:
Cal 287
T Fat 7 g
21% Calories from Fat
Prot 4 g
Carbo 55 g
Fiber 2 g
Chol 3 mg
Sod 159 mg

³/₄ cup evaporated milk
¹/₃ cup orange juice
3 cups miniature marshmallows
1 1-pound package graham crackers, crushed
1 teaspoon cinnamon
¹/₂ teaspoon nutmeg
¹/₄ teaspoon ground cloves
1¹/₂ cups raisins
³/₄ cup chopped dates
1 cup chopped walnuts
1¹/₂ cups mixed candied fruit

Combine evaporated milk, orange juice and marshmallows in bowl. Let stand for several minutes. Mix cracker crumbs, cinnamon, nutmeg and cloves in large bowl. Add raisins, dates, walnuts and candied fruit; mix well. Stir in marshmallow mixture. Press firmly into 9-inch tube pan lined with waxed paper. Chill, tightly covered, for 2 days or longer. May garnish with additional candied fruit and nuts or substitute orange liqueur for orange juice. May press into 3 miniature loaf pans if preferred.

Shirley J. Haller, John I. Sabin Chapter

Grandma's Fruitcake

Yield:
20 servings
Utensil:
bundt pan

Approx Per Serving:
Cal 245
T Fat 6 g
22% Calories from Fat
Prot 3 g
Carbo 46 g
Fiber 2 g
Chol 11 mg
Sod 91 mg

1 cup raisins
¹/₂ cup brandy
1 package date nut bread mix
1 cup flaked coconut
1 cup chopped red and green candied cherries
¹/₂ cup chopped candied pineapple
¹/₂ cup chopped moist figs
¹/₂ cup chopped walnuts
¹/₂ cup chopped pecans
¹/₂ cup orange juice
1 egg

Soak raisins in brandy in bowl overnight. Combine date nut bread mix, coconut, cherries, pineapple, figs, walnuts and pecans in bowl; mix well. Drain raisins, reserving brandy. Add orange juice and enough additional brandy to reserved brandy to measure 1 cup. Beat egg in bowl. Add orange juice mixture; mix well. Add raisins and egg mixture to batter; mix well. Spoon into 6-cup bundt pan sprayed with nonstick cooking spray. Bake at 350 degrees for 50 minutes or until toothpick inserted in center comes out clean. Remove to wire rack to cool. May bake in 2 loaf pans. May decorate top with cherries and nuts before baking if desired.

Sally L. Ritchie, George S. Ladd Chapter

GRANDMA'S GINGERBREAD

| Yield: |
| 15 servings |
| Utensil: |
| cake pan |

3¹/₂ cups sifted cake
  flour
2 teaspoons baking soda
1 teaspoon cinnamon
1 tablespoon ginger
¹/₂ teaspoon cloves

1 cup sugar
2 eggs
³/₄ cup oil
1 cup blackstrap
  molasses
1 cup buttermilk

**Approx Per
Serving:**
Cal 292
T Fat 12 g
37% Calories
from Fat
Prot 3 g
Carbo 44 g
Fiber 1 g
Chol 29 mg
Sod 157 mg

Combine flour and baking soda in mixer bowl. Add cinnamon, ginger, cloves, sugar, eggs, oil, molasses and buttermilk in order listed, mixing well after each addition. Spoon into greased 9x13-inch cake pan. Bake at 325 degrees until gingerbread tests done. Cool on wire rack.

Ruth Flores, Sierra Pacific Chapter

GRAHAM CRACKER CAKE

| Yield: |
| 15 servings |
| Utensil: |
| tube pan |

³/₄ cup milk
1 teaspoon vinegar
3 tablespoons butter,
  softened
⁷/₈ cup sugar
3 egg yolks
1 teaspoon vanilla extract

2¹/₄ cups graham cracker
  crumbs
2¹/₂ teaspoons baking
  powder
¹/₂ teaspoon salt
3 egg whites, stiffly beaten
¹/₈ teaspoon salt

**Approx Per
Serving:**
Cal 166
T Fat 6 g
30% Calories
from Fat
Prot 3 g
Carbo 26 g
Fiber <1 g
Chol 51 mg
Sod 291 mg

Mix milk with vinegar in bowl; let stand until sour. Cream butter in mixer bowl until light. Add sugar gradually, beating until fluffy. Beat in egg yolks and vanilla. Combine cracker crumbs, baking powder and salt in bowl. Add to batter ¹/₃ at a time, mixing well after each addition. Add milk; mix well. Fold in egg whites and salt. Spoon into greased tube pan. Bake at 350 degrees for 30 minutes. Remove to wire rack to cool.

Pam Miller, De Anza Chapter

HILLBILLY CAKE

Yield:
15 servings
Utensil:
cake pan

Approx Per Serving:
Cal 353
T Fat 13 g
31% Calories from Fat
Prot 3 g
Carbo 59 g
Fiber 1 g
Chol 45 mg
Sod 251 mg

½ cup melted butter
1½ cups sugar
2 cups flour
2 eggs
2 teaspoons baking soda
½ teaspoon salt
1 20-ounce can crushed
  pineapple
1 cup packed brown
  sugar
1 cup chopped pecans

Combine butter, sugar, flour, eggs, baking soda, salt and pineapple in bowl; mix well. Spoon into greased and floured 9x13-inch cake pan. Sprinkle with mixture of brown sugar and pecans. Bake at 350 degrees for 40 minutes. Cool on wire rack.

Harold McCoy, John I. Sabin Chapter

LEMON-LIME BUTTER CAKE

Yield:
16 servings
Utensil:
2 cake pans

Approx Per Serving:
Cal 437
T Fat 24 g
49% Calories from Fat
Prot 4 g
Carbo 53 g
Fiber <1 g
Chol 117 mg
Sod 298 mg

1 2-layer package
  yellow cake mix
½ cup melted butter
¾ cup fresh lime juice
¼ cup water
4 eggs
¼ teaspoon lemon extract
3 tablespoons vanilla
  extract
¼ cup melted butter
2 to 3 cups
  confectioners' sugar
2 to 3 tablespoons lime
  juice
1 tablespoon vanilla
  extract
2 cups whipping cream,
  whipped

Combine cake mix, ½ cup butter, ¾ cup lime juice, water, eggs, lemon extract and 3 tablespoons vanilla in mixer bowl; mix until smooth. Spoon into 2 greased and floured 9-inch cake pans. Bake at 350 degrees for 35 to 45 minutes or until layers test done. Cool in pans for 10 minutes. Invert layers onto plates. Pierce holes in layers. Mix ¼ cup butter, confectioners' sugar, 2 to 3 tablespoons lime juice and 1 tablespoon vanilla in bowl. Drizzle over layers. Cool completely. Spread whipped cream between layers and over top and side of cake. Garnish with lemon and lime slices.

Aundrea De Cou, Los Amigos Chapter

MARBLE CAKE

Yield:
16 servings
Utensil:
bundt pan

Approx Per
Serving:
Cal 392
T Fat 21 g
46% Calories
from Fat
Prot 4 g
Carbo 52 g
Fiber 1 g
Chol 53 mg
Sod 272 mg

1 2-layer package
   yellow cake mix
1 4-ounce package
   vanilla instant
   pudding mix
4 eggs

²/₃ cup oil
1 cup boiling water
1 5¹/₂-ounce can
   chocolate syrup
2 cups semisweet
   chocolate chips

Combine cake mix, pudding mix, eggs, oil and water in mixer bowl; mix well. Spoon ³/₄ of the batter into greased and floured bundt or tube pan. Stir chocolate syrup into remaining batter. Drizzle over batter in pan. Cut through with knife to marbleize. Sprinkle with chocolate chips. Bake at 325 degrees for 50 to 60 minutes or until toothpick inserted in center comes out clean. Cool in pan for 20 to 30 minutes. Remove, right side up, to serving plate. Do not use pudding-recipe cake mix for this cake.

Robin Cuthbert, John I. Sabin Chapter

MAYONNAISE CAKE

Yield:
15 servings
Utensil:
cake pan

Approx Per
Serving:
Cal 225
T Fat 7 g
28% Calories
from Fat
Prot 3 g
Carbo 39 g
Fiber 1 g
Chol 5 mg
Sod 321 mg

2¹/₂ cups flour
1¹/₄ cups sugar
2 teaspoons baking soda
¹/₂ cup baking cocoa
¹/₂ teaspoon salt

1¹/₄ cups mayonnaise-
   type salad dressing
1¹/₄ cups warm water
1 teaspoon vanilla extract

Sift flour, sugar, baking soda, cocoa and salt together 3 times. Combine salad dressing, water and vanilla in mixer bowl; beat until smooth. Add dry ingredients; mix well. Spoon into greased 9x13-inch cake pan. Bake at 350 degrees for 45 minutes. Cool on wire rack.

Rusty Kamman, Mission Chapter

PERSIMMON CAKE

Yield:
16 servings
Utensil:
bundt pan

Approx Per Serving:
Cal 377
T Fat 17 g
42% Calories from Fat
Prot 4 g
Carbo 47 g
Fiber 1 g
Chol 67 mg
Sod 293 mg

1 2-layer package spice cake mix
1 4-ounce package vanilla instant pudding mix
5 eggs
²/₃ cup oil
¹/₂ teaspoon baking soda
1¹/₂ cups mashed persimmon pulp
1 cup rum
1 cup golden raisins
²/₃ cup chopped walnuts

Combine cake mix, pudding mix, eggs, oil, baking soda, persimmon pulp and rum; mix well. Stir in raisins and walnuts. Spoon into greased and floured bundt pan. Bake at 350 degrees for 1 hour. Cool in pan for 30 minutes. Remove, right side up, to serving plate.

Robin Cuthbert, John I. Sabin Chapter

FROSTED PINEAPPLE TEA CAKES

Yield:
16 servings
Utensil:
muffin pan

Approx Per Serving:
Cal 286
T Fat 13 g
38% Calories from Fat
Prot 3 g
Carbo 43 g
Fiber 1 g
Chol 31 mg
Sod 206 mg

2 cups sifted flour
1 teaspoon baking powder
¹/₂ teaspoon baking soda
1 teaspoon salt
¹/₂ cup shortening
¹/₂ cup sugar
¹/₂ cup packed brown sugar
2 eggs
¹/₂ cup crushed pineapple, drained
¹/₂ cup water
1 teaspoon vanilla extract
1 cup semisweet chocolate chips
2 tablespoons melted butter
1¹/₂ cups sifted confectioners' sugar
2 tablespoons crushed pineapple with syrup

Sift first 4 ingredients into bowl. Cream shortening, sugar and brown sugar in mixer bowl until light. Beat in eggs 1 at a time. Mix in ¹/₂ cup pineapple. Beat in dry ingredients alternately with water. Stir in vanilla and chocolate chips. Fill paper-lined muffin cups half full. Bake at 350 degrees for 20 to 25 minutes. Cool on wire rack. Blend butter with ¹/₂ cup confectioners' sugar in mixer bowl. Add 1 cup confectioners' sugar alternately with 2 tablespoons pineapple, mixing well after each addition. Spread on tea cakes.

Bob Rezak, John I. Sabin Chapter

POTATO CAKE

Yield:
12 servings
Utensil:
loaf pan

Approx Per Serving:
Cal 518
T Fat 29 g
49% Calories from Fat
Prot 8 g
Carbo 61 g
Fiber 3 g
Chol 114 mg
Sod 267 mg

1 cup butter, softened
2 cups sugar
1/2 cup milk
4 eggs, beaten
1 cup mashed cooked
  potatoes
2 1/2 cups flour
1 cup grated chocolate
2 teaspoons baking
  powder
1/2 teaspoon nutmeg
1/2 teaspoon cinnamon
1 cup chopped walnuts

Combine butter, sugar and milk in mixer bowl; mix until smooth. Beat in eggs. Add potatoes, flour, chocolate, baking powder, nutmeg and cinnamon; mix well. Stir in walnuts. Spoon into greased and floured 5x10-inch loaf pan. Bake at 300 degrees for 2 hours. Remove to wire rack to cool. May frost as desired. My grandmother always used seven-minute frosting. May bake in 2 layer cake pans if preferred.

Lucille I. McCarthy, John I. Sabin Chapter

COCONUT CREAM POUND CAKE

Yield:
16 servings
Utensil:
bundt pan

Approx Per Serving:
Cal 277
T Fat 15 g
47% Calories from Fat
Prot 3 g
Carbo 33 g
Fiber 1 g
Chol 46 mg
Sod 285 mg

1 2-layer package white
  cake mix
1 cup sour cream
1/2 cup water
1/2 cup margarine,
  softened
3 eggs
1 cup shredded coconut
1 teaspoon coconut
  extract
1/2 cup confectioners'
  sugar
2 1/2 teaspoons hot water
1/2 teaspoon coconut
  extract

Combine cake mix, sour cream, water, margarine, eggs, coconut and 1 teaspoon coconut extract in mixer bowl; mix until smooth. Spoon into greased and floured bundt pan. Bake at 350 degrees for 45 to 50 minutes or until cake tests done. Cool in pan for 10 minutes. Remove to wire rack to cool completely. Blend confectioners' sugar, hot water and 1/2 teaspoon coconut flavoring in bowl. Drizzle over cake.

Barbara Von Dohlen, John I. Sabin Chapter

CREAM CHEESE POUND CAKE

Yield:
16 servings
Utensil:
tube pan

**Approx Per
Serving:**
Cal 450
T Fat 25 g
*48% Calories
from Fat*
Prot 5 g
Carbo 54 g
Fiber 1 g
Chol 142 mg
Sod 214 mg

1½ cups butter, softened
8 ounces cream cheese,
  softened
3 cups sugar
3 cups cake flour
6 eggs
1 tablespoon vanilla
  extract

Cream butter and cream cheese in mixer bowl until light. Add sugar, beating until fluffy. Add flour, eggs and vanilla; mix well. Spoon into greased and floured tube or bundt pan. Place in cold oven; set oven temperature to 300 degrees. Bake for 1 hour or until wooden pick inserted in center comes out clean. Cool in pan for 10 minutes. Remove to wire rack to cool completely.

Julia Jacobs, Los Amigos Chapter

EGGNOG POUND CAKE

Yield:
16 servings
Utensil:
bundt pan

**Approx Per
Serving:**
Cal 229
T Fat 10 g
*41% Calories
from Fat*
Prot 3 g
Carbo 31 g
Fiber <1 g
Chol 14 mg
Sod 260 mg

2 tablespoons
  margarine, softened
½ cup sliced almonds
1 2-layer package
  yellow cake mix
1½ cups eggnog
¼ cup melted margarine
2 tablespoons rum
½ teaspoon nutmeg

Spread 2 tablespoons margarine in bundt pan. Press almonds into flutes of pan. Combine cake mix, eggnog, melted margarine, rum and nutmeg in bowl; mix well. Spoon into prepared pan. Bake at 350 degrees for 45 to 55 minutes or until wooden pick inserted in center comes out clean. Cool in pan for 10 minutes. Invert onto wire rack to cool completely.

Diane Bolz, George S. Ladd Chapter

WHIPPED CREAM POUND CAKE

Yield:
16 servings
Utensil:
tube pan

Approx Per Serving:
Cal 406
T Fat 20 g
43% Calories from Fat
Prot 5 g
Carbo 54 g
Fiber 1 g
Chol 145 mg
Sod 134 mg

1 cup butter, softened
3 cups sugar
7 eggs, at room temperature
3 cups cake flour
1 cup whipping cream
2 teaspoons vanilla extract

Cream butter and sugar in mixer bowl until light and fluffy. Beat in eggs 1 at a time. Sift flour twice. Add half the flour, whipping cream, remaining flour and vanilla to creamed mixture, mixing well after each addition. Spoon into greased and floured 10-inch tube pan. Place in cold oven; set oven temperature to 350 degrees. Bake for 1 hour to 1 hour and 10 minutes or until knife inserted in center comes out clean. Cool in pan for 5 minutes. Remove to wire rack to cool completely. May store, well wrapped, for several days.

Brenda McCoy, John I. Sabin Chapter

PRUNE CAKE

Yield:
16 servings
Utensil:
tube pan

Approx Per Serving:
Cal 360
T Fat 20 g
49% Calories from Fat
Prot 5 g
Carbo 43 g
Fiber 1 g
Chol 42 mg
Sod 206 mg

2 cups flour
2 cups sugar
1 teaspoon baking soda
1 teaspoon cinnamon
1 teaspoon nutmeg
1 teaspoon cloves
1 teaspoon salt
1 cup milk
1 cup oil
3 eggs
1 cup cooked prunes
1 cup chopped walnuts

Mix flour, sugar, baking soda, cinnamon, nutmeg, cloves and salt in bowl. Add milk, oil, and eggs; mix well. Stir in prunes and walnuts. Spoon into greased and floured tube pan. Bake at 375 degrees for 1 hour. Cool in pan for 10 minutes. Remove to wire rack to cool completely.

Edythe Laughlin, Silver State Chapter

BACARDI RUM CAKE

Yield:
16 servings
Utensil:
tube pan

Approx Per Serving:
Cal 423
T Fat 22 g
49% Calories from Fat
Prot 4 g
Carbo 47 g
Fiber 1 g
Chol 69 mg
Sod 310 mg

1 cup chopped pecans
1 2-layer package yellow cake mix
1 4-ounce package vanilla instant pudding mix
4 eggs
1/2 cup cold water
1/2 cup oil
1/2 cup dark rum
1/2 cup butter
1/4 cup water
1 cup sugar
1/2 cup dark rum

Sprinkle pecans in greased 10-inch tube pan. Combine cake mix, pudding mix, eggs, 1/2 cup cold water, oil and 1/2 cup rum in mixer bowl; mix until smooth. Spoon into prepared pan. Bake at 325 degrees for 1 hour. Cool in pan on wire rack. Invert onto serving plate. Melt butter in saucepan. Stir in 1/4 cup water and sugar. Cook for 5 minutes, stirring frequently. Stir in 1/2 cup rum. Pierce top of cake. Brush glaze evenly over top and side of cake.

Martha Blissitt, John I. Sabin Chapter

RUM CAKE

Yield:
16 servings
Utensil:
bundt pan

Approx Per Serving:
Cal 385
T Fat 17 g
43% Calories from Fat
Prot 4 g
Carbo 47 g
Fiber <1 g
Chol 53 mg
Sod 295 mg

3/4 cup chopped walnuts
1 2-layer package yellow cake mix
1 4-ounce package vanilla instant pudding mix
1/2 cup oil
1/2 cup water
4 eggs
1/2 cup dark rum
1/4 cup margarine
1/4 cup water
1 cup sugar
1/2 cup dark rum

Sprinkle walnuts into greased and floured 10-cup bundt pan. Combine cake mix, pudding mix, oil, 1/2 cup water, eggs and 1/2 cup rum in large mixer bowl. Beat at medium speed for 2 minutes. Spoon into prepared pan. Bake at 350 degrees for 45 minutes or until cake tests done. Remove to wire rack to cool. Combine margarine, 1/4 cup water and sugar in small saucepan. Cook over medium heat until sugar dissolves, stirring constantly; remove from heat. Stir in 1/2 cup rum. Pierce cake. Spoon glaze over cake.

Ann Bell, Los Amigos Chapter

CHOCOLATE BEER SAUERKRAUT CAKE

Yield:
16 servings
Utensil:
2 cake pans

Approx Per Serving:
Cal 233
T Fat 9 g
35% Calories from Fat
Prot 3 g
Carbo 33 g
Fiber 1 g
Chol 62 mg
Sod 248 mg

²/₃ cup butter, softened
1¹/₂ cups sugar
1 teaspoon vanilla extract
3 eggs
¹/₂ cup baking cocoa
2¹/₄ cups flour
1 teaspoon baking soda

1 teaspoon baking powder
¹/₄ teaspoon salt
1 cup beer
²/₃ cup chopped sauerkraut, rinsed, drained

Cream butter and sugar in mixer bowl until light and fluffy. Add vanilla. Beat in eggs 1 at a time. Mix cocoa, flour, baking soda, baking powder and salt together. Add to batter alternately with beer, mixing well after each addition. Stir in sauerkraut. Spoon into 2 greased and floured 9-inch cake pans. Bake at 350 degrees for 40 minutes. Remove to wire rack to cool. Frost as desired.

Rusty Kamman, Mission Chapter

SAUERKRAUT CAKE

Yield:
15 servings
Utensil:
cake pan

Approx Per Serving:
Cal 248
T Fat 10 g
35% Calories from Fat
Prot 4 g
Carbo 37 g
Fiber 2 g
Chol 43 mg
Sod 506 mg

1 16-ounce can sauerkraut
²/₃ cup margarine, softened
1¹/₂ cups sugar
3 eggs

2 teaspoons vanilla extract
2¹/₄ cups flour
¹/₂ cup baking cocoa
1 teaspoon baking soda
1 teaspoon salt
1 cup cold water

Rinse sauerkraut and squeeze dry. Chop fine. Cream margarine in mixer bowl until light. Add sugar, beating until fluffy. Beat in eggs 1 at a time. Add vanilla. Mix flour, cocoa, baking soda and salt together. Add to batter alternately with water, mixing well after each addition. Stir in sauerkraut. Spoon into 9x13-inch cake pan. Bake at 350 degrees for 35 minutes. Cool on wire rack. Garnish with confectioners' sugar and serve with whipped cream.

Betty Menk Gray, John I. Sabin Chapter

SAUERKRAUT SURPRISE CAKE

Yield:
15 servings
Utensil:
cake pan

Approx Per Serving:
Cal 400
T Fat 17 g
36% Calories from Fat
Prot 4 g
Carbo 63 g
Fiber 2 g
Chol 71 mg
Sod 344 mg

½ cup butter, softened
1½ cups sugar
3 eggs
1 teaspoon vanilla extract
2 cups sifted flour
1 teaspoon baking powder
1 teaspoon baking soda
½ cup baking cocoa
¼ teaspoon salt
1 cup water
1   8-ounce can chopped sauerkraut, rinsed, drained
1 recipe Chocolate Frosting (page 234)

Cream ½ cup butter and sugar in mixer bowl until light and fluffy. Beat in eggs 1 at a time. Add 1 teaspoon vanilla. Sift flour, baking powder, baking soda, cocoa and salt together. Add to creamed mixture alternately with water, mixing well after each addition. Stir in sauerkraut. Spoon into greased and floured 9x13-inch cake pan. Bake at 350 degrees for 35 to 40 minutes or until cake tests done. Cool in pan on wire rack. Spread with Chocolate Frosting.

Toni Earl, Silver State Chapter

PORTUGUESE SPICE CAKE

Yield:
16 servings
Utensil:
tube pan

Approx Per Serving:
Cal 381
T Fat 19 g
43% Calories from Fat
Prot 4 g
Carbo 52 g
Fiber 2 g
Chol 0 mg
Sod 239 mg

1 cup raisins
3 cups water
2 cups sugar
1 cup oil
3 cups flour
1 teaspoon salt
2 teaspoons baking soda
1 teaspoon cloves
1 teaspoon allspice
1 teaspoon cinnamon
1 tablespoon vanilla extract
1 cup chopped walnuts

Combine raisins and water in saucepan. Bring to a boil. Let stand until cool. Drain, reserving 2 cups water. Beat sugar and oil in mixer bowl until light. Sift flour, salt, baking soda and spices together. Add to sugar mixture alternately with reserved raisin water, mixing well after each addition. Stir in vanilla, walnuts and raisins. Pour into greased tube pan. Bake at 375 degrees for 1 hour and 10 minutes or until cake tests done. Remove to wire rack to cool.

Shirley Rocha, George S. Ladd Chapter

STRAWBERRY CAKE

Yield:
12 servings
Utensil:
cake pan

Approx Per Serving:
Cal 554
T Fat 27 g
43% Calories from Fat
Prot 5 g
Carbo 75 g
Fiber 1 g
Chol 92 mg
Sod 353 mg

1 2-layer package white cake mix
1 3-ounce package strawberry gelatin
3 tablespoons flour
1/2 cup water
3/4 cup oil
4 eggs
1 10-ounce package frozen strawberries, thawed
1/2 cup melted butter
3 cups (or more) confectioners' sugar

Combine cake mix, gelatin and flour in mixer bowl. Add water, oil and eggs; beat well. Stir in 3/4 of the strawberries. Pour into greased and floured 9x13-inch cake pan. Bake at 375 degrees for 30 minutes or until cake tests done. Let stand until cool. Combine remaining strawberries, butter and enough confectioners' sugar to make icing of spreading consistency in mixer bowl; mix well. Spread over cake.

Thelma Keller, John I. Sabin Chapter

STRAWBERRY GELATIN CAKE

Yield:
16 servings
Utensil:
tube pan

Approx Per Serving:
Cal 313
T Fat 14 g
40% Calories from Fat
Prot 3 g
Carbo 44 g
Fiber 1 g
Chol 53 mg
Sod 231 mg

1 2-layer package strawberry cake mix
1 3-ounce package strawberry gelatin
4 eggs
3/4 cup cold water
3/4 cup oil
1 10-ounce package frozen strawberries in syrup, thawed
1 cup confectioners' sugar

Combine cake mix, gelatin, eggs and water in mixer bowl. Beat for 3 minutes. Add oil. Beat for 3 minutes. Pour into greased and floured tube pan. Bake at 350 degrees for 35 minutes or until cake tests done. Let stand until cool. Combine strawberries and confectioners' sugar in bowl; mix well. Drizzle over cake.

Linda Lim, Los Amigos Chapter

STRAWBERRY SHORTCUT CAKE

Yield:
12 servings
Utensil:
cake pan

Approx Per Serving:
Cal 556
T Fat 31 g
49% Calories from Fat
Prot 5 g
Carbo 68 g
Fiber 2 g
Chol 80 mg
Sod 300 mg

1 2-layer package white cake mix
3 eggs
1 cup oil
3/4 cup water
3 10-ounce packages frozen sweetened strawberries, thawed
1 3-ounce package strawberry gelatin
2 cups miniature marshmallows
1 cup whipping cream, whipped

Combine cake mix, eggs, oil and water in mixer bowl. Beat at high speed for 2 minutes. Combine strawberries and gelatin in bowl; mix well. Sprinkle marshmallows over bottom of greased 9x13-inch cake pan. Pour batter over marshmallows. Spoon strawberry mixture evenly over batter. Bake at 350 degrees for 40 minutes or until cake tests done. Let stand until completely cool. Cut into squares. Invert onto serving plates. Top with whipped cream. Marshmallows will rise to top and strawberries will settle to bottom during baking.

Shelly Brown, George S. Ladd Chapter

TURTLE CAKE

Yield:
12 servings
Utensil:
cake pan

Approx Per Serving:
Cal 640
T Fat 36 g
49% Calories from Fat
Prot 7 g
Carbo 77 g
Fiber 1 g
Chol 81 mg
Sod 577 mg

1 14-ounce package caramels
1/2 cup butter
1/2 cup sweetened condensed milk
1 2-layer package German chocolate cake mix
1 cup chopped pecans
1 cup chocolate chips

Melt caramels with butter and condensed milk in saucepan; mix well. Set aside to cool. Prepare cake mix using package directions. Pour half the batter into greased and floured 9x13-inch cake pan. Bake at 350 degrees for 15 minutes. Pour caramel mixture over top. Sprinkle pecans and chocolate chips over caramel layer. Spread remaining batter over top. Bake for 15 minutes longer or until cake tests done. Let stand until cool. Cut into squares.

Doris Dahl, George S. Ladd Chapter

CREAM CHEESE FROSTING

Yield:
15 servings
Utensil:
bowl

Approx Per
Serving:
Cal 135
T Fat 8 g
49% Calories
from Fat
Prot 1 g
Carbo 16 g
Fiber 0 g
Chol 23 mg
Sod 64 mg

8 ounces cream cheese,
  softened
3 tablespoons butter,
  softened

1 teaspoon vanilla extract
2 cups confectioners'
  sugar

Beat cream cheese, butter and vanilla in mixer bowl until light and fluffy. Add confectioners' sugar; mix well.

Jan Moore, John I. Sabin Chapter

CARROT CAKE FROSTING

Yield:
15 servings
Utensil:
bowl

Approx Per
Serving:
Cal 301
T Fat 18 g
51% Calories
from Fat
Prot 1 g
Carbo 36 g
Fiber 0 g
Chol 50 mg
Sod 148 mg

1 cup butter, softened
8 ounces cream cheese,
  softened
1 1-pound package
  confectioners' sugar

2 teaspoons vanilla
  extract
1 teaspoon rum or
  almond extract

Cream butter and cream cheese in mixer bowl until smooth. Add confectioners' sugar and flavorings; mix well. May tint orange with 3 drops of red food coloring and 14 drops of yellow food coloring if desired.

Bonnie Boelens, John I. Sabin Chapter

CHOCOLATE FROSTING

Yield:
15 servings
Utensil:
saucepan

Approx Per Serving:
Cal 186
T Fat 9 g
40% Calories from Fat
Prot 1 g
Carbo 29 g
Fiber <1 g
Chol 12 mg
Sod 67 mg

1 cup chocolate chips
1/4 cup butter
1/2 cup sour cream
1/4 teaspoon salt

1 teaspoon vanilla extract
2 1/2 to 2 3/4 cups
   confectioners' sugar

Melt chocolate chips with butter in saucepan over low heat; remove from heat. Stir in sour cream, salt and vanilla. Add enough confectioners' sugar to make of desired consistency, mixing well.

Toni Earl, Silver State Chapter

MARSHMALLOW FROSTING WITHOUT MARSHMALLOWS

Yield:
16 servings
Utensil:
saucepan

Approx Per Serving:
Cal 40
T Fat 0 g
0% Calories from Fat
Prot <1 g
Carbo 10 g
Fiber 0 g
Chol 0 mg
Sod 9 mg

1/2 cup sugar
1/4 cup light corn syrup
2 tablespoons water

2 egg whites
1 teaspoon vanilla extract

Combine sugar, corn syrup and water in saucepan; cover. Bring to a rolling boil over medium heat, stirring occasionally; uncover. Cook to 242 degrees on candy thermometer; do not stir. Beat egg whites until stiff peaks form. Pour hot syrup in very thin stream into egg whites, beating constantly at high speed until very stiff peaks form. Add vanilla. Beat until blended. May store in airtight container in refrigerator for 3 days.

June A. Schelb, Mission Chapter

Candy

ALMOND BRITTLE

Yield:
30 servings
Utensil:
baking sheet

Approx Per Serving:
Cal 236
T Fat 19 g
68% Calories from Fat
Prot 2 g
Carbo 17 g
Fiber 1 g
Chol 0 mg
Sod 144 mg

2 cups sugar
2 cups margarine
2 cups almonds

½ cup chocolate chips, melted
¼ cup chopped walnuts

Combine sugar, margarine and almonds in heavy saucepan. Bring to a boil, stirring constantly. Cook over medium heat for 30 to 40 minutes or until golden brown, stirring constantly. Oil in margarine will separate but eventually mixes. Pour onto 10x15-inch baking sheet. Let stand for 5 minutes. Spread melted chocolate chips over top; sprinkle with walnuts. Cool to room temperature. Break into serving pieces.

Linda Colon, Silver State Chapter

PEANUT BRITTLE

Yield:
30 servings
Utensil:
baking sheet

Approx Per Serving:
Cal 169
T Fat 7 g
37% Calories from Fat
Prot 4 g
Carbo 24 g
Fiber 1 g
Chol 0 mg
Sod 72 mg

2 cups sugar
1 cup light corn syrup
½ teaspoon salt

1 pound raw peanuts
½ teaspoon baking soda

Combine sugar, corn syrup and salt in heavy saucepan. Bring to a boil, stirring constantly. Boil for 5 minutes, stirring constantly. Remove from heat. Stir in peanuts. Boil for 10 minutes longer or until golden brown, stirring constantly. Remove from heat. Stir in baking soda. Pour onto 10x15-inch baking sheet. Cool to room temperature. Break into serving pieces.

Cathy Harper, Silver State Chapter

MICROWAVE PEANUT BRITTLE

Yield:
30 servings
Utensil:
baking sheet

Approx Per Serving:
Cal 114
T Fat 5 g
38% Calories from Fat
Prot 3 g
Carbo 16 g
Fiber 1 g
Chol 1 mg
Sod 34 mg

2 cups unsalted peanuts
1½ cups sugar
½ cup corn syrup
½ cup water
⅛ teaspoon salt
1 tablespoon butter
1 teaspoon baking soda
1 teaspoon vanilla extract

Combine peanuts, sugar, corn syrup, water and salt in large microwave-safe bowl. Microwave, uncovered, on High for 5 minutes; stir. Microwave on High for 13 minutes. Add butter, baking soda and vanilla; stir just until mixed. Pour onto buttered 10x15-inch baking sheet. Cool to room temperature. Break into serving pieces.

Alice Milovich, Silver State Chapter

CARAMEL CORN

Yield:
64 servings
Utensil:
baking pan

Approx Per Serving:
Cal 103
T Fat 5 g
38% Calories from Fat
Prot 1 g
Carbo 16 g
Fiber 1 g
Chol 12 mg
Sod 118 mg

3 cups packed brown sugar
¾ cup light corn syrup
1½ cups butter
½ teaspoon cream of tartar
1½ teaspoons salt
1½ teaspoons baking soda
6 to 8 quarts popped popcorn

Combine brown sugar, corn syrup, butter, cream of tartar and salt in heavy saucepan. Bring to a boil, stirring constantly. Cook over medium heat to hard-ball stage or 250 to 268 degrees on candy thermometer, stirring frequently. Remove from heat. Stir in baking soda. Place popped popcorn in large baking pan. Pour syrup over popcorn, stirring to coat popcorn. Bake at 200 degrees for 1 hour, stirring every 15 minutes. Pour onto waxed paper to cool, stirring to separate popcorn.

Linda Rowe, George S. Ladd Chapter

OVEN CARAMEL CORN

Yield:
64 servings
Utensil:
roasting pan

**Approx Per
Serving:**
Cal 74
T Fat 3 g
*36% Calories
from Fat*
Prot 1 g
Carbo 12 g
Fiber 1 g
Chol 0 mg
Sod 78 mg

2 cups packed brown
  sugar
1 cup margarine
1/2 cup light corn syrup
1 teaspoon butter
  flavoring

1 teaspoon burnt sugar
  flavoring
1 teaspoon salt
1/2 teaspoon baking soda
8 quarts popped popcorn

Combine brown sugar, margarine, corn syrup, butter flavoring, burnt sugar flavoring and salt in heavy saucepan. Bring to a boil, stirring constantly. Boil for 5 minutes, stirring occasionally. Remove from heat. Stir in baking soda. Pour popcorn into large roasting pan. Pour syrup over popcorn, stirring to coat popcorn. Bake at 250 degrees for 1 hour, stirring every 15 minutes. Pour onto waxed paper to cool, stirring to separate popcorn.

Evelyn Mess, John I. Sabin Chapter

CARAMEL

Yield:
16 servings
Utensil:
baking dish

**Approx Per
Serving:**
Cal 99
T Fat 2 g
*20% Calories
from Fat*
Prot 2 g
Carbo 18 g
Fiber 1 g
Chol 8 mg
Sod 32 mg

1 14-ounce can
  sweetened condensed
  milk

1 fresh pineapple

Pour sweetened condensed milk into 8-inch square glass baking dish. Cover dish with foil; place in larger pan half filled with hot water. Bake at 425 degrees for 1 hour or until thickened and caramel-colored. Cool to room temperature. Chill in refrigerator. Cut into servings. Serve with fresh cut pineapple. This method of cooking sweetened condensed milk is recommended by the manufacturer which does not recommend cooking sweetened condensed milk in the can.

Stephen J. Huysentruyt, Sierra Pacific Chapter

CAPTAIN CRUNCH CANDY

Yield:
42 servings
Utensil:
waxed paper

Approx Per
Serving:
Cal 71
T Fat 5 g
55% Calories
from Fat
Prot 1 g
Carbo 7 g
Fiber <1 g
Chol 0 mg
Sod 51 mg

2 cups white chocolate
  chips
1½ cups Captain
  Crunch cereal
1½ cups Rice Krispies
  cereal
1 cup unsalted dry
  roasted peanuts

Melt white chocolate chips in top of double boiler over boiling water, stirring occasionally. Combine cereals and peanuts in large bowl; toss to mix. Pour melted white chocolate over mixture, stirring to coat cereal and peanuts. Drop by teaspoonfuls onto waxed paper, pressing lightly into shape with fingers. Cool until set.

Marjorie D. Chrystal, John I. Sabin Chapter

CHOCOLATE PEANUT BUTTER BALLS

Yield:
90 servings
Utensil:
waxed paper

Approx Per
Serving:
Cal 111
T Fat 7 g
53% Calories
from Fat
Prot 2 g
Carbo 12 g
Fiber <1 g
Chol 0 mg
Sod 75 mg

1 cup melted margarine
3 cups crushed crisp rice
  cereal
1 1-pound package
  confectioners' sugar
1 teaspoon vanilla extract
2 cups crunchy-style
  peanut butter
2 cups semisweet
  chocolate chips
⅓ stick paraffin

Combine margarine, cereal, confectioners' sugar, vanilla and peanut butter in mixer bowl; mix well. Melt chocolate chips and paraffin together in double boiler over boiling water, stirring occasionally. Shape cereal mixture into balls; dip in chocolate to coat. Place candy on waxed paper until set.

Jennifer Crane, Los Amigos Chapter

CHOCOLATE PEANUT BUTTER DROPS

Yield:
70 servings
Utensil:
baking sheet

Approx Per
Serving:
Cal 134
T Fat 9 g
60% Calories
from Fat
Prot 3 g
Carbo 12 g
Fiber 1 g
Chol 8 mg
Sod 68 mg

2 cups peanut butter
2¹/₂ cups confectioners'
　sugar
¹/₃ 1-pound package
　graham crackers,
　crushed

1 cup melted butter
12 ounces semisweet
　chocolate
8 ounces milk chocolate

Combine peanut butter, confectioners' sugar, graham cracker crumbs and butter in bowl; mix well. Shape into 1-inch balls. Place on foil-lined baking sheet. Freeze until very firm. Melt chocolate in double boiler over boiling water, stirring occasionally. Place frozen peanut butter balls on pick; dip in chocolate until coated. Place on foil-lined baking sheet, removing picks. Let stand until chocolate is set.

Shirley J. Haller, John I. Sabin Chapter

FAMOUS FUDGE

Yield:
16 servings
Utensil:
baking pan

Approx Per
Serving:
Cal 300
T Fat 14 g
40% Calories
from Fat
Prot 2 g
Carbo 46 g
Fiber 1 g
Chol 42 mg
Sod 60 mg

2 cups chocolate chips
¹/₂ cup butter
1 1-pound package
　confectioners' sugar

1 teaspoon vanilla extract
2 eggs

Combine chocolate chips and butter in 1-quart microwave-safe bowl. Microwave on High until melted; stir to mix. Combine confectioners' sugar, vanilla and eggs in bowl; mix well. Add chocolate mixture; mix well. Pour into buttered 8-inch square baking pan. Freeze until very firm. May substitute mint flavored chocolate chips for chocolate chips and add peanut butter, marshmallows or nuts.

Bonnie Funk, George S. Ladd Chapter

BETTY'S FAMOUS FANTASY FUDGE

Yield:
16 servings
Utensil:
baking pan

Approx Per
Serving:
Cal 432
T Fat 22 g
43% Calories
from Fat
Prot 2 g
Carbo 62 g
Fiber 1 g
Chol 3 mg
Sod 123 mg

3 cups sugar
3/4 cup margarine
2/3 cup evaporated milk
2 cups semisweet
  chocolate chips
1 7-ounce jar
  marshmallow creme
1 cup chopped pecans
1 teaspoon vanilla extract

Combine sugar, margarine and evaporated milk in heavy 2 1/2-quart saucepan. Bring to a boil, stirring constantly. Cook over medium heat for 5 minutes or to 234 degrees on candy thermometer, soft-ball stage, stirring constantly. Remove from heat. Stir in chocolate chips until melted. Add marshmallow creme, pecans and vanilla; mix well. Pour into greased 9-inch square baking pan. Cool to room temperature; cut into squares.

Karen Celaya, Sierra Pacific Chapter

HEALTHY CANDY

Yield:
30 servings
Utensil:
baking pan

Approx Per
Serving:
Cal 64
T Fat 3 g
44% Calories
from Fat
Prot 2 g
Carbo 8 g
Fiber 1 g
Chol 0 mg
Sod 18 mg

1/2 cup peanut butter
1/2 cup honey
1 cup wheat germ
1 3-ounce can coconut

Combine peanut butter, honey and wheat germ in bowl; mix well. Shape into small balls with buttered fingers. Roll balls in coconut to coat. Place on waxed paper-lined baking pan. Chill in refrigerator until firm.

Dorothy Hamata, Mission Chapter

OATMEAL FUDGE CANDY

Yield:
36 servings
Utensil:
waxed paper

2 cups sugar
1/2 cup baking cocoa
1/2 cup peanut butter
1/2 cup milk

1/2 cup butter
3 cups oats
1 teaspoon vanilla extract

Combine sugar, cocoa, peanut butter, milk and butter in saucepan. Bring to a boil, stirring frequently. Boil for 2 minutes, stirring constantly. Stir in oats and vanilla. Drop by teaspoonfuls onto waxed paper.

Carol Holmes, John I. Sabin Chapter

Approx Per
Serving:
Cal 118
T Fat 5 g
37% Calories
from Fat
Prot 2 g
Carbo 17 g
Fiber 1 g
Chol 7 mg
Sod 38 mg

CANDIED ORANGE PEEL

Yield:
24 servings
Utensil:
waxed paper

6 large oranges
3 cups sugar
1/4 cup orange liqueur

1/2 cup crystallized sugar
1 cup melted chocolate

Trim ends from oranges; cut oranges into quarters. Remove rind; cut into 1/4-inch wide strips. Place orange rind in deep saucepan. Add water to cover by 2 inches. Bring to a boil, stirring occasionally. Boil for 5 minutes, stirring occasionally; drain. Repeat 3 times with fresh water each time; drain well. Place rind in large skillet. Sprinkle with 3 cups sugar. Cook over very low heat for 1½ hours, stirring occasionally. Stir in orange liqueur. Cook for 30 minutes longer, stirring occasionally. Remove to wire rack. Chill in refrigerator until coating is set. Roll in 1/2 cup crystallized sugar; dip 1 end in melted chocolate. Place between sheets of waxed paper. Store in refrigerator. May cook rind in stages over 2 day period.

Linda Wright, Sierra Pacific Chapter

Approx Per
Serving:
Cal 149
T Fat 3 g
15% Calories
from Fat
Prot 1 g
Carbo 32 g
Fiber 1 g
Chol 0 mg
Sod 1 mg

PECAN TURTLES

Yield:
36 servings
Utensil:
baking sheet

Approx Per Serving:
Cal 139
T Fat 8 g
49% Calories from Fat
Prot 1 g
Carbo 18 g
Fiber <1 g
Chol 2 mg
Sod 43 mg

1/2 cup margarine
1 cup packed light brown sugar
1/8 teaspoon salt
1/2 cup light corn syrup
2/3 cup sweetened condensed milk
1 1/2 cups pecan pieces
1/2 teaspoon vanilla extract
1 cup semisweet chocolate chips, melted

Melt margarine in saucepan over low heat. Add brown sugar, salt, corn syrup and condensed milk; mix well. Simmer for 15 to 20 minutes or to 245 degrees on candy thermometer, firm-ball stage, stirring frequently. Stir in pecans and vanilla. Drop by tablespoonfuls onto greased baking sheet. Cool until firm. Dip in melted chocolate to coat. Let stand until chocolate sets.

Shelly Brown, George S. Ladd Chapter

MASHED POTATO CANDY

Yield:
24 servings
Utensil:
bowl

Approx Per Serving:
Cal 154
T Fat 6 g
31% Calories from Fat
Prot 3 g
Carbo 25 g
Fiber 1 g
Chol <1 mg
Sod 57 mg

1/2 cup cold mashed potatoes
1/4 teaspoon vanilla extract
1 1-pound package confectioners' sugar
1 cup peanut butter

Combine mashed potatoes and vanilla in bowl; mix well. Add confectioners' sugar, a small amount at a time until mixture is the consistency of bread dough. Roll out on confectioners' sugar coated surface. Spread with peanut butter. Roll as for jelly roll to enclose peanut butter. Cut into slices; place on waxed paper. Chill in refrigerator until set.

Rusty Kamman, Mission Chapter

ROCKY ROAD CANDY LOGS

Yield:
60 servings
Utensil:
baking sheet

Approx Per
Serving:
Cal 57
T Fat 4 g
52% Calories
from Fat
Prot <1 g
Carbo 7 g
Fiber <1 g
Chol 0 mg
Sod 23 mg

2 cups chocolate
  chips
½ cup butter

1 10-ounce package
  colored miniature
  marshmallows

Melt chocolate chips and butter together in saucepan over low heat. Cool for several minutes or until mixture will not melt marshmallows. Stir in marshmallows. Divide into 2 portions. Shape each portion into 15-inch log on waxed paper. Roll waxed paper to enclose candy log. Place on baking sheet. Chill in refrigerator until firm. Cut into ½-inch slices.

Doris Dahl, George S. Ladd Chapter

ENGLISH TOFFEE

Yield:
30 servings
Utensil:
baking sheet

Approx Per
Serving:
Cal 275
T Fat 22 g
67% Calories
from Fat
Prot 4 g
Carbo 20 g
Fiber 3 g
Chol 20 mg
Sod 67 mg

1 cup butter
1 cup sugar
3 tablespoons water
1 tablespoon light corn
  syrup

1 pound almonds, finely
  chopped
1 pound chocolate

Combine butter, sugar, water and corn syrup in heavy saucepan. Simmer to 300 degrees on candy thermometer, hard-crack stage, stirring frequently. Remove from heat. Stir in ½ cup chopped almonds. Pour onto baking sheet. Cool to room temperature. Melt chocolate in double boiler over hot water, stirring occasionally. Pour half the chocolate over candy, spreading to coat surface. Sprinkle with half the remaining chopped almonds. Let stand until set. Turn candy. Coat with remaining chocolate; sprinkle with remaining chopped almonds. Let stand until set. Break into servings. This candy ages well in airtight container in refrigerator.

Cathy Harper, Silver State Chapter

Cookies

BROWNIES

Yield:
16 servings
Utensil:
baking pan

Approx Per Serving:
Cal 141
T Fat 8 g
51% Calories from Fat
Prot 2 g
Carbo 16 g
Fiber 1 g
Chol 42 mg
Sod 58 mg

½ cup butter, softened
1 cup sugar
2 eggs, at room temperature
2 squares unsweetened baking chocolate, melted

½ cup sifted flour
Salt to taste
1½ teaspoons vanilla extract

Combine butter, sugar and eggs in mixer bowl; beat until smooth. Add chocolate; mix well. Sift in flour and salt. Add vanilla; mix well. Spoon into 9x10-inch baking pan lined with waxed paper. Bake at 400 degrees for 15 minutes or just until brownies test done; do not overbake. Remove from pan immediately; discard waxed paper. Cut into squares.

Dolores Syme, John I. Sabin Chapter

FUDGY BROWNIES

Yield:
20 servings
Utensil:
baking pan

Approx Per Serving:
Cal 136
T Fat 9 g
59% Calories from Fat
Prot 1 g
Carbo 14 g
Fiber 1 g
Chol 34 mg
Sod 54 mg

2 squares unsweetened chocolate
½ cup butter
⅔ cup flour
1 cup sugar

½ teaspoon baking powder
2 eggs
1 teaspoon vanilla extract
½ cup chopped pecans

Melt chocolate with butter in saucepan over very low heat, stirring to blend well; remove from heat. Combine flour, sugar, baking powder and eggs in mixer bowl; beat until smooth. Stir in chocolate mixture and vanilla. Add pecans; mix well. Spread in greased 8x8-inch baking pan. Bake at 350 degrees for 20 to 30 minutes or until brownies test done. Cool on wire rack. Cut into squares.

Connie Papillon, Los Amigos Chapter

HEAVENLY ROCKY ROAD FUDGE BARS

Yield:
36 servings
Utensil:
baking dish

**Approx Per
Serving:**
Cal 156
T Fat 10 g
*57% Calories
from Fat*
Prot 2 g
Carbo 16 g
Fiber 1 g
Chol 33 mg
Sod 62 mg

1/2 cup butter
1 ounce unsweetened
  chocolate
1 cup sugar
1 cup flour
1/2 cup chopped pecans
1 teaspoon baking
  powder
1 teaspoon vanilla extract
2 eggs
6 ounces cream cheese,
  softened

1/2 cup sugar
2 tablespoons flour
1/4 cup butter, softened
1 egg
1/2 teaspoon vanilla
  extract
1/4 cup chopped pecans
1 cup chocolate chips
2 cups miniature
  marshmallows
Rocky Road Fudge
  Frosting

Grease and flour 9x13-inch baking dish. Melt butter and chocolate in saucepan over low heat, stirring occasionally. Add 1 cup sugar, 1 cup flour, 1/2 cup pecans, baking powder, 1 teaspoon vanilla and 2 eggs; mix well. Spread in prepared baking dish. Combine cream cheese, 1/2 cup sugar, 2 tablespoons flour, 1/4 cup butter, 1 egg, 1/2 teaspoon vanilla and 1/4 cup pecans in bowl; mix well. Spread over mixture; sprinkle with chocolate chips. Bake at 350 degrees for 20 to 35 minutes or until toothpick inserted in center comes out clean. Sprinkle with miniature marshmallows. Bake for 2 minutes longer. Pour Rocky Road Fudge Frosting over marshmallows, stirring to swirl together. Cool to room temperature. Cut into servings.

Rocky Road Fudge Frosting

*Nutritional
information for
Rocky Road
Fudge Frosting
is included
above.*

1/4 cup butter
1 ounce unsweetened
  chocolate
2 ounces cream cheese,
  softened

1/4 cup milk
1 1-pound package
  confectioners' sugar
1 teaspoon vanilla extract

Combine butter, chocolate, cream cheese and milk in saucepan. Cook over low heat until butter and chocolate are melted, stirring frequently. Stir in confectioners' sugar and vanilla.

Mrs. E. C. Danielson, John I. Sabin Chapter

TURTLE BROWNIES

Yield:
24 servings
Utensil:
baking pan

Approx Per Serving:
Cal 327
T Fat 18 g
48% Calories from Fat
Prot 3 g
Carbo 41 g
Fiber 1 g
Chol 4 mg
Sod 241 mg

1 14-ounce package caramels
1/3 cup evaporated milk
1 2-layer package German chocolate cake mix
1/3 cup evaporated milk
3/4 cup margarine, softened
1 cup chopped pecans
2 cups semisweet chocolate chips

Melt caramels with 1/3 cup evaporated milk in double boiler, stirring to mix well. Combine cake mix, 1/3 cup evaporated milk and margarine in bowl; mix well. Stir in pecans. Press half the mixture into greased 9x13-inch baking pan. Bake at 350 degrees for 6 minutes. Sprinkle with chocolate chips. Spread with caramel mixture. Crumble remaining chocolate mixture over top. Bake for 15 to 20 minutes or until brownies test done. Cool slightly on wire rack; cut into bars.

Shelly Brown, George S. Ladd Chapter

CHESS BARS

Yield:
24 servings
Utensil:
baking pan

Approx Per Serving:
Cal 255
T Fat 10 g
33% Calories from Fat
Prot 2 g
Carbo 41 g
Fiber 0 g
Chol 47 mg
Sod 200 mg

1 2-layer white or yellow cake mix
1/2 cup melted butter
1 egg
2 eggs
8 ounces cream cheese, softened
1 1-pound package confectioners' sugar

Combine cake mix, butter and 1 egg in bowl; mix well. Press over bottom of greased 9x13-inch baking pan. Combine 2 eggs, cream cheese and confectioners' sugar in mixer bowl; mix until smooth. Spread over first layer. Bake at 325 degrees for 35 to 40 minutes or until set. Cool on wire rack; cut into bars.

Jo Hearn, Los Amigos Chapter

JAM CRUMBLE

Yield:
16 servings
Utensil:
glass dish

Approx Per
Serving:
Cal 260
T Fat 9 g
31% Calories
from Fat
Prot 3 g
Carbo 43 g
Fiber 1 g
Chol 23 mg
Sod 174 mg

³/₄ cup butter, softened
1 cup packed dark
  brown sugar
1³/₄ cups flour
¹/₂ teaspoon baking soda
1¹/₂ cups quick-cooking
  oats
¹/₂ teaspoon salt
³/₄ cup jam

Cream butter and brown sugar in mixer bowl until fluffy. Add flour, baking soda, oats and salt; mix well. Press half the mixture into greased 8x8-inch glass dish. Microwave on High for 3¹/₂ minutes. Spread evenly with jam. Crumble remaining oats mixture over top; press down lightly. Microwave on High for 5 minutes. Let stand for 5 minutes. Cut into bars or squares.

Edna Garlock, De Anza Chapter

LEMON BARS

Yield:
40 servings
Utensil:
baking dish

Approx Per
Serving:
Cal 136
T Fat 7 g
44% Calories
from Fat
Prot 2 g
Carbo 18 g
Fiber 1 g
Chol 21 mg
Sod 61 mg

1³/₄ cups flour
¹/₂ cup confectioners'
  sugar
1 cup margarine
¹/₂ cup finely ground
  walnuts
4 eggs
2 cups sugar
5 tablespoons flour
6 tablespoons lemon
  juice
1 tablespoon vanilla
  extract
1 cup coconut

Mix 1³/₄ cups flour and confectioners' sugar in bowl. Cut in margarine until crumbly. Stir in walnuts. Press into greased and floured 9x13-inch baking dish. Bake at 350 degrees for 25 minutes. Combine eggs, sugar, 5 table-spoons flour, lemon juice and vanilla in mixer bowl; beat until smooth. Spoon over hot baked layer; sprinkle with coconut. Bake for 20 minutes longer. Cool on wire rack; cut into bars. May substitute butter for half the margarine.

Marge Frawner, John I. Sabin Chapter

LEMON SNOW BARS

Yield:
20 servings
Utensil:
baking pan

Approx Per Serving:
Cal 109
T Fat 5 g
42% Calories from Fat
Prot 1 g
Carbo 15 g
Fiber <1 g
Chol 34 mg
Sod 50 mg

1 cup flour
¼ cup confectioners' sugar
½ cup butter
2 eggs
¾ cup sugar

3 tablespoons lemon juice
2 tablespoons flour
¼ teaspoon baking powder

Mix 1 cup flour and confectioners' sugar in bowl. Cut in butter. Press into greased 8x8-baking pan. Bake at 350 degrees for 10 to 12 minutes or until light brown. Beat eggs with sugar and lemon juice in mixer bowl until thick and lemon-colored. Add mixture of 2 tablespoons flour and baking powder; mix well. Spoon over baked layer. Bake for 20 to 25 minutes or until golden brown. Cool on wire rack. Cut into bars. Garnish with confectioners' sugar.

Diana Bauman, Los Amigos Chapter

LEMON SQUARES

Yield:
24 servings
Utensil:
baking pan

Approx Per Serving:
Cal 199
T Fat 9 g
39% Calories from Fat
Prot 2 g
Carbo 29 g
Fiber <1 g
Chol 36 mg
Sod 137 mg

2 cups flour
1 cup margarine, softened
½ cup confectioners' sugar
2 cups sugar
¼ cup flour

1 teaspoon baking powder
4 eggs, slightly beaten
Grated rind and juice of 2 lemons
¼ teaspoon salt

Combine 2 cups flour, margarine and confectioners' sugar in bowl; mix well. Press into 9x13-inch baking pan sprayed with nonstick cooking spray. Bake at 325 degrees for 25 minutes. Combine sugar, ¼ cup flour, baking powder, eggs, lemon rind, lemon juice and salt in blender container; process until smooth. Spoon over baked layer. Bake for 25 minutes or until set. Cool on wire rack for 1 hour. Cut into squares.

Marion H. Dodge, John I. Sabin Chapter

PEANUT BUTTER FINGERS

Yield:
28 servings
Utensil:
baking pan

Approx Per
Serving:
Cal 177
T Fat 10 g
48% Calories
from Fat
Prot 4 g
Carbo 20 g
Fiber 1 g
Chol 17 mg
Sod 119 mg

$\frac{1}{2}$ cup butter, softened
$\frac{1}{2}$ cup sugar
$\frac{1}{2}$ cup packed brown
  sugar
1 egg
$\frac{1}{3}$ cup peanut butter
$\frac{1}{2}$ teaspoon vanilla
  extract
1 cup sifted flour
$\frac{1}{4}$ teaspoon baking soda
$\frac{1}{2}$ teaspoon salt
1 cup quick-cooking oats
1 cup chocolate chips
$\frac{1}{2}$ cup confectioners'
  sugar
$\frac{1}{2}$ cup peanut butter
2 to 4 tablespoons
  evaporated milk

Cream butter, sugar and brown sugar in mixer bowl until light and fluffy. Beat in egg, $\frac{1}{3}$ cup peanut butter and vanilla. Add flour, baking soda and salt; mix well. Mix in oats. Spread in greased 9x13-inch baking pan. Bake at 350 degrees for 20 to 25 minutes or until light brown. Sprinkle with chocolate chips. Let stand on wire rack for 5 minutes; spread chocolate evenly. Cool for 15 to 20 minutes. Beat confectioners' sugar and $\frac{1}{2}$ cup peanut butter with enough evaporated milk in bowl to make of desired consistency. Spread over cooled layer. Let stand until set. Cut into bars.

Eleanor Elliott, Silver State Chapter

SOUR CREAM RAISIN BARS

Yield:
16 servings
Utensil:
baking pan

Approx Per
Serving:
Cal 428
T Fat 18 g
36% Calories
from Fat
Prot 5 g
Carbo 65 g
Fiber 3 g
Chol 50 mg
Sod 209 mg

2 cups raisins
1$\frac{1}{2}$ cups water
1 cup packed brown sugar
1 cup margarine
1$\frac{3}{4}$ cups oats
1 teaspoon baking soda
1$\frac{3}{4}$ cups flour
3 egg yolks, slightly
  beaten
1$\frac{1}{2}$ cups sour cream
1 cup sugar
$\frac{1}{3}$ cup cornstarch
1 teaspoon vanilla extract
$\frac{1}{4}$ teaspoon nutmeg

Cook raisins in water in saucepan for 10 minutes; drain. Combine brown sugar, margarine, oats, baking soda and flour in large bowl; mix with pastry blender. Press 3$\frac{1}{3}$ cups mixture evenly over bottom of greased 9x13-inch baking pan. Bake at 350 degrees for 7 minutes. Mix next 4 ingredients in double boiler. Cook over boiling water until thickened, stirring constantly. Stir in raisins, vanilla and nutmeg. Spread over baked layer. Crumble remaining oats mixture over top. Bake for 25 to 30 minutes or until set. Chill in refrigerator. Cut into 16 large bars.

Nancy L. Fry, Silver State Chapter

THE BEST TOFFEE BARS

Yield:
16 servings
Utensil:
baking pan

Approx Per Serving:
Cal 233
T Fat 17 g
64% Calories from Fat
Prot 2 g
Carbo 20 g
Fiber 1 g
Chol 44 mg
Sod 101 mg

1 cup butter, softened
1 cup sugar
1 egg yolk
1 cup flour
1 teaspoon cinnamon
1 egg white, beaten
1 cup chopped pecans

Cream butter and sugar in mixer bowl until light and fluffy. Beat in egg yolk. Add mixture of flour and cinnamon; mix well. Press mixture into baking pan. Brush with beaten egg white. Sprinkle with pecans; press in lightly. Bake at 250 degrees for 1 hour. Cut into bars immediately. Cool in pan on wire rack.

Karolyn Tillisch Aznoe, John I. Sabin Chapter

APPLESAUCE RAISIN COOKIES

Yield:
36 servings
Utensil:
cookie sheet

Approx Per Serving:
Cal 88
T Fat 3 g
32% Calories from Fat
Prot 1 g
Carbo 14 g
Fiber <1 g
Chol 6 mg
Sod 90 mg

1   2-layer package
    applesauce cake mix
1/2 cup raisins
2 tablespoons water
2 tablespoons oil
1 egg
1/2 cup chopped pecans

Combine cake mix, raisins, water, oil, egg and pecans in mixer bowl; mix well. Drop by teaspoonfuls 2 inches apart onto greased cookie sheet. Bake at 375 degrees for 10 minutes. Remove to wire rack to cool immediately. May substitute spice cake mix for applesauce cake mix.

Velda Wheeler, John I. Sabin Chapter

CARROT COOKIES

Yield:
48 servings
Utensil:
cookie sheet

Approx Per
Serving:
Cal 90
T Fat 5 g
46% Calories
from Fat
Prot 1 g
Carbo 12 g
Fiber <1 g
Chol 5 mg
Sod 37 mg

1 cup shortening
3/4 cup sugar
1 egg, beaten
1 cup mashed cooked
carrots
1/2 teaspoon lemon
extract
1 teaspoon vanilla extract
1 teaspoon baking
powder

2 cups flour
1/2 teaspoon salt
21/2 teaspoons butter,
softened
11/2 cups confectioners'
sugar
11/2 tablespoons orange
juice
2 teaspoons grated
orange rind

Cream shortening and sugar in mixer bowl until light and fluffy. Beat in egg, carrots and flavorings. Add mixture of baking powder, flour and salt; mix well. Drop by teaspoonfuls 1 inch apart onto greased cookie sheet. Bake at 350 degrees for 12 to 15 minutes or until golden brown. Blend butter and confectioners' sugar in mixer bowl. Add orange juice and orange rind; mix until smooth. Spread on warm cookies. Cool on wire rack. May substitute milk for orange juice and 3/4 teaspoon vanilla for orange rind.

Lee Stevens, Sierra Pacific Chapter

COWBOY COOKIES

Yield:
36 servings
Utensil:
cookie sheet

Approx Per
Serving:
Cal 171
T Fat 8 g
41% Calories
from Fat
Prot 2 g
Carbo 24 g
Fiber 1 g
Chol 12 mg
Sod 65 mg

2 cups flour
1/2 teaspoon baking
powder
1 teaspoon baking soda
1/2 teaspoon salt
1 cup shortening
1 cup sugar

1 cup packed brown
sugar
2 eggs
2 cups oats
1 cup chocolate chips
1 teaspoon vanilla extract

Mix flour, baking powder, baking soda and salt in bowl. Combine shortening, sugar, brown sugar and eggs in mixer bowl; beat until light. Add to dry ingredients; mix well. Stir in oats, chocolate chips and vanilla. Drop by teaspoonfuls onto greased cookie sheet. Bake at 350 degrees for 15 minutes. Remove to wire rack to cool.

Cindy Willyard, Sierra Pacific Chapter

GUMDROP COOKIES

Yield:
36 servings
Utensil:
cookie sheet

Approx Per Serving:
Cal 121
T Fat 5 g
38% Calories from Fat
Prot 1 g
Carbo 18 g
Fiber <1 g
Chol 0 mg
Sod 94 mg

1   2-layer package yellow cake mix
3 egg whites
1/2 cup oil
1 cup chopped gumdrops
1/2 cup chopped almonds

Combine cake mix, egg whites and oil in mixer bowl; mix well. Stir in gumdrops and almonds. Drop by teaspoonfuls onto cookie sheet sprayed with nonstick cooking spray. Bake at 350 degrees for 12 to 15 minutes or until light brown. Remove to wire rack to cool.

Ethel Pedersen, Los Amigos Chapter

KITCHEN SINK COOKIES

Yield:
100 servings
Utensil:
cookie sheet

Approx Per Serving:
Cal 67
T Fat 3 g
44% Calories from Fat
Prot 1 g
Carbo 9 g
Fiber <1 g
Chol 9 mg
Sod 49 mg

1 cup butter, softened
1 cup sugar
1 cup packed brown sugar
2 eggs
2 cups flour
1 teaspoon baking powder
1 teaspoon baking soda
1/2 teaspoon salt
1 teaspoon vanilla extract
1 cup quick-cooking oats
1 cup crushed cornflakes
1 cup chocolate chips
1 cup chopped walnuts

Cream butter, sugar and brown sugar in mixer bowl until light and fluffy. Beat in eggs 1 at a time. Sift in flour, baking powder, baking soda and salt; mix well. Stir in vanilla, oats, cereal, chocolate chips and walnuts. Shape into balls. Place on lightly greased cookie sheet; flatten with fork dipped in flour. Bake at 375 degrees until light brown. Remove to wire rack to cool.

Georgia Hansen, John I. Sabin Chapter

LEMON DROPS

Yield:
60 servings
Utensil:
cookie sheet

Approx Per Serving:
Cal 72
T Fat 3 g
41% Calories from Fat
Prot 1 g
Carbo 10 g
Fiber <1 g
Chol 15 mg
Sod 39 mg

1 cup butter, softened
1 cup sugar
2 eggs
2³/4 cups flour
³/4 teaspoon baking soda

1   6-ounce can frozen
lemonade concentrate,
thawed
¹/4 cup sugar

Cream butter and 1 cup sugar in mixer bowl until light and fluffy. Beat in eggs 1 at a time. Sift flour and baking soda together. Add to creamed mixture alternately with ¹/2 cup lemonade concentrate, mixing well after each addition. Drop by teaspoonfuls 1¹/2 inches apart onto ungreased baking sheet. Bake at 350 degrees for 10 minutes or until edges are golden brown. Brush warm cookies with remaining lemonade concentrate; sprinkle lightly with ¹/4 cup sugar. Remove to wire rack to cool.

Shirley J. Haller, John I. Sabin Chapter

EASIEST LEMON COOKIES

Yield:
36 servings
Utensil:
cookie sheet

Approx Per Serving:
Cal 85
T Fat 2 g
24% Calories from Fat
Prot 1 g
Carbo 16 g
Fiber 0 g
Chol 6 mg
Sod 96 mg

1   2-layer package
pudding-recipe lemon
cake mix
4 ounces whipped topping

1 egg
1 cup confectioners'
sugar

Combine cake mix, whipped topping and egg in bowl; mix well. Shape into balls. Roll in confectioners' sugar. Place on greased cookie sheet. Bake at 350 degrees for 13 to 15 minutes or until light brown. Remove to wire rack to cool.

Elaine Simmerson, John I. Sabin Chapter

COCONUT OATMEAL COOKIES

Yield:
60 servings
Utensil:
cookie sheet

Approx Per Serving:
Cal 89
T Fat 4 g
39% Calories from Fat
Prot 1 g
Carbo 13 g
Fiber <1 g
Chol 7 mg
Sod 82 mg

1 cup margarine, softened
1 cup sugar
1 cup packed brown sugar
2 eggs
2 teaspoons vanilla extract

2 cups flour
1 teaspoon baking powder
1 teaspoon salt
1 cup oats
1½ cups coconut

Combine margarine, sugar, brown sugar, eggs and vanilla in bowl; mix until smooth. Add flour, baking powder and salt; mix well. Stir in oats and coconut. Drop by teaspoonfuls onto greased cookie sheet. Bake at 350 degrees for 10 minutes or until light brown. Remove to wire rack to cool.

Barbara Von Dohlen, John I. Sabin Chapter

PEANUT BUTTER COOKIES

Yield:
48 servings
Utensil:
cookie sheet

Approx Per Serving:
Cal 74
T Fat 4 g
53% Calories from Fat
Prot 1 g
Carbo 8 g
Fiber <1 g
Chol 10 mg
Sod 45 mg

1 cup butter, softened
3 rounded tablespoons peanut butter
½ teaspoon vanilla extract

1 cup sugar
2 cups sifted flour
½ teaspoon baking soda
Salt to taste

Cream butter and peanut butter in mixer bowl until light. Add vanilla and sugar; beat until smooth. Sift in flour, baking soda and salt; mix with hands. Shape into 1-inch balls. Place on greased cookie sheet; flatten with fork. Bake at 325 degrees for 15 to 20 minutes or until light brown. Remove to wire rack to cool.

Bonnie DiBenedetto, John I. Sabin Chapter

Brown Sugar Peanut Butter Cookies

Yield:
48 servings
Utensil:
cookie sheet

Approx Per Serving:
Cal 134
T Fat 7 g
45% Calories from Fat
Prot 2 g
Carbo 17 g
Fiber 1 g
Chol 5 mg
Sod 58 mg

¹/₂ cup butter, softened
¹/₂ cup shortening
1 cup peanut butter
1 cup packed brown sugar
1 cup sugar
1 teaspoon vanilla extract
1 teaspoon baking soda
1 tablespoon milk
3 cups flour

Cream butter, shortening, peanut butter, brown sugar, sugar and vanilla in mixer bowl until light and fluffy. Add mixture of baking soda and milk; mix well. Mix in flour. Shape into small balls. Place on greased cookie sheet; flatten with fork. Bake at 350 degrees for 12 minutes. Remove to wire rack to cool.

Sue Austin, George S. Ladd Chapter

Persimmon Oatmeal Cookies

Yield:
36 servings
Utensil:
cookie sheet

Approx Per Serving:
Cal 123
T Fat 6 g
42% Calories from Fat
Prot 2 g
Carbo 17 g
Fiber 1 g
Chol 12 mg
Sod 102 mg

³/₄ cup margarine, softened
1¹/₂ cups sugar
2 eggs
1 teaspoon baking soda
1 cup persimmon pulp
1 teaspoon vanilla extract
1¹/₂ cups flour
¹/₂ teaspoon nutmeg
¹/₂ teaspoon cloves
1 teaspoon cinnamon
¹/₂ teaspoon salt
1¹/₂ cups quick-cooking oats
¹/₂ cup coconut
¹/₂ cup chopped pecans

Cream margarine and sugar in mixer bowl until light and fluffy. Beat in eggs. Add mixture of baking soda and persimmon; mix well. Add vanilla, flour, nutmeg, cloves, cinnamon and salt; mix well. Stir in oats, coconut and pecans. Drop by teaspoonfuls onto greased cookie sheet. Bake at 375 degrees for 11 to 12 minutes or until light brown. Remove to wire rack to cool.

Sharon Cousins, John I. Sabin Chapter

PINEAPPLE DROP COOKIES

Yield:
60 servings
Utensil:
cookie sheet

Approx Per Serving:
Cal 63
T Fat 3 g
44% Calories from Fat
Prot 1 g
Carbo 8 g
Fiber <1 g
Chol 4 mg
Sod 24 mg

1/2 cup shortening
1 cup packed brown sugar
1 egg
3/4 cup crushed pineapple
1 teaspoon vanilla extract

2 cups sifted flour
1 1/2 teaspoons baking powder
1/4 teaspoon baking soda
1/4 teaspoon salt
1 cup chopped pecans

Cream shortening in mixer bowl until light. Add brown sugar gradually, beating until fluffy. Beat in egg. Add pineapple and vanilla; mix well. Sift flour, baking powder, baking soda and salt together. Add to creamed mixture; mix well. Mix in pecans. Drop by teaspoonfuls onto greased cookie sheet. Bake at 450 degrees for 10 to 12 minutes or until light brown. Remove to wire rack to cool.

Doris Dahl, George S. Ladd Chapter

RUM BALLS

Yield:
24 servings
Utensil:
bowl

Approx Per Serving:
Cal 89
T Fat 4 g
40% Calories from Fat
Prot 1 g
Carbo 13 g
Fiber <1 g
Chol 2 mg
Sod 15 mg

1 cup vanilla wafer crumbs
1 cup confectioners' sugar
2 tablespoons baking cocoa
1 cup chopped pecans

1 1/2 tablespoons white corn syrup
1/4 cup rum
1/2 cup confectioners' sugar

Combine cookie crumbs, 1 cup confectioners' sugar, cocoa and pecans in bowl; mix well. Add mixture of corn syrup and rum; mix well. Shape into balls. Roll in 1/2 cup confectioners' sugar. Store in airtight container in refrigerator. May substitute bourbon for rum. This recipe is from my Grandma Strong.

Sue Austin, George S. Ladd Chapter

Pies

CANDY BAR PIE

Yield:
8 servings
Utensil:
pie plate

Approx Per
Serving:
Cal 328
T Fat 25 g
67% Calories
from Fat
Prot 3 g
Carbo 26 g
Fiber 2 g
Chol 13 mg
Sod 58 mg

1¹/₃ cups grated coconut
2 tablespoons melted
   butter
1 teaspoon instant coffee
   granules

2 tablespoons water
1 7¹/₂-ounce chocolate
   candy bar
4 cups whipped topping

Mix coconut and butter in bowl. Press into 8-inch pie plate. Bake at 325 degrees for 10 minutes or until coconut is golden brown. Cool to room temperature. Dissolve coffee granules in water in small saucepan. Add chocolate. Heat over low heat until chocolate melts, stirring to mix well. Cool to room temperature. Fold in whipped topping. Spoon into prepared pie plate. Freeze for several hours to overnight. Garnish with chocolate curls or toasted slivered almonds.

Donna Sue Boatright, Los Amigos Chapter

CHOCOLATE PIE

Yield:
8 servings
Utensil:
pie plate

Approx Per
Serving:
Cal 557
T Fat 39 g
61% Calories
from Fat
Prot 6 g
Carbo 51 g
Fiber 2 g
Chol 169 mg
Sod 433 mg

1 cup butter, softened
1¹/₂ cups sugar
3 squares unsweetened
   chocolate, melted

2 teaspoons vanilla extract
¹/₄ teaspoon salt
4 eggs
1 baked pie shell

Cream butter and sugar in mixer bowl until light and fluffy. Add chocolate, vanilla and salt; mix well. Add eggs 1 at a time, beating for 5 minutes after each addition. Spoon into pie shell. Chill for 4 hours.

Jann Dunkleberger, De Anza Chapter

CHOCOLATE CREAM PIE

Yield:
8 servings
Utensil:
pie plate

Approx Per Serving:
Cal 607
T Fat 47 g
65% Calories from Fat
Prot 7 g
Carbo 48 g
Fiber 3 g
Chol 105 mg
Sod 208 mg

15 Oreo cookies
¼ cup melted butter
¾ cup milk
2½ cups miniature marshmallows
1 8-ounce chocolate bar with almonds, broken

2 squares unsweetened chocolate, broken
2 tablespoons baking cocoa
2 cups whipping cream, whipped

Process cookies in blender until crushed. Mix with butter in 10-inch deep dish pie plate. Press firmly over bottom and side of plate. Chill for 1 hour. Combine milk, marshmallows, candy bar and chocolate squares in saucepan. Heat until melted, stirring to mix well. Stir in cocoa. Cool to room temperature. Fold in whipped cream. Spoon into prepared pie plate.

Lucille Stancil, De Anza Chapter

COOKIES AND CREAM PIE

Yield:
8 servings
Utensil:
pie plate

Approx Per Serving:
Cal 547
T Fat 34 g
56% Calories from Fat
Prot 6 g
Carbo 55 g
Fiber 2 g
Chol 76 mg
Sod 274 mg

18 Oreo cookies, finely crushed
⅓ cup melted butter
1 pint coffee ice cream, softened

1 16-ounce can chocolate fudge ice cream topping
1 cup whipping cream
1 tablespoon white Crème de Cacao

Mix cookie crumbs with butter in 9-inch pie plate; press firmly over bottom and side of plate. Freeze until firm. Spread ice cream in prepared pie plate. Top with fudge topping. Freeze until serving time. Whip cream in mixer bowl until soft peaks form. Fold in Crème de Cacao. Spread over pie. Garnish with chopped nuts.

Dorothy Coats, John I. Sabin Chapter

CREAM CHEESE PIE

Yield:
8 servings
Utensil:
pie plate

Approx Per Serving:
Cal 431
T Fat 29 g
60% Calories from Fat
Prot 7 g
Carbo 37 g
Fiber <1 g
Chol 128 mg
Sod 283 mg

14 graham crackers, finely crushed
1/4 cup melted butter
12 ounces cream cheese, softened
2 eggs, beaten
3/4 cup sugar
2 teaspoons vanilla extract
1/2 teaspoon lemon juice
1 cup sour cream
3 1/2 tablespoons sugar
1 teaspoon vanilla extract

Mix cracker crumbs and butter in 9-inch pie plate; press over bottom and side of plate. Beat cream cheese in mixer bowl until light. Add eggs, 3/4 cup sugar, 2 teaspoons vanilla and lemon juice; beat until smooth. Spoon into prepared pie plate. Bake at 350 degrees for 15 to 20 minutes or until set. Cool for 5 minutes. Blend sour cream with 3 1/2 tablespoons sugar and 1 teaspoon vanilla in bowl. Spread over pie. Bake for 10 minutes longer. Cool to room temperature. Chill overnight.

Dorothy Coats, John I. Sabin Chapter

TIPSY ICE CREAM PIE

Yield:
8 servings
Utensil:
pie plate

Approx Per Serving:
Cal 477
T Fat 28 g
55% Calories from Fat
Prot 5 g
Carbo 47 g
Fiber <1 g
Chol 86 mg
Sod 283 mg

1/4 cup butter
1 1/2 cups chocolate wafer crumbs
1/4 cup sugar
1 pint vanilla ice cream, softened
1 pint chocolate ice cream, softened
1/4 cup Cognac
1/4 cup light rum
1 cup whipping cream
2 tablespoons confectioners' sugar
1/4 cup grated bittersweet chocolate

Melt butter in large skillet; remove from heat. Stir in cookie crumbs and sugar. Press over bottom and side of 9-inch pie plate. Bake at 450 degrees for 5 minutes. Chill in refrigerator. Layer vanilla ice cream, chocolate ice cream, Cognac and rum in prepared pie plate. Chill in freezer. Whip cream in mixer bowl until soft peaks form. Fold in confectioners' sugar. Spread over pie. Top with grated chocolate. Freeze until firm. Wrap in foil and store in freezer. Let stand at room temperature for 20 minutes before serving.

Judy Meeker, De Anza Chapter

EGGNOG PIE

Yield:
8 servings
Utensil:
pie plate

Approx Per Serving:
Cal 662
T Fat 55 g
75% Calories from Fat
Prot 10 g
Carbo 33 g
Fiber 3 g
Chol 199 mg
Sod 117 mg

2¹/₂ cups ground pecans
¹/₃ cup sugar
¹/₄ cup melted butter
1¹/₂ tablespoons unflavored gelatin
3 tablespoons brandy
4 egg yolks
¹/₃ cup sugar
1¹/₃ cups milk
¹/₄ cup dark rum
1¹/₂ teaspoons vanilla extract
4 egg whites
Salt to taste
³/₄ cup whipping cream, whipped
Rum Whipped Cream

Mix pecans, ¹/₃ cup sugar and butter in 9-inch pie plate. Press over bottom and side of plate. Bake at 375 degrees for 15 minutes. Cool to room temperature. Soften gelatin in brandy in bowl. Beat egg yolks with ¹/₃ cup sugar in mixer bowl. Scald milk in heavy saucepan. Stir a small amount of hot milk into egg yolks; stir egg yolks into hot milk. Cook over medium-low heat until mixture is thick enough to coat spoon, stirring constantly; do not boil. Remove from heat. Stir in gelatin, ¹/₄ cup rum and vanilla. Spoon into bowl. Set into larger bowl of ice. Let stand until cool but not set, stirring occasionally. Beat eggs whites with salt in mixer bowl until stiff peaks form. Fold in whipped cream. Fold into cooled custard. Spoon into prepared pie plate. Spread Rum Whipped Cream over pie. Chill in refrigerator. Let stand at room temperature for 30 minutes before serving. Garnish with chocolate curls.

Rum Whipped Cream

Nutritional information for Rum Whipped Cream is included above.

1 cup whipping cream
¹/₄ cup confectioners' sugar
2 tablespoons dark rum

Whip cream with confectioners' sugar and rum in mixer bowl until soft peaks form.

Dorothy Coats, John I. Sabin Chapter

FUDGE BROWNIE PIE

Yield:
8 servings
Utensil:
pie plate

*Approx Per
Serving:*
Cal 583
T Fat 38 g
*56% Calories
from Fat*
Prot 9 g
Carbo 57 g
Fiber 2 g
Chol 86 mg
Sod 369 mg

1 unbaked 9-inch pie
  shell
1 cup semisweet
  chocolate chips
1/4 cup butter
1/2 cup baking mix

1 14-ounce can
   sweetened condensed
   milk
2 eggs
1 teaspoon vanilla extract
1 cup chopped pecans

Bake pie shell at 375 degrees for 10 minutes. Reduce oven temperature to 325 degrees. Melt chocolate chips with butter in saucepan over low heat. Combine with baking mix, condensed milk, eggs and vanilla in large mixer bowl; beat until smooth. Stir in pecans. Spoon into pie shell. Bake for 35 to 45 minutes or until center is set. Serve warm or at room temperature with ice cream if desired.

Leone Burke, Mission Chapter

GRASSHOPPER PIE

Yield:
8 servings
Utensil:
pie plate

*Approx Per
Serving:*
Cal 334
T Fat 19 g
*52% Calories
from Fat*
Prot 3 g
Carbo 36 g
Fiber <1 g
Chol 51 mg
Sod 147 mg

14 Oreo cookies, finely
   crushed
2 tablespoons melted
  butter
24 marshmallows

1/2 cup milk
1/4 cup Crème de Menthe
2 tablespoons Crème de
  Cacao
2 cups whipped cream

Mix cookie crumbs with melted butter in 9-inch pie plate; press over bottom and side of plate. Melt marshmallows with milk in saucepan, stirring to mix well. Stir in Crème de Menthe and Crème de Cacao. Fold in 1 cup whipped cream. Spoon into prepared pie plate. Chill until firm. Top with remaining whipped cream. May tint filling with green food coloring if desired.

Dorothy Coats, John I. Sabin Chapter

KEY LIME PIE

Yield:
8 servings
Utensil:
pie plate

Approx Per Serving:
Cal 407
T Fat 13 g
28% Calories from Fat
Prot 4 g
Carbo 70 g
Fiber 1 g
Chol 80 mg
Sod 262 mg

1   9-inch graham cracker pie shell
1¼ cups sugar
¼ cup cornstarch
¼ cup lime juice
3 egg yolks
1½ cups boiling water
3 egg whites
6 tablespoons sugar

Bake pie shell at 350 degrees for 8 minutes. Increase oven temperature to 425 degrees. Cool pie shell to room temperature. Combine 1¼ cups sugar, cornstarch, lime juice and egg yolks in saucepan. Add boiling water gradually, stirring to mix well. Bring to a boil. Cook for 4 minutes or until thickened, stirring constantly. Place in large pan of ice. Let stand until cool. Spoon into pie shell. Beat egg whites at high speed in mixer bowl until frothy. Add 6 tablespoons sugar 1 tablespoon at a time, beating constantly until stiff peaks form. Spread over pie. Bake for 4 minutes or until golden brown. Chill for 8 hours.

Betty Menk Gray, John I. Sabin Chapter

PUMPKIN PIES

Yield:
16 servings
Utensil:
2 pie plates

Approx Per Serving:
Cal 322
T Fat 16 g
43% Calories from Fat
Prot 7 g
Carbo 41 g
Fiber 1 g
Chol 75 mg
Sod 369 mg

4 eggs
1   29-ounce can pumpkin
¾ cup sugar
¾ cup packed brown sugar
1 teaspoon salt
2 teaspoons cinnamon
¼ cup melted butter
1 teaspoon ginger
½ teaspoon cloves
2   13-ounce cans evaporated milk
2 unbaked 9-inch pie shells

Beat eggs slightly in mixer bowl. Add pumpkin, sugar, brown sugar, salt, cinnamon, butter, ginger, cloves and evaporated milk in order listed, mixing until smooth. Spoon into pie shells. Bake at 425 degrees for 15 minutes. Reduce oven temperature to 350 degrees. Bake for 45 minutes longer or until knife inserted in center comes out clean. This was my Grandmother's recipe; it originally called for a lump of butter.

Susan Keirn, John I. Sabin Chapter

STRAWBERRY PIE

Yield:
8 servings
Utensil:
pie plate

Approx Per
Serving:
Cal 242
T Fat 8 g
28% Calories
from Fat
Prot 2 g
Carbo 43 g
Fiber 2 g
Chol 0 mg
Sod 206 mg

1 cup sugar
3 tablespoons cornstarch
1/4 teaspoon salt
2 cups fresh strawberries

1 baked pie shell
2 cups fresh whole
  strawberries

Mix sugar, cornstarch and salt in saucepan. Add 2 cups strawberries; mash well. Cook over medium heat until thickened and clear, stirring constantly. Cool to room temperature. Line pie shell with 2 cups whole strawberries. Pour cooled mixture over top. Chill until serving time. Garnish with whipped cream.

Ruth Flores, Sierra Pacific Chapter

CHOCOLATE PECAN TASSIES

Yield:
36 servings
Utensil:
muffin pan

Approx Per
Serving:
Cal 96
T Fat 7 g
59% Calories
from Fat
Prot 1 g
Carbo 9 g
Fiber <1 g
Chol 16 mg
Sod 36 mg

3 ounces cream cheese,
  softened
1/2 cup butter, softened
1 cup flour
1 square unsweetened
  chocolate

1 tablespoon butter
3/4 cup packed brown
  sugar
1 egg
1 teaspoon vanilla extract
1 cup chopped pecans

Blend cream cheese and 1/2 cup butter in mixer bowl. Add flour; mix until smooth. Chill, wrapped in plastic wrap, for 1 hour. Melt chocolate and 1 tablespoon butter in saucepan. Stir in brown sugar, egg and vanilla. Cook until thickened, stirring constantly. Stir in pecans. Shape chilled dough into 36 balls. Press each ball into miniature muffin cup to form shells. Spoon filling into prepared shells. Bake at 350 degrees for 20 minutes. Cool in pan on wire rack for 10 to 15 minutes. Remove to serving plate. Garnish with confectioners' sugar.

Karen Rubio, John I. Sabin Chapter

No-Salt Seasoning

Salt is an acquired taste and can be significantly reduced in the diet by learning to use herbs and spices instead. When using fresh herbs, use 3 times the amount of dried herbs. Begin with small amounts to determine your favorite tastes. A dash of fresh lemon or lime juice can also wake up your taste buds.

Herb Blends to Replace Salt

Combine all ingredients in small airtight container. Add several grains of rice to prevent caking.

No-Salt Surprise Seasoning — 2 teaspoons garlic powder and 1 teaspoon each of dried basil, oregano and dehydrated lemon juice.

Pungent Salt Substitute — 3 teaspoons dried basil, 2 teaspoons each of summer savory, celery seed, cumin seed, sage and marjoram, and 1 teaspoon lemon thyme; crush with mortar and pestle.

Spicy No-Salt Seasoning — 1 teaspoon each cloves, pepper and coriander, 2 teaspoons paprika and 1 tablespoon dried rosemary; crush with mortar and pestle.

Herb Complements

Beef — bay leaf, chives, cumin, garlic, hot pepper, marjoram, rosemary

Pork — coriander, cumin, garlic, ginger, hot pepper, savory, thyme

Poultry — garlic, oregano, rosemary, savory, sage

Cheese — basil, chives, curry, dill, marjoram, oregano, parsley, sage, thyme

Fish — chives, coriander, dill, garlic, tarragon, thyme

Fruit — cinnamon, coriander, cloves, ginger, mint

Bread — caraway, marjoram, oregano, poppy seed, rosemary, thyme

Salads — basil, chives, tarragon, parsley, sorrel

Vegetables — basil, chives, dill, tarragon, marjoram, mint, parsley, pepper

Basic Herb Butter

Combine 1 stick unsalted butter, 1 to 3 tablespoons dried herbs or twice that amount of minced fresh herbs of choice, 1/2 teaspoon lemon juice and white pepper to taste. Let stand for 1 hour or longer before using.

Basic Herb Vinegar

Heat vinegar of choice in saucepan; do not boil. Pour into bottle; add 1 or more herbs of choice and seal bottle. Let stand for 2 weeks before using.

MICROWAVE TIPS

* Always choose the minimum cooking time. Remember that food continues to cook after it is removed from the microwave.
* Keep your microwave clean. Built-up grease or food spatters in the microwave can slow cooking times.
* When poaching or frying an egg in a browning dish, always prick the center of the yolk with a fork to keep the egg from exploding.
* Do not try to hard-cook eggs *in the shell* in a microwave. They will build up pressure and burst.
* Do not use metal dishes or aluminum foil except as specifically recommended by the manufacturer of your microwave.
* Never use a foil tray over 3/4 inch deep in your microwave.
* When heating TV-style dinners, remove the foil cover, then place tray back in carton. Food will heat only from the top.
* Be sure to prick potatoes before baking to allow steam to escape.
* Cut a small slit in pouch-packed frozen foods before heating in microwave to allow steam to escape.
* When microwaving more than one item, arrange them in a circle near edges of the oven.
* Cover foods that need to be steamed or tenderized.
* Do not pop popcorn in a low-voltage microwave or without a microwave-approved corn popper.

Did You Know You Can...?

(Use HIGH setting for the following unless otherwise indicated.)

* Use your microwave oven to melt chocolate, to soften cream cheese and to soften or melt butter.
* Roast shelled nuts for 6 to 10 minutes, stirring frequently.
* Peel fruit or tomatoes by placing in 1 cup hot water. Microwave for 30 to 45 seconds; remove skins easily.
* Plump dried fruit by placing it in a dish with 1 to 2 teaspoons water. Cover tightly with plastic wrap. Microwave for 1/2 to 1 1/2 minutes.
* Precook barbecued ribs or chicken in the microwave until almost done, then place on the grill to sear and add a charcoal flavor.
* Soften brown sugar by placing it in a dish with a slice of bread or apple and microwaving for 30 to 45 seconds, stirring once.
* Dry bread for crumbs or croutons. Place cubed or crumbled bread on paper towels. Microwave for 6 to 7 minutes, stirring occasionally.
* Warm baby food or baby bottles by removing metal lid and microwaving for 10 to 20 seconds. Be sure to test temperature before feeding baby.
* Freshen chips and crackers by microwaving for 15 to 30 seconds. Let stand for 2 to 3 minutes.
* Dry herbs by placing on paper towels and microwaving for 2 to 3 minutes or until herbs are dry.
* Ripen an avocado by microwaving on LOW for 2 to 4 minutes.

Quantities to Serve 100

Baked beans	5 gallons
Beef	40 pounds
Beets	30 pounds
Bread	10 loaves
Butter	3 pounds
Cabbage for slaw	20 pounds
Cakes	8 cakes
Carrots	33 pounds
Cauliflower	18 pounds
Cheese	18 pounds
Chicken for chicken pie	40 pounds
Coffee	3 pounds
Cream	3 quarts
Fruit cocktail	1 gallon
Fruit juice	4 (No. 10) cans
Fruit salad	20 quarts
Ground beef	30 to 36 pounds
Ham	40 pounds
Ice cream	4 gallons
Lettuce	20 heads
Meat loaf	24 pounds
Milk	6 gallons
Nuts	3 pounds
Olives	1¾ pounds
Oysters	18 quarts
Pickles	2 quarts
Pies	17 pies
Potatoes	35 pounds
Roast pork	40 pounds
Rolls	200 rolls
Salad dressing	3 quarts
Scalloped potatoes	5 gallons
Soup	5 gallons
Sugar cubes	3 pounds
Tomato juice	4 (No. 10) cans
Vegetables	4 (No. 20) cans
Vegetable salad	20 quarts
Whipping cream	4 pints
Wieners	25 pounds

GLOSSARY OF COOKING TECHNIQUES

Bake: To cook by dry heat in an oven, or under hot coals.

Bard: To cover lean meats with bacon or pork fat before cooking to prevent dryness.

Baste: To moisten, especially meats, with melted butter, pan drippings, sauce, etc. during cooking time.

Beat: To mix ingredients by vigorous stirring or with electric mixer.

Blanch: To immerse, usually vegetables or fruit, briefly into boiling water to inactivate enzymes, loosen skin, or soak away excess salt.

Blend: To combine 2 or more ingredients, at least 1 of which is liquid or soft, to produce a mixture that has a smooth uniform consistency quickly.

Boil: To heat liquid until bubbly; the boiling point for water is about 212 degrees, depending on the altitude and the atmospheric pressure.

Braise: To cook, especially meats, covered, in a small amount of liquid.

Brew: To prepare a beverage by allowing boiling water to extract the flavor and/or the color from certain substances.

Broil: To cook by direct exposure to intense heat such as a flame or an electric heating unit.

Caramelize: To melt sugar in a heavy pan over low heat until golden, stirring constantly.

Chill: To cool in the refrigerator or in cracked ice.

Clarify: To remove impurities from melted butter or margarine by allowing sediment to settle, then pouring off clear yellow liquid. Other fats may be clarified by straining.

Cream: To blend shortening, butter, margarine, usually softened, or sometimes oil, with a granulated or crushed ingredient until the mixture is soft and creamy. Usually described in method as light and fluffy.

Curdle: To congeal milk with rennet or heat until solid lumps or curds are formed.

Cut in: To disperse solid shortening into dry ingredients with a knife or pastry blender. Texture of the mixture should resemble coarse cracker meal. Described in method as crumbly.

Decant: To pour a liquid such as wine or melted butter carefully from 1 container into another leaving the sediment in the original container.

Deep-fry: To cook in a skillet or deep pan containing hot cooking oil. Deep-fried foods are generally completely immersed in the hot oil.

Deglaze: To heat stock, wine or other liquid in the pan in which meat has been cooked, mixing with pan juices and sediment to form a gravy or sauce base.

Degorger: To remove strong flavors or impurities before cooking, i.e. soaking ham in cold water or sprinkling vegetables with salt, then letting stand for a period of time and pressing out excess fluid.

Degrease: To remove accumulated fat from surface of hot liquids.

Dice: To cut into small cubes about 1/4-inch in size. Do not use dice unless ingredient can truly be cut into cubes.

Dissolve: To create a solution by thoroughly mixing a solid or granular substance with a liquid until no sediment remains.

Dredge: To coat completely with flour, bread crumbs, etc.

Filet: To remove bones from meat or fish. (Pieces of meat, fish or poultry from which bones have been removed are called filets.)

Flambé: To pour warmed Brandy or other spirits over food in a pan, then ignite and continue cooking briefly.

Fold in: To blend a delicate frothy mixture into a heavier one so that none of the lightness or volume is lost. Using a rubber spatula, turn under and bring up and over, rotating bowl 1/4 turn after each folding motion.

Fry: To cook in a pan or skillet containing hot cooking oil. The oil should not totally cover the food.

Garnish: To decorate or enhance food before serving.

Glaze: To cover or coat with sauce, syrup, egg white or a jellied substance. After applying, it becomes firm, adding color and flavor.

Grate: To rub food against a rough, perforated utensil to produce slivers, chunks, curls, etc.

Gratiné: To top a sauced dish with crumbs, cheese or butter, then brown under a broiler.

Grill: To broil, usually over hot coals or charcoal.

Grind: To cut, crush, or force through a chopper to produce small bits.

Infuse: To steep herbs or other flavorings in a liquid until liquid absorbs flavor.

Julienne: To cut vegetables, fruit, etc. into long thin strips.

Knead: To press, fold and stretch dough until smooth and elastic. Method usually notes time frame or result.

Lard: To insert strips of fat or bacon into lean meat to keep it moist and juicy during cooking. Larding is an internal basting technique.

Leaven: To cause batters and doughs to rise, usually by means of a chemical leavening agent. This process may occur before or during baking.

Marinate: To soak, usually in a highly seasoned oil-acid solution, to flavor and/or tenderize food.

Melt: To liquefy solid foods by action of heat.

Mince: To cut or chop into very small pieces.

Mix: To combine ingredients to distribute uniformly.

Mold: To shape into a particular form.

Panbroil: To cook in a skillet or pan using a very small amount of fat to prevent sticking.

Panfry: To cook in a skillet or pan containing only a small amount of fat.

Parboil: To partially cook in boiling water. Most parboiled foods require additional cooking with or without other ingredients.

Parch: To dry or roast slightly through exposure to intense heat.

Pit: To remove the hard inedible seed from peaches, plums, etc.

Plank: To broil and serve on a board or wooden platter.

Plump: To soak fruits, usually dried, in liquid until puffy and softened.

Poach: To cook in a small amount of gently simmering liquid.

Preserve: To prevent food spoilage by pickling, salting, dehydrating, smoking, boiling in syrup, etc. Preserved foods have excellent keeping qualities when properly prepared and stored.

Purée: To reduce the pulp of cooked fruit and vegetables to a smooth and thick liquid by straining or blending.

Reduce: To boil stock, gravy or other liquid until the volume is reduced, the liquid is thickened and the flavor is intensified.

Refresh: To place blanched drained vegetables or other food in cold water to halt cooking process.

Render: To cook meat or meat trimmings at low temperature until fat melts and can be drained and strained.

Roast: (1) To cook by dry heat either in an oven or over hot coals. (2) To dry or parch by intense heat.

Sauté: To cook in a skillet containing a small amount of hot cooking oil. Sautéed foods should never be immersed in the cooking oil and should be stirred frequently.

Scald: (1) To heat a liquid almost to the boiling point. (2) To soak, usually vegetables or fruit, in boiling water until the skins are loosened.

Scallop: To bake with a sauce in a casserole. The food may either be mixed or layered with the sauce.

Score: To make shallow cuts diagonally in parallel lines, especially in meat.

Scramble: To cook and stir simultaneously, especially eggs.

Shirr: To crack eggs into individual buttered baking dishes, then bake or broil until whites are set. Chopped meats or vegetables, cheese, cream or bread crumbs may also be added.

Shred: To cut or shave food into slivers.

Shuck: To remove the husk from corn or the shell from oysters, clams, etc.

Sieve: To press a mixture through a closely meshed metal utensil to make it homogeneous.

Sift: To pass, usually dry ingredients, through a fine wire mesh in order to produce a uniform consistency.

Simmer: To cook in or with a liquid at or just below the boiling point.

Skewer: (1) To thread, usually meat and vegetables, onto a sharpened rod (as in shish kabob). (2) To fasten the opening of stuffed fowl closed with small pins.

Skim: To ladle or spoon off excess fat or scum from the surface of a liquid.

Smoke: To preserve or cook through continuous exposure to wood smoke for a long time.

Steam: To cook with water vapor in a closed container, usually in a steamer, on a rack, or in a double boiler.

Sterilize: To cleanse and purify through exposure to intense heat.

Stew: To simmer, usually meats and vegetables, for a long period of time. Also used to tenderize meats.

Stir-fry: To cook small pieces of vegetables and/or meat in a small amount of oil in a wok or skillet over high heat, stirring constantly, until tender-crisp.

Strain: To pass through a strainer, sieve, or cheesecloth in order to break down or remove solids or impurities.

Stuff: To fill cavities especially those of meats, vegetables and poultry.

Toast: To brown and crisp, usually by means of direct heat or to bake until brown.

Toss: To mix lightly with lifting motion using 2 forks or spoons.

Whip: To beat a mixture until air has been thoroughly incorporated and the mixture is light and fluffy, the volume is greatly increased, and the mixture holds its shape.

Wilt: To apply heat to cause dehydration, color change and a droopy appearance.

GRANDMOTHER'S "RECEET" FOR DOING FAMILY WASH

Husbands, the next time your wives complain about doing the family wash, show them this. It was "Grandmother's Receet" for washday back in those days before modern laundry equipment was avilable.

1. Build fire in back yard to heet keetle of rain water.
2. Set tubs so smoke won't blow in eyes if wind is pert.
3. Shave one hole cake lie soap in billin water.
4. Sort things, make three piles. 1 pile white, 1 pile cullord, 1 pile work britches and rags.
5. Stur flour in cold water to smooth then thin down with billin water.
6. Rub dirty spots en board. Scrub hard. Then bile, Tub cullord but don't bile—just rench and starch.
7. Take white things out of kettle with broom stick handle then rench, blew and starch.
8. Spred tee towels on grass.
9. Hang old rags on fence.
10. Pore rench water in flower bed.
11. Scrub porch with hot soapy water.
12. Turn tubs upside down.
13. Go put on cleen dress—smooth hair with side combs—brew cup of tee —set and rest a spell and count your blessins.

Gals, hang this up above your automatic electric washer and dryer and when things look bleak, read it again.

HERBS

Use fresh whole herbs when possible. When fresh herbs are not available, use whole dried herbs that can be crushed just while adding. Store herbs in airtight containers away from the heat of the stove. Fresh herbs may be layered between paper towels and dried in the microwave on HIGH for 2 minutes or until dry.

Basil	Can be chopped and added to cold poultry salads. If the recipe calls for tomatoes or tomato sauce, add a touch of basil for a rich flavor.
Bay leaf	The basis of many French seasonings. It is added to soups, stews, marinades and stuffings.
Bouquet garni	A bundle of parsley, thyme and bay leaves tied together and added to stews, soups or sauces. Other herbs and spices may be added to the basic herbs.
Chervil	One of the traditional *fines herbes* used in French cooking. (The others are tarragon, parsley and chives.) It is good in omelets and soups.
Chives	Available fresh, dried or frozen, it can be substituted for raw onion or shallot in nearly any recipe.
Garlic	One of the oldest herbs in the world, it must be carefully handled. For best results, press or crush the garlic clove.
Marjoram	An aromatic herb of the mint family, it is good in soups, sauces, stuffings and stews.
Mint	Use fresh, dried or ground with vegetables, desserts, fruits, jelly, lamb or tea. Fresh sprigs of mint make attractive aromatic garnishes.
Oregano	A staple, savory herb in Italian, Spanish, Greek and Mexican cuisines. It is very good in dishes with a tomato foundation, especially in combination with basil.
Parsley	Use this mild herb as fresh sprigs or dried flakes to flavor or garnish almost any dish.
Rosemary	This pungent herb is especially good in poultry and fish dishes and in such accompaniments as stuffings.
Saffron	Use this deep orange herb, made from the dried stamens of a crocus, sparingly in poultry, seafood and rice dishes.
Sage	This herb is a perennial favorite with all kinds of poultry and stuffings.
Tarragon	One of the *fines herbes*. Goes well with all poultry dishes whether hot or cold.
Thyme	Usually used in combination with bay leaf in soups, stews and sauces.

SPICES

Spices should be stored in airtight containers away from the heat of the stove or in the refrigerator. Add ground spices toward the end of the cooking time to retain maximum flavor. Whole spices may be added at the beginning but should have a small amount of additional spices added near the end of cooking time also.

Allspice	Pungent aromatic spice, whole or in powdered form. It is excellent in marinades, particularly in game marinade, or in curries.
Caraway seed	Use the whole seeds in breads, especially rye, and with cheese, sauerkraut and cabbage dishes.
Celery seed	Use whole or ground in salad dressings, sauces, pickles or meat, cheese, egg and fish dishes.
Chili powder	Made from dried red chili peppers, this spice ranges from mild to fiery depending on the type of chili pepper used. Used especially in Mexican cooking, it is a delicious addition to eggs, dips and sauces.
Cinnamon	Ground from the bark of the cinnamon tree, it is delicious in desserts as well as savory dishes.
Coriander	Seed used whole or ground, this slightly lemony spice adds an unusual flavor to soups, stews, chili dishes, curries and desserts.
Curry powder	A blend of several spices, this gives Indian cooking its characteristic flavor.
Cumin	A staple spice in Mexican cooking. Use in meat, rice, cheese, egg and fish dishes.
Ginger	The whole root used fresh, dried or ground is a sweet, pungent addition to desserts or oriental-style dishes.
Mustard (dry)	Ground mustard seed brings a sharp bite to sauces or may be sprinkled sparingly over poultry or other foods.
Nutmeg	Use the whole spice or a bit of freshly ground for flavor in beverages, breads and desserts. A sprinkle on top is both a flavor enhancer and an attractive garnish.
Pepper	Black and white pepper from the pepperberry or peppercorn, whether whole, ground or cracked, is the most commonly used spice in or on any food.
Poppy seed	Use these tiny, nutty-flavored seeds in salad dressings, breads, cakes or as a flavorful garnish for cheese, rolls or noodle dishes.
Turmeric	Ground from a root related to ginger, this is an essential in curry powder. Also used in pickles, relishes, cheese and egg dishes.

EQUIVALENT CHART

	When the recipe calls for	Use
Baking	1/2 cup butter	4 ounces
	2 cups butter	1 pound
	4 cups all-purpose flour	1 pound
	4 1/2 to 5 cups sifted cake flour	1 pound
	1 square chocolate	1 ounce
	1 cup semisweet chocolate chips	6 ounces
	4 cups marshmallows	1 pound
	2 1/4 cups packed brown sugar	1 pound
	4 cups confectioners' sugar	1 pound
	2 cups granulated sugar	1 pound
Cereal – Bread	1 cup fine dry bread crumbs	4 to 5 slices
	1 cup soft bread crumbs	2 slices
	1 cup small bread cubes	2 slices
	1 cup fine cracker crumbs	28 saltines
	1 cup fine graham cracker crumbs	15 crackers
	1 cup vanilla wafer crumbs	22 wafers
	1 cup crushed cornflakes	3 cups uncrushed
	4 cups cooked macaroni	8 ounces uncooked
	3 1/2 cups cooked rice	1 cup uncooked
Dairy	1 cup shredded cheese	4 ounces
	1 cup cottage cheese	8 ounces
	1 cup sour cream	8 ounces
	1 cup whipped cream	1/2 cup heavy cream
	2/3 cup evaporated milk	1 small can
	1 2/3 cups evaporated milk	1 13-ounce can
Fruit	4 cups sliced or chopped apples	4 medium
	1 cup mashed bananas	3 medium
	2 cups pitted cherries	4 cups unpitted
	2 1/2 cups shredded coconut	8 ounces
	4 cups cranberries	1 pound
	1 cup pitted dates	1 8-ounce package
	3 to 4 tablespoons lemon juice plus 1 tablespoon grated lemon rind	1 lemon
	1/3 cup orange juice plus 2 teaspoons grated orange rind	1 orange
	4 cups sliced peaches	8 medium
	2 cups pitted prunes	1 12-ounce package
	3 cups raisins	1 15-ounce package

	When the recipe calls for	Use
Meats	4 cups chopped cooked chicken 3 cups chopped cooked meat 2 cups cooked ground meat	1 5-pound chicken 1 pound, cooked 1 pound, cooked
Nuts	1 cup chopped nuts	4 ounces shelled 1 pound unshelled
Vegetables	2 cups cooked green beans 2½ cups lima beans or red beans 4 cups shredded cabbage 1 cup grated carrot 8 ounces fresh mushrooms 1 cup chopped onion 4 cups sliced or chopped potatoes 2 cups canned tomatoes	½ pound fresh or 1 16-ounce can 1 cup dried, cooked 1 pound 1 large 1 4-ounce can 1 large 4 medium 1 16-ounce can

Measurement Equivalents

1 tablespoon = 3 teaspoons 2 tablespoons = 1 ounce 4 tablespoons = ¼ cup 5⅓ tablespoons = ⅓ cup 8 tablespoons = ½ cup 12 tablespoons = ¾ cup 16 tablespoons = 1 cup 1 cup = 8 ounces or ½ pint 4 cups = 1 quart 4 quarts = 1 gallon	1 6½ to 8-ounce can = 1 cup 1 10½ to 12-ounce can = 1¼ cups 1 14 to 16-ounce can = 1¾ cups 1 16 to 17-ounce can = 2 cups 1 18 to 20-ounce can = 2½ cups 1 29-ounce can = 3½ cups 1 46 to 51-ounce can = 5¾ cups 1 6½ to 7½-pound can or Number 10 = 12 to 13 cups

Metric Equivalents

Liquid	Dry
1 teaspoon = 5 milliliters 1 tablespoon = 15 milliliters 1 fluid ounce = 30 milliliters 1 cup = 250 milliliters 1 pint = 500 milliliters	1 quart = 1 liter 1 ounce = 30 grams 1 pound = 450 grams 2.2 pounds = 1 kilogram

NOTE: The metric measures are approximate benchmarks for purposes of home food preparation.

SUBSTITUTION CHART

	Instead of	Use
Baking	1 teaspoon baking powder	¼ teaspoon baking soda plus ½ teaspoon cream of tartar
	1 tablespoon cornstarch (for thickening)	2 tablespoons flour or 1 tablespoon tapioca
	1 cup sifted all-purpose flour	1 cup plus 2 tablespoons sifted cake flour
	1 cup sifted cake flour	1 cup minus 2 tablespoons sifted all-purpose flour
	1 cup dry bread crumbs	¾ cup cracker crumbs
Dairy	1 cup buttermilk	1 cup sour milk or 1 cup yogurt
	1 cup heavy cream	¾ cup skim milk plus ⅓ cup butter
	1 cup light cream	⅞ cup skim milk plus 3 tablespoons butter
	1 cup sour cream	⅞ cup sour milk plus 3 tablespoons butter
	1 cup sour milk	1 cup milk plus 1 tablespoon vinegar or lemon juice or 1 cup buttermilk
Seasoning	1 teaspoon allspice	½ teaspoon cinnamon plus ⅛ teaspoon cloves
	1 cup catsup	1 cup tomato sauce plus ½ cup sugar plus 2 tablespoons vinegar
	1 clove of garlic	⅛ teaspoon garlic powder or ⅛ teaspoon instant minced garlic or ¾ teaspoon garlic salt or 5 drops of liquid garlic
	1 teaspoon Italian spice	¼ teaspoon each oregano, basil, thyme, rosemary plus dash of cayenne pepper
	1 teaspoon lemon juice	½ teaspoon vinegar
	1 tablespoon mustard	1 teaspoon dry mustard
	1 medium onion	1 tablespoon dried minced onion or 1 teaspoon onion powder
Sweet	1 1-ounce square chocolate	¼ cup cocoa plus 1 teaspoon shortening
	1⅔ ounces semisweet chocolate	1 ounce unsweetened chocolate plus 4 teaspoons granulated sugar
	1 cup honey	1 to 1¼ cups sugar plus ¼ cup liquid or 1 cup corn syrup or molasses
	1 cup granulated sugar	1 cup packed brown sugar or 1 cup corn syrup, molasses or honey minus ¼ cup liquid

INDEX

Index

Index

This Cookbook Is A Perfect Gift For Holidays, Weddings, Anniversaries and Birthdays.

★ ★

You may order as many of our Cookbooks as you wish for the price of $10.00 each, plus $2.00 postage and handling per cookbook ordered.

CUSTOMER INFORMATION: (Please Print)

Name _____

Address _____

City/State/Zip _____

Phone   (   )   _____

Please send _____ copies of *Gold & Silver Palates*

@ $10.00 each copy **plus** $2.00 shipping and handling (per copy)
TOTAL AMOUNT ($12.00 x #books) = $ _____

Enclosed is my check for $ _____
(Payable to Telephone Pioneers)

Mail Order Form To:
John I. Sabin Chapter
3675 T Street, Room 119
P.O. Box 15038
Sacramento, CA 95851

(Please Print All Information)

SHIP TO: (Person receiving shipment)	**SHIP TO:** (Person receiving shipment)
Name _____	Name _____
Address _____	Address _____
City _____	City _____
State _____ Zip _____	State _____ Zip _____
Phone ( ) _____	Phone ( ) _____
Gift Card From _____	Gift Card From _____

Telephone Pioneers of America

ANSWERING THE CALL OF THOSE IN NEED

REGION 2